THE FATHERS
OF THE CHURCH

A NEW TRANSLATION

VOLUME 79

THE FATHERS
OF THE CHURCH

A NEW TRANSLATION

ST. AUGUSTINE

TRACTATES ON THE GOSPEL OF JOHN 11–27

Translated by

JOHN W. RETTIG
Xavier University
Cincinnati, Ohio

THE CATHOLIC UNIVERSITY OF AMERICA PRESS
Washington, D.C.

LIBRARY OF CONGRESS CATALOGING-IN-PUBLICATION DATA
Augustine, Saint, Bishop of Hippo.
    Tractates on the Gospel of John.

    (The Fathers of the church ; v. 78–79)
    Includes bibliographies and indexes.
    Translation of: In Evangelium Iohannis tractatus.
Tractatus 1–27.
        Contents: [1] 1–10—[2] 11–27.
        1. Bible. N.T. John—Sermons—Early works to 1800.
    2. Sermons, Latin—Translations into English—Early
    works to 1800. 3. Sermons, English—Translations
    from Latin—Early works to 1800. I. Title. II. Series:
    Fathers of the church : v. 78, etc.
    BR60.F3A8246 [BS2615] 270 s [226'.506]   87–18387
    ISBN 0–8132–0078–4 (v. 1)
    ISBN 0–8132–0079–2 (v. 2)

CONTENTS

ABBREVIATIONS

AC	Antike und Christentum Kultur- und religionsgeschichtliche Studien. Münster, 1929–.
ACW	Ancient Christian Writers. New York, New York/Mahwah, New Jersey: Newman Press, 1946–.
BA	Bibliothèque augustinienne. Oeuvres de saint augustin. Paris, 1936–.
BAC	Biblioteca de Autores Cristianos. Madrid, 1946–.
CCD	Confraternity of Christian Doctrine. Translations of the Old and New Testaments.
CCL	Corpus Christianorum Series Latina. Turnhout, 1953–.
CSEL	Corpus Scriptorum Ecclesiasticorum Latinorum. Vienna, 1866–.
DACL	*Dictionnaire d'archéologie chrétienne et de liturgie.* Paris, 1907–1953.
DCD	*De Civitate Dei.*
DDC	*De Doctrina Christiana.*
DDQ	*De Diversis Quaestionibus LXXXIII.*
DThC	*Dictionnaire de théologie catholique.* Paris, 1935.
En in Ps	*Enarrationes in Psalmos.*
FOTC	The Fathers of the Church. New York and Washington, D.C., 1947–.
GCS	Die Griechischen Christlichen Schriftsteller. Berlin, 1897–.
JBC	*The Jerome Biblical Commentary.* Ed. R. Brown, J. Fitzmyer, R. Murphy. Englewood Cliffs, New Jersey, 1968.
JThS	*Journal of Theological Studies.*
LF	A Library of the Fathers of the Holy Catholic Church. Ed. E. B. Pusey, J. Keble, and J. H. Newman. Oxford, 1837–1861.
LNPF	A Select Library of Nicene and Post-Nicene Fathers of the Christian Church. Ed. P. Schaff and H. Wace. Buffalo and New York, 1888. Rep. 1956.
LXX	*Septuagint.* Ed. A. Rahlfs. 2 vols. Stuttgart, 1935.
NAB	*The New American Bible.* Paterson, New Jersey, 1970.
NBA	Nuova Biblioteca Agostiniana. Rome, 1967–.
NCE	*The New Catholic Encyclopedia.* New York, 1967.
ODCC²	*The Oxford Dictionary of the Christian Church.* 2d ed. Ed. F. L. Cross and E. A. Livingstone. Oxford, 1984.

PG   Migne, J.-P., ed. Patrologiae Cursus Completus: Series Graeca. Paris, 1857–1866.

PL   Migne, J.-P., ed. Patrologiae Cursus Completus: Series Latina. Paris, 1878–1890.

RAug   *Recherches augustiniennes.*

REAug   *Revue des études augustiniennes.*

RSR   *Recherches de science religieuse.*

SC   Sources chrétiennes. Paris, 1942–.

SPM   Stromata Patristica et Mediaevalia 1. *Sancti Aurelii Augustini Sermones selecti duodeviginti.* Ed. C. Lambot. Utrecht, 1950.

TLL   Thesaurus Linguae Latinae. Leipzig, 1900–.

Tr in Io Ep   *Tractates on the First Epistle of John.*

VigC   *Vigiliae Christianae.*

BIBLIOGRAPHY

Texts and Translations

Berrouard, M.-F. *Homélies sur l'évangile de saint Jean, I–XVI.* BA 71 (1969) and *XVII–XXXIII.* BA 72 (1977).

Browne, H. *Homilies on the Gospel According to St. John, and His First Epistle by S. Augustine, Bishop of Hippo.* LF 26 (1848) and 29 (1849).

Caillau, A. et al. (edd.). A. Aur. *Augustini Hipponensis Episcopi In Joannis Evangelium Tractatus CXXIV* Patres Ecclesiae 121, 122, 123. *Augustinus* 14, 15, 16. Paris, 1842.

Gandolfo, E., Tarulli, V. *Commento al Vangelo di s. Giovanni.* NBA 24 (1968).

Gibb, J. *Lectures or Tractates on the Gospel According to St. John.* Vol. 1, *Tractates 1–37.* The Works of Aurelius Augustine. Vol. 10. Edinburgh, 1873.

————, Innes, J. *St. Augustin: Lectures or Tractates on the Gospel According to St. John.* LNPF 7, ser. 1. 1888. Reprint. Grand Rapids, Michigan: Wm. B. Eerdmans, 1983.

Migne, J.-P. *In Joannis Evangelium Tractatus CXXIV.* PL 35.1375–1970. This 1861 edition is a reprint of the edition of the Benedictines of St. Maur, S. *Aurelii Augustini Opera.* Ed. J. Blampin, P. Coustant, et al. Vol. 3, pars altera. Paris, 1680.

Pontet, M. *Sermons sur saint Jean.* Namur, 1958.

Prieto, T. *Obras de San Agustín, XIII: Tratados sobre el Evangelio de San Juan (I–XXXV).* BAC 139 (1955).

Rabanal, V. *Obras de San Agustín, XIV: Tratados sobre el Evangelio de San Juan (XXXVI–CXXIV).* BAC 165 (1957).

Willems, R., ed. *Sancti Aurelii Augustini In Iohannis Evangelium Tractatus CXXIV.* CCL 36 (1954).

Other Patristic Texts and Translations

Augustine, St. *De Baptismo contra Donatistas.* PL 43.107–124 (1865); CSEL 51.19–141. Ed. M. Petschenig (1908).

————. *Contra Litteras Petiliani.* PL 43.245–383 (1865); CSEL 52.3–27. Ed. M. Petschenig (1909).

————. *De Civitate Dei.* CCL 47 and 48. Ed. B. Dombart and A. Kalb (1955).

————. *De Diversis Quaestionibus LXXXIII.* CCL 44A. Ed. A. Mutzenbecher (1975).

————. *De Doctrina Christiana.* CCL 32. Ed. J. Martin (1962); FOTC 5.19–235. Tr. J. Gavigan (1947).

————. *Enarrationes in Psalmos.* CCL 38–40. Ed. E. Dekkers and J. Fraipont (1956); ACW 29 and 30 (Psalms 1–37). Tr. Dame S. Hebgin and Dame F. Corrigan (1960, 1961).

————. *Epistulae.* PL 33; CSEL 34.1 (1895), 34.2 (1898), 44 (1904), 57

(1911), 58 (1923), 88 (1981); FOTC 12, 18, 20, 30, 32. Tr. W. Parsons (1951–1956).

―――. *De Haeresibus*. CCL 46.263–345. Ed. R. Vander Plaetse and C. Beukers (1969).

Concilia Africae A.345–A.525. CCL 149. Ed. C. Munier (1974).

Optatus of Milevis. *De Schismate Donatistarum*. CSEL 26. Ed. K. Ziwsa (1893).

Possidius, *Vita du S. Agostino*. Ed. M. Pellegrino. *Verba Seniorum* 4. Alba, 1955.

―――. *Indiculus*. Ed. A. Wilmart, "Operum S. Augustini Elenchus a Possidio Eiusdem Discipulo Calamensi Episcopo Digestus." *Miscellanea Agostiniana*. Vol. 2. Rome, 1931. Pp. 149–233.

Bible(s)

The Anchor Bible. Ed. R. Brown. *The Gospel According to John* (i–xii) and (xiii–xxi). Vols. 29 and 29A. New York, 1966, 1970.

Évangile selon saint Jean. 8th ed. M.-J. Lagrange. Paris, 1948.

The Gospel According to John. 2d ed. Ed. C. Barrett. Philadelphia, 1978.

The Gospel According to Saint John. R. Schnackenburg. Tr. C. Hastings. New York, 1980.

The Holy Bible Translated from the Latin Vulgate. Douay Rheims Version. Old Testament originally published at Douay (1609), New Testament originally published at Rheims (1582). Baltimore, 1899.

The Jerome Biblical Commentary. Ed. R. Brown, J. Fitzmyer, and R. Murphy. Englewood Cliffs, New Jersey, 1968.

The Jerusalem Bible. Ed. A. Jones et al. New York, 1966.

The New American Bible. Tr. Members of the Catholic Bible Association of America. Paterson, New Jersey, 1970.

The New Testament of Our Lord and Savior Jesus Christ. Translated from the Latin Vulgate. Confraternity of Christian Doctrine. New York, 1941.

Novum Testamentum Graece et Latine. 7th ed. Ed. A. Merk. Rome, 1951.

The Old Testament. Confraternity of Christian Doctrine. New York, 1965.

Septuaginta. Ed. A. Rahlfs. 2 vols. Stuttgart, 1935.

The Septuagint Version of the Old Testament and Apochrypha with an English Version and with Various Readings and Critical Notes. Tr. L. Benton. London, n.d.

Other Works

Agaësse, P. *Saint Augustin. Commentaire de la première épître de s. Jean*. SC 75 (1961, 1966²).

"Apollinarius and Apollinarianism." ODCC², 70–71.

Ayers, R. "Language Theory and Analysis in Augustine." *Scottish Journal of Theology* 29 (1976) 1–12.

―――. *Language, Logic, and Reason in the Church Fathers*. Hildesheim, 1981.

Balmus, C. *Étude sur le style de saint Augustin dans les Confessions et la Cité de Dieu*. Paris, 1930.

Batiffol, P. *Le catholicisme de saint Augustin*. 3d ed. Paris, 1920.

Bardy, G. "Tractare, Tractatus." RSR 33 (1946) 211–235.

Battenhouse, R., ed. *A Companion to the Study of St. Augustine*. New York, 1955.

Berrouard, M.-F. "La date des Tractatus I–LIV In Ioannis Evangelium de saint Augustin." RAug 7 (1971) 105–168.

————. "Saint Augustin et la ministère de la prédication." RAug 2 (1962) 447–501.

————. "Pour une refléxion sur le 'sacramentum' augustinien. La Manne et l'Eucharistie dans le tractatus XXVI, 11–12 in Ioannis Evangelium," *Forma Futuri: Studi in onore del Cardinale Michele Pellegrino.* Turin, 1975. Pp. 830–844.

————. "L'être sacramental de l'eucharistie selon saint Augustin: Commentaire de Io 6, 60–63 dans le Tractatus XXVII, 1–6 et 11–12 in Ioannis Evangelium." *Nouvelle revue théologique* 99 (1977) 702–721.

Blackman, E. *Marcion and His Influence.* London, 1948.

Brown, P. *Augustine of Hippo.* Berkeley, 1967.

————. *Religion and Society in the Age of Augustine.* New York, 1972.

————. *The World of Late Antiquity.* London, 1971.

Bubacz, B. *St. Augustine's Theory of Knowledge: A Contemporary Analysis.* New York, 1981.

Burkitt, F. *The Religion of the Manichees.* Cambridge, 1925.

————. *The Old Latin and the Itala.* Cambridge, 1896.

Burnaby, J. *Amor Dei.* London, 1938.

Burns, J. "Augustine's Role in the Imperial Action against the Pelagians." JThS 30, n.s. (1979) 67–83.

Camelot, P.-T. "Realisme et symbolisme dans la doctrine eucharistique de saint Augustin." *Revue des sciences philosophiques et théologiques* 31 (1947) 394–410.

Chadwick, H. *Augustine.* New York, 1986.

Chiovaro, F. "Apollinarianism." NCE 1.665–667.

Comeau, M. *Saint Augustin, exégète du quatrième évangile.* Paris, 1930.

Courcelle, P. "La littérature latine d'époque patristique." *Actes du premier congrès de la Fédération Internationale des Associations d'Études Classiques.* Paris, 1951. Pp. 287–307.

————. *Les Confessions de saint Augustin dans le tradition littéraire.* Paris, 1963.

De Bruyne, D. "Le Dies Festus Januarium du Tractatus Quintus S. Augustini in Joannis Evangelium." *Revue Bénédictine* 43 (1931) 347.

De Clercq, V. "Arianism." NCE 1.791–794.

Decret, F. *Aspects du Manichéisme dans l'Afrique romaine.* Paris, 1970.

Deferrari, R. "Verbatim Reports of Augustine's Unwritten Sermons." *Transactions and Proceedings of the American Philological Association* 46 (1915) 35–45.

————. "On the Date and Order of Delivery of St. Augustine's Tractates on the Gospel and Epistles of St. John." *Classical Philology* 12 (1917) 191–194.

————. "St. Augustine's Method of Composing and Delivering Sermons." *The American Journal of Philology* 43 (1922) 97–123, 193–219.

De Plinval, G. *Pelage. Ses écrits, sa vie et sa réforme.* Lausanne, 1943.

Dölger, F. "Konstantin der Grosse und der Manichaismus, Sonne und Christus in Manichaismus." AC 2 (1930) 301–314.

Doyle, G. "St. Augustine's Tractates on the Gospel of John Compared with the Rhetorical Theory of the De Doctrina Christiana." Ph.D. diss., University of North Carolina, 1975. Cf. *Dissertation Abstracts International* 37.3 (1976) 1525-A.

————. "Augustine's Sermonic Method." *The Westminster Theological Journal* 39 (1977) 213–238.

Evans, G. *Augustine on Evil.* Cambridge, 1982.

Fairweather, E. "Saint Augustine's Interpretation of Infant Baptism." *Augustinus Magister* 2. Paris, 1954. Pp. 897–903.

Finaert, G. *L'Évolution littéraire de saint Augustin.* Collection d'études latines 17. Paris, 1939.

Ferguson, J. *Pelagius. A Historical and Theological Study.* Cambridge, 1956.

———. "Aspects of Early Christianity in North Africa." *Africa in Classical Antiquity.* Ibadan, 1969. Pp. 182–191.

Frend, W. *The Donatist Church.* Oxford, 1952.

———. *Martyrdom and Persecution in the Early Church.* Oxford, 1965.

Gallay, J. "Dilige et quod vis fac." RSR 43 (1955) 545–555.

Gaudemet, J. *L'Église dans l'empire romain (iv–v siécles).* Paris, 1958.

Gilson, E. *The Christian Philosophy of St. Augustine.* Tr. L. Lynch. New York, 1960.

Gonzalez, C. I. "María en el comentario de San Agustín al Evangelio de San Juan." *Estudios Eclesiásticos* 61 (1986) 395–419.

Grabowski, S. *The Church. An Introduction to the Theology of St. Augustine.* St. Louis, 1957.

Hagendahl, H. *Augustine and the Latin Classics.* Stockholm, 1967.

Hamman, A.-G. *La vie quotidienne en Afrique du Nord au temps de saint Augustin.* Paris, 1979.

Hardy, R. *Actualité de la révélation divine. Une étude des "Tractatus in Ioannis Euangelium" de saint Augustin.* Théologie Historique 28. Paris, 1974.

Haring, N. "St. Augustine's Use of the Word *Character.*" *Mediaeval Studies* 14 (1952) 79–97.

Jackson, B. Darrell. "The Theory of Signs in St. Augustine's *De Doctrina Christiana.* REAug 15 (1969) 9–49.

Jones, A. *The Later Roman Empire 284–602.* Oxford, 1964.

Keleher, J. *Saint Augustine's Notion of Schism in the Donatist Controversy.* Mundelein, 1961.

Kelly, J. *Early Christian Creeds.* 3d ed. New York, 1981.

———. *Early Christian Doctrines.* 5th ed. New York, 1976.

Knox, R. "Donatist and Circumcellion." *Enthusiasm.* New York, 1950. Pp. 50–70.

Koenen, L. "Augustine and Manicheism in Light of the Cologne Mani codex." *Illinois Classical Studies* 3 (1978) 154–195.

La Bonnardière, A.-M. *Recherches de chronologie augustinienne.* Paris, 1965.

Lamirande, E. *Church, State, and Toleration: An Intriguing Change of Mind in Augustine.* Villanova, Pa., 1975.

Lehman, P. "The Anti-Pelagian Writings." In *A Companion to the Study of St. Augustine.* Ed. R. Battenhouse. New York, 1955. Pp. 203–234.

Le Landais, M. "Deux années de prédication de saint Augustin: introduction à la lecture de l'*In Ioannem.*" *Études augustiniennes.* Théologie 28 (Paris, 1953) 7–95.

Mandouze, A. *Saint Augustin: L'aventure de la raison et de la grâce.* Paris, 1968.

Markus, R. "St. Augustine on Signs." *Phronesis* 2 (1957) 60–83.

———. *Saeculum. History and Society in the Theology of St. Augustine.* Cambridge, 1970.

Marrou, H.-I. *Saint Augustin et le fin de la culture antique.* Paris, 1938.

———. *A History of Education in Antiquity.* Tr. G. Lamb. New York, 1956.

Metzger, B. *The Early Versions of the New Testament.* Oxford, 1977.

Milne, C. *A Reconstruction of the Old Latin Text of the Gospels Used by Saint Augustine.* Cambridge, 1926.

Mohrmann, C. *Die Altchristliche Sondersprache in den Sermones des hl. Augustin* 1. 2d ed. Amsterdam, 1965.

———. "Saint Augustin prédicateur." *La Maison-Dieu* 39 (1954) 83–96.

———. "Praedicare—Tractare—Sermo." Ibid. 97–107.

———. *Études sur le latin du chrétiens I and II.* Rome, 1958, 1961.

Monceaux, P. *Histoire littéraire de l'Afrique chrétienne depuis les origines jusqu'à l'invasion arabe.* 7 vols. See esp. vols. 4–7. Paris, 1901–1923.

Moon, A. *The De Natura Boni of Augustine.* Catholic University of America Patristic Studies 88. Washington, D.C., 1955.

Morris, J. "Pelagian Literature." *JThS* 16 (1965) 25–60.

Nash, R. *The Light of the Mind. St. Augustine's Theory of Knowledge.* Lexington, 1969.

O'Brien, M. *Titles of Address in Christian Latin Epistolography to 543 A.D.* Washington, D.C., 1930.

O'Connell, R. *Art and the Christian Intelligence in St. Augustine.* Cambridge, Mass., 1978.

O'Donnell, J. *Augustine.* Boston, 1985.

O'Malley, T. *Tertullian and the Bible.* Latinitas Christianorum Primaeva 21. Nijmegen-Utrecht, 1967.

Pelikan, J. (ed.). *"Our Lord's Sermon on the Mount."* In *The Preaching of St. Augustine.* Tr. F. Cardman. Philadelphia, 1973.

Petre, H. *Caritas: Étude sur le vocabulaire de la charité chrétienne.* Specilegium Sacrum Lovaniense Études et Documents 22. Louvain, 1948.

Poque, S. *Le langage symbolique dans la prédication d'Augustin d'Hippone.* Paris, 1984.

———. "Trois semaines de prédication à Hippone en février-mars 407." *RAug* 7 (1971) 169–187.

Pontet, M. *L'exégèse de s. Augustin prédicateur.* Paris, 1945.

Pope, H. "Saint Augustine's *Tractatus in Ioannem:* A Neglected Classic." *The Ecclesiastical Review* 49 (1913) 161–172.

Portalié, E. *A Guide to the Thought of Saint Augustine.* Tr. R. Bastian. Chicago, 1960.

Prestige, G. *God in Patristic Thought.* London, 1949.

Raven, C. *Apollinarianism.* Cambridge, 1923.

Reardon, B. "The Relation of Philosophy to Faith in the Teaching of St. Augustine." *Studia Patristica* 2 (1957) 288–294.

Rondet, H. "La croix sur le front." *RSR* 42 (1954) 388–394.

Sage, M. *Cyprian.* Cambridge, Mass., 1975.

Saint-Martin, J. "La prédestination d'après les pères latins, particulièrement d'après saint Augustin." *DThC* 12.2832–2896.

Schildenberger, J. "Die Itala der hl. Augustinus." *Colligere fragmenta: Festschrift Alban Dold.* Ed. B. Fischer and V. Fiola. Beuron, 1952. Pp. 84–102.

Schmitt, E. *Le mariage chrétien dans l'oeuvre de saint Augustin: Une théologie baptismale de la vie conjugale.* Paris, 1983.

Schumacher, W. *Spiritus and Spiritualis: A Study in the Sermons of St. Augustine.* Mundelein, Ill., 1957.

Siedlecki, E. *A Patristic Synthesis of John VI, 54–55.* Mundelein, Ill., 1956.

Sparrow Simpson, E. *St. Augustine and African Church Divisions.* London, 1910.

Straw, C. "Augustine as Pastoral Theologian: The Exegesis of the Parables of the Field and the Threshing Floor." *Augustinian Studies* 14 (1983) 129–151.

Tengstrom, E. *Donatisten und Katholiken.* Goeteburg, 1964.

TeSelle, E. *Augustine the Theologian.* New York, 1970.

Testard, M. *Saint Augustin et Cicéron.* Paris, 1958.

Van der Meer, F. *Augustine the Bishop.* Tr. B. Battershaw and G. Lamb. New York, 1961.

Weismann, F. J. "Christo, Verbo creador y redentor, en la controversia anti-donatista de los 'Tractatus in Johannis Evangelium' I–XVI de San Agustin." *Stromata* 42 (1986) 301–328.

West, R. *St. Augustine.* New York, 1933.

Widengren, G. *Mani and Manichaeism.* Tr. C. Kessler. London, 1965.

Willis, G. *Saint Augustine and the Donatist Heresy.* London, 1950.

Wright, D. "Tractatus 20–22 of St. Augustine's *In Iohannem.*" JThS 15 n.s. (1964) 317–330.

———. "The Manuscripts of St. Augustine's *Tractatus in Evangelium Iohannis.* A Preliminary Survey." RAug 8 (1972) 55–143.

Zarb, S. "Chronologia Tractatuum S. Augustini in Euangelium primamque Epistolam Ioannis Apostoli." *Angelicum* 10 (1933) 50–110.

INTRODUCTION

INTRODUCTION

HIS SECOND VOLUME of Augustine's *In Ioannis Evangelium Tractatus CXXIV* contains *Tractates* 11 to 27. All of these sermons were also delivered to his congregation at Hippo Regius[1] and show the same devoted pastoral care that Augustine directed to those people of God entrusted to him as their pastor.[2] Because of the theological profundity of John's Gospel these sermons, too, reflect especially theological concerns, though spiritual and moral matters are not in any way disregarded. That fullness of scriptural exegesis which characterizes the tractate as a species of the sermon is found here.

The constant presence of Manichaeism[3] in North Africa and the urgent pressures exerted by the Donatist schismatics[4] are still apparent in the earlier *Tractates* in this group, *Tractates* 11 to 16. But then the doctrinal focus shifts somewhat and Trinitarian and Christological matters become more prominent. Not only are the Arians[5] given greater attention, but several Christological heresies of lesser importance, the Apollarinarists,[6] Photinus of Sirmium,[7] and the Sabellians,[8] are brought into the argument. The doctrinal content of the sermons, however, is determined as much by the requirements of the scriptural exegesis as by Augustine's current theological concerns.

The first twelve *Tractates* were part of a large group of thirty-eight sermons that were delivered as a unit. Le

---

1. See FOTC 78, Introduction (33)–(35), (37), (39)–(44).
2. Id. (1) and (4).
3. Id. (16) and (17).
4. Id. (19)–(24).
5. Id. (31).
6. See *Tractate* 23.6.
7. See *Tractate* 26.5.
8. See *Tractate* 29.7.

Landais[9] has shown that *En in Ps* 95 and 119 to 133 were intercalated with *Tractates* 1 to 12. Augustine himself tells us that the ten *Tractates on the First Epistle of John* were preached after *Tractate* 12 and before *Tractate* 13.[10] La Bonnardière[11] demonstrates that *En in Ps* 21.2 was given after *Tractate* 12 and before the ten *Tractates on the Epistle*. Le Landais dates the whole collection of *Tractates on the Gospel* and *Epistle* and these *Enarrationes* on the Psalms as beginning in 414 A.D. and ending in 416 A.D. But La Bonnardière more convincingly puts this group in 406 and 407 A.D., and *Tractates* 13 to 16 in 407 and 408 A.D.; the remaining *Tractates* in this volume she would put after 418 A.D. She considers *Tractates* 17 to 23 as a unit.

But Wright[12] and Berrouard[13] have shown that *Tractates* 20, 21, and 22 do not belong to the planned sequence of sermons on John's Gospel, but were added at a later time. Berrouard dates these three sermons in 418–419 A.D. and a group made up of *Tractates* 17 to 19 and 23 to 54 he would put between 413 and 416 A.D., probably in 414 A.D. He agrees with La Bonnardière on the dating and grouping of *Tractates* 1 to 16.

The translation of Augustine's scriptural quotations has been conformed as far as his Latin text allows to the Douay Rheims version since that translation is closest to Augustine's biblical texts. Two modifications have been made in this prac-

9. M. Le Landais, "Deux années de prédication de saint Augustin: introduction à la lecture de l'*In Ioannem*," *Études augustiniennes* Théologie 28 (Paris, 1953) 7–95. See FOTC 78, Introduction (37) and (38).

10. *Tr in Io Ep*, prologue. See P. Agaësse, *Saint Augustin commentaire de la première épître de S. Jean*, SC 75.104–107.

11. A.-M. La Bonnardière, *Recherches de chronologie augustinienne* (Paris, 1965). See FOTC 78, Introduction (39)–(44). The intercalated series of sermons was as follows: *En in Ps* 119 and 120; *Tractate* 1; *En in Ps* 121; *Tractate* 2; *En in Ps* 122 and 123; *Tractate* 3; *En in Ps* 124 and 125; *Tractate* 4; *En in Ps* 126; *Tractates* 5 and 6; *En in Ps* 127; *Tractate* 7; *En in Ps* 128 and 129; *Tractates* 8, 9, and 10; *En in Ps* 130, 131, and 95; *Tractate* 11; *En in Ps* 132–133 (listed as two *enarrationes* but preached as a single sermon); *Tractate* 12; *En in Ps* 21.2; *Tractates on the First Epistle* 1–10.

12. D. Wright, "Tractatus 20–22 of St. Augustine's *In Iohannem*," JThS 15 n. s. (1964) 317–330. See FOTC 78, Introduction (46).

13. M.-F. Berrouard, "La date des Tractatus I–LIV In Ioannis Evangelium de saint Augustin," RAug 7 (1971) 105–168. See FOTC 78, Introduction (47).

tice, however. First, the wording has been made more contemporary, and secondly, sometimes words, phrases, or entire sentences have been taken from the *New American Bible* or the Confraternity of Christian Doctrine revision of the Challoner Rheims version of the New Testament where these translations seemed better suited to the contemporary ear.

TRACTATES
11–27

TRACTATE 11

On John 2.23–25 and 3.1–5

PPORTUNELY HAS THE LORD arranged for us on this day the sequence of this reading. For I trust that you, my beloved people, have noticed that we have undertaken to examine and discuss the gospel according to John in sequence. Opportunely, therefore, it has happened that you heard today from the gospel that "unless a man be born again of water and the Holy Spirit, he will not see the kingdom of God."[1] For it is the time for us to exhort you who are still catechumens, who believe in Christ in such a way that you still carry your own sins. But no one, burdened with sins, will see the kingdom of Heaven; for unless he has been forgiven them, he will not reign with Christ.

(2) But they cannot be forgiven except for him who has been born again of water and the Holy Spirit. But let us observe what all the words mean so that those who are slow to act may find here with what great solicitude they must hasten to put aside their burden. For if they were carrying some heavy pack, either of stone, or of wood, or of something even profitable, if they were carrying grain, wine, or money, they would run to put down their burdens. They are carrying a pack of sins and they are reluctant to run. One must run to put down this pack; it weighs [him] down and drowns [him].

2. Look, you heard that "when" the Lord Jesus Christ "was at Jerusalem at the Passover upon the feast day, many believed in his name, seeing the signs which he did." "Many believed in his name." And what follows? "But Jesus himself

---

1. Jn 3.3 and 5 are conflated here.

9

did not trust himself to them."[2] What does this mean, then, that they were believing "in his name" and "Jesus himself did not trust himself to them"? Is it perhaps that they had not believed in him and were feigning that they believed, and therefore Jesus did not trust himself to them? But the Evangelist would not say, "Many believed in his name," unless he were bearing true witness to them. It is a great thing, therefore, and a remarkable one that men believe in Christ and Christ does not trust himself to men.

(2) Especially since he is the Son of God, he certainly suffered willingly; and if he were unwilling, he would never suffer, who, if he were unwilling, would not even be born. But if he wanted only this, that he only be born and not die, he could do whatever he wanted because he is the omnipotent Son of the omnipotent Father. Let us prove it from the facts themselves. For when they wanted to take hold of him, he went away from them. The gospel says, "And when they wanted to hurl him down from the summit of a hill, he went away from them" unharmed.[3] And when they came to arrest him after he had already been sold by the traitor Judas when that man thought he had it in his power to hand over his master and Lord, there, too, the Lord showed that he was suffering voluntarily, not of necessity. For when the Jews wanted to arrest him, "He said to them, 'Whom do you seek?' But they said, 'Jesus of Nazareth.' And he said, 'I am he.' When they heard this, they drew back and fell down."[4]

(3) By casting them down in answering them, he showed his power so that by being arrested by them he might show his will. Therefore that he suffered was an act of mercy. For he was delivered up for our sins and he rose again for our justification.[5] Hear his words: "I have the power to lay down my life and I have the power to take it up again. No one takes

2. Both "believe" and "trust" are the same word in Latin, *credere*, a subtle use of word connotations that is untranslatable. The Greek text of John exhibits the same usage in the Greek verb *pisteúein*. Both "believe" and "trust," of course, involve faith.

3. Cf. Lk 4.29–30.   4. Cf. Jn 18.4–6.

5. Cf. Rom 4.25.

it from me, but I lay it down of myself that I may take it up again."[6] Therefore, since he had such great power, since he was preaching it in words, was showing it in deeds, what does it mean that Jesus did not trust himself to them, as if they were going to harm him against his will, as if they were going to do something to him against his will, especially since they had already believed in his name?

(4) And the Evangelist says, "They believed in his name," about the very men about whom he says, "But Jesus did not trust himself to them." Why? "Since he knew all men, and because he did not need anyone to give testimony of man, for he himself knew what was in man." The artist knew more what was in his work than the work [knew] what was in itself. The creator of man knew what was in man, which created man himself did not know. Do we not prove this about Peter, that he did not know what was in himself when he said, "even to death with you"?[7] Hear that the Lord knew what was in man. You with me even to death? "Amen, amen, I say to you, before the cock crows, you will deny me three times."[8] The man, therefore, did not know what was in himself, but the creator of the man knew what was in the man.

(5) Nevertheless many believed in his name and Jesus himself did not trust himself to them. What are we saying, brothers? Perhaps the subsequent words will indicate to us what the mystery of these words means. That men had believed in him is clear, is true; no one doubts it, the gospel says it, the truthful Evangelist attests it. Likewise that Jesus himself was not trusting himself to them, this, too, is clear and no Christian doubts it, because both this gospel says it and the same truthful Evangelist attests it. Why then did they believe in his name and Jesus did not trust himself to them? Let us see the subsequent words.

3. "Now there was a man of the Pharisees, Nicodemus by name, a ruler of the Jews. This man came to him at night and said to him, 'Rabbi.'" You already know that Rabbi

6. Cf. Jn 10.17–18.
7. Cf. Lk 22.33; Mt 26.35; Mk 14.31; Jn 13.37.
8. Cf. Mt 26.34; Mk 14.30; Lk 22.34; Jn 13.38.

means "Teacher." " 'We know that you have come as a teacher from God, for no one can do these signs you do unless God be with him.' " Therefore, this Nicodemus was one of those who had believed in his name, seeing the signs and wonders which he was doing.

(2) For earlier [the gospel] said this: "Now when he was at Jerusalem at the Passover on the feast day, many believed in his name." Why did they believe? [The gospel] continues and says, "seeing the signs and wonders which he was doing." And about Nicodemus what does it say? "There was a ruler of the Jews, by name Nicodemus. This man came to him at night and said to him, 'Rabbi, we know that you have come as a teacher from God.' " This man, too, therefore, had believed in his name. And for what reason had he himself believed? [The gospel] continues, "For no one can do these signs that you do unless God be with him." Therefore if Nicodemus was one of those many who had believed in his name, let us now consider in this Nicodemus why Jesus did not trust himself to them.

(3) "Jesus answered and said to him, 'Amen, amen, I say to you, unless a man be born again, he cannot see the kingdom of God.' " Therefore Jesus trusts himself to those who have been born again. Look, those men believed in him, and Jesus did not trust himself to them. Such are all catechumens; they themselves now believe in Christ's name, but Jesus does not trust himself to them.

(4) Pay attention, my beloved people, and understand. If we say to a catechumen, "Do you believe in Christ?" he answers, "I do believe" and signs himself. He already carries the cross of Christ on his forehead and is not ashamed of the Lord's cross.[9] Look, he has believed in his name. Let us ask him, "Do you eat the flesh of the Son of man and drink the blood of the Son of man?" He does not know what we are saying because Jesus has not trusted himself to him.

4. Therefore, since Nicodemus was of that number, he came to the Lord; but he came at night, and perhaps this is

9. Cf. *Tractate* 3.2.

a relevant consideration. He came to the Lord, and he came at night; he came to light, and he came in darkness. But what do they who have been born again of water and the Holy Spirit hear from the Apostle? "You were once darkness, but now light in the Lord. Walk as children of the light."[10]

(2) And again, "But let us, who are of the day, be sober."[11] They who have been born again, therefore, were of the night and are of the day; they were darkness and are light. Jesus now trusts himself to them, and they do not come to Jesus at night as Nicodemus did; they do not seek the day in darkness. For now, too, such men profess; Jesus has approached them and worked salvation in them, because he said, "Unless a man eats my flesh and drinks my blood, he will not have life in him."[12] And because catechumens have the sign of the cross on their foreheads, they are already from the great house; but let them become sons from servants. For they are not to be thought of as nothing who already belong to the great house.

(3) But when did the people of Israel eat manna? When they crossed the Red Sea. But what does the Red Sea signify? Hear the Apostle: "For I would not have you ignorant, brothers, that our fathers were all under the cloud, and all passed through the sea."[13] Why did they pass through the sea? As if you were asking him, he continued and said, "and all were baptized through Moses in the cloud and the sea."[14] If, therefore, the figure of the sea has such value, how much value has the actuality of baptism? If that which was done figuratively led the people who had been crossed over to manna, what will Christ make manifest to us in the truth of his baptism, when his people have been crossed over through him? Through his baptism he has crossed over the believers, and all their sins, enemies pursuing them, so to speak, were destroyed, just as all the Egyptians perished in that sea.

(4) Where does he cross over to, brothers? Where does Jesus, whose figure Moses represented, who was crossing over

---

10. Cf. Eph 5.8.
11. Cf. 1 Thes 5.8.
12. Cf. Jn 6.54 (NAB 6.53).
13. 1 Cor 10.1.
14. 1 Cor 10.2.

through the sea, [where does Jesus] cross over to through baptism? Where does he cross over to? To manna. What is manna? "I am," he said, "the living bread who have come down from heaven."[15] The faithful, already crossed over through the Red Sea, receive the manna. Why the Red Sea? A sea, yes, but why also red? That Red Sea signified the baptism of Christ. How is the baptism of Christ red unless consecrated by the blood of Christ? Where, then, does he lead the believers and the baptized? To manna.

(5) Look, I say manna. It is well known what the Jews, that people of Israel, received; it is well known what God rained upon them from the sky. And the catechumens do not know what Christians receive! Let them pass over through the Red Sea; let them eat manna so that, as they have believed in Jesus' name, so Jesus may trust himself to them.

5. Pay attention, then, my brothers, to what answers that man who came to Jesus at night gives. Although he came to Jesus, yet, because he came at night, he still speaks from the darkness of his flesh. He does not understand what he hears from the Lord; he does not understand what he hears from the light "which enlightens every man who comes into the world."[16] The Lord already said to him, "Unless a man be born again, he will not see the kingdom of God."

(2) "Nicodemus said to him, 'How can a man be born when he is old?'" The Spirit speaks to him, and he understands flesh; he understands his own flesh because he does not yet understand Christ's flesh. For when the Lord Jesus said, "Unless a man eats my flesh and drinks my blood, he will not have life in him," some who were following him were scandalized and said among themselves, "This saying is hard. Who can listen to it?"[17] For they thought Jesus was saying this, that they could cut him up in pieces like a lamb, cook him, and eat him; shuddering at his words, they went away and

15. Cf. Jn 6.51. But it should be noted that in the Latin the relative clause is in the first person: "I am the living bread, [I] who have come down from heaven."

16. Cf. Jn 1.9.

17. Cf. Jn 6.54 and 61 (NAB 6.53 and 60).

followed him no more. So the Evangelist says, "And the Lord himself remained with the Twelve; and they said to him 'Lord, look, they have departed from you.' And he said, 'Do you also wish to go away?'"[18] He wanted to show that he was necessary for them, they were not necessary for Christ.

(3) Let no one suppose that he puts Christ in fear when he is told that he should be a Christian, as if Christ will be more blessed if you are a Christian. To be a Christian is good for you; but now if you are not a Christian, it will not be an evil for Christ. Hear the word of the Psalm: "I have said to the Lord, 'You are my God, for you do not need my goods.'"[19] Thus "You are my God, for you do not need my goods." If you are without God, you will be less; if you are with God, God will not be greater. He is not greater with you, but you are less without him. Therefore grow in him; do not withdraw yourself so that, as it were, he may be diminished. You will be remade if you approach; you will be diminished if you retire. If you approach, he remains undiminished; and if you fall, he remains undiminished.

(4) Therefore when he had said to the apostles, "Do you also wish to go away?" Peter, that rock, answered with the voice of all, "Lord, to whom shall we go? You have the words of everlasting life."[20] The flesh of the Lord was well savored in his mouth. But the Lord explained to them, and said, "It is the spirit that gives life."[21] When he had said, "Unless a man eats my flesh and drinks my blood, he will not have life in him," that they might not understand it in terms of the flesh, he said, "It is the Spirit that gives life; but the flesh profits nothing. The words that I have spoken to you are spirit and life."[22]

6. This Nicodemus who had come to Jesus at night did not understand this spirit and this life. Jesus said to him, "Unless a man be born again, he will not see the kingdom of God."

18. Cf. Jn 6.67–68. Only the last part of the attributed quotation is actually in the text of John.
19. Cf. Ps 15.2.
20. Cf. Jn 6.68–69 (NAB 6.67–68).
21. Cf. Jn 6.65 (NAB 6.63).   22. Ibid.

And that man, understanding his own flesh, in whose mouth the flesh of Christ was not yet savored, said, "How can a man, when he is old, be born again? Can he enter a second time into his mother's womb and be born?" He knew only one birth from Adam and Eve; he did not yet know [the birth] from God and the Church. He knew only the parents who beget for death; he did not yet know the parents who beget for life. He knew only the parents who beget those who will succeed them; he did not yet know the parents who, living forever, beget those who will remain. Therefore, although there are two births, he knew one. One is from earth, the other from heaven; one is from the flesh, the other from the Spirit; one is from mortality, the other from eternity; one is from male and female, the other from God and Church. But these two are each single; neither the one nor the other can be repeated.

(2) Nicodemus rightly understood birth of the flesh; so too, understand, you, birth of the spirit, just as Nicodemus understood birth of the flesh. What did Nicodemus understand? "Can a man enter a second time into the womb of his mother and be born?" So, whoever says to you that you may be born a second time spiritually, answer what Nicodemus said, "Can a man enter a second time into the womb of his mother and be born?" I have already been born from Adam; Adam cannot beget me a second time. I have already been born from Christ; Christ cannot beget me a second time. Just as the womb cannot be sought again, so neither can baptism.

7. He who is born from the Catholic church is born, as it were, from Sara, a free woman; he who is born from heresy, as it were, is born from a bond woman, but still from the seed of Abraham. My beloved people, observe how great a mystery [is here].

(2) God gives witness and says, "I am the God of Abraham, the God of Isaac, and the God of Jacob."[23] Were there not other patriarchs? Was not Noe a holy man before these, who alone in the whole human race together with his whole house

23. Cf. Ex 3.6.

deserved to be delivered from the Flood, in whom and in his sons the Church is represented? They escape the Flood, with wood carrying them.[24] And then afterwards [come] the great men whom we know, whom Holy Scripture commends, Moses faithful in all his house.[25] And those three are named, as if they alone were deserving of him: "I am the God of Abraham, the God of Isaac, and the God of Jacob; this is my name forever."[26]

(3) An enormous mystery! The Lord has the power to open both our mouths and your hearts that we may be able to speak as he has deigned to reveal and that you may be able to grasp as it is advantageous for you.

8. Therefore those patriarchs are three, Abraham, Isaac, and Jacob. You already know that the sons of Jacob were twelve and from them are the people of Israel because Jacob himself is Israel and the people of Israel are the twelve tribes belonging to the twelve sons of Israel. Abraham, Isaac, and Jacob, three fathers and one people. Three fathers, as it were, in the beginning of the people; three fathers in whom the people was prefigured. And the earlier people itself [is] the present people. For in the people of the Jews the people of the Christians was prefigured. There a figure, here the truth; there a shadow, here the body, as the Apostle says, "Now these things happened to them in figure." It is the Apostle's voice and he says, "They were written for us, upon whom the end of the world has come."[27]

(2) Let your mind recur to Abraham, Isaac, and Jacob. In those three we find free women giving birth and bondwomen giving birth; we find there the progeny of free women, we find there also the progeny of bondwomen. The bondwoman signifies nothing good. "Cast out the bondwoman," [Scripture] says, "and her son; for the son of the bondwoman will not be heir with the son of the free woman."[28] The Apostle mentions this;[29] and in these two sons of Abraham the Apostle says was a figure of the two testaments, Old and New. To

24. Cf. Gn 7.7.
25. Cf. Nm 12.7: Heb 3.2.
26. Cf. Ex 3.6 and 15.
27. Cf. 1 Cor 10.11.
28. Cf. Gn 21.10.
29. Cf. Gal 4.21–31.

the Old Testament belong the lovers of temporal things, the lovers of the world; to the New Testament belong the lovers of eternal life. Therefore that Jerusalem on earth was a shadow of the heavenly Jerusalem, the mother of us all, which is in heaven. And these are the Apostle's words. And about that city from which we are sojourners you know many things, you have already heard many things. Now we find something remarkable in these births, that is, in these offspring, in these procreations of free women and bondwomen, namely four types of men; and in these four types of men is comprised the figure of the Christian people, so that what was said in regard to these three is not astonishing: "I am the God of Abraham, the God of Isaac, and the God of Jacob."[30]

(3) For notice, brothers, among all Christians, either good are born from evil, or evil are born from good, or good from good, or evil from evil; you cannot find more than these four types. I shall repeat them again. Pay attention, retain [them]. Stir your hearts; don't be slothful. Take in, lest you be taken in,[31] how there are four types of all Christians. Either good are born from good, or evil are born from evil, or evil from good, or good from evil. I think that it is clear. Good from good, if both those who baptize are good and those who are baptized believe rightly and are numbered rightly in the members of Christ. Evil from evil, if both those who baptize are evil and those who are baptized approach God with double-dealing heart and do not keep those moral practices which they hear in the Church that they may be there, not chaff, but grain. For how many they are, you know, my beloved people. The good from the evil; sometimes an adulterer baptizes and he who is baptized is justified. The evil from the good; sometimes they who baptize are saints but they who are baptized are unwilling to keep the way of God.

9. I think, brothers, that it is well known in the Church and that what we are saying is manifested by daily examples; but let us consider in our forefathers that they had these four

30. Cf. Ex 3.6.
31. I.e., "Understand, so that you may not be deceived, . . ."

types also. The good from the good; Ananias baptized Paul.[32] What about the evil from the evil? The Apostle mentions certain preachers of the gospel whom he says were accustomed to proclaim the gospel impurely, whom he tolerates in the Christian community, and says, "But what of it? Provided only that in every way, whether by occasion or by truth Christ is being proclaimed, and in this I rejoice."[33] Was he malevolent and did he rejoice in another's evil?[34] No, but because truth was being preached by evil men, and Christ was being preached by the mouths of evil men, if they baptized any like themselves, evil baptized evil; if they baptized any such as the Lord admonishes when he says, "Do what they say; but do not do what they do,"[35] evil baptized good. The good baptized the evil, as Simon Magus was baptized by Philip, a holy man.[36]

(2) These four types, therefore, my brothers, are well known. Look, I repeat them again. Hold fast to them, count them, pay attention to them. Beware those types which are evil; hold fast to those which are good. The good are born from the good when holy men are baptized by holy men; the evil from the evil when both they who baptize and they who are baptized live wickedly and impiously; the good from the evil when they who baptize are evil and they who are baptized are good; and the evil from the good when they who baptize are good and they who are baptized are evil.

10. How do we find these types in these three names; "I am the God of Abraham, the God of Isaac, and the God of Jacob"?[37] We take bondwomen among the evil; we take free women among the good. Free women bear good men; Sara bore Isaac.[38] Bondwomen bear evil men; Agar bore Ismael.[39] We have in Abraham alone both that type when good [are] from good and that type when evil [are] from evil.

(2) Where are the evil from the good prefigured? Rebecca, the wife of Isaac, was a free woman; read it; she bore twins, one was good, the other evil. You have Scripture saying clearly

---

32. Cf. Acts 9.10–18.
33. Cf. Phil 1.17–18.
34. Cf. *Tractate* 5.19.
35. Cf. Mt 23.3.
36. Cf. Acts 8.13.
37. Cf. Ex 3.6.
38. Cf. Gn 21.2–3.
39. Cf. Gn 16.15.

by the voice of God, "I loved Jacob, but hated Esau."[40] Rebecca begot these two, Jacob and Esau; one of them is chosen, the other is reproached; one succeeds to the inheritance, the other is disinherited. God does not make his people from Esau, but he makes it from Jacob. One seed, but they who were conceived were different; one womb, but they who were born were different. Can it be said that the woman who bore Esau as a free woman bore Jacob as a woman not free? They were wrestling in the womb of their mother, and it was said to Rebecca, when they were wrestling there, "Two peoples are in your womb."[41] Two men, two peoples, a good people, an evil people; but still they are wrestling in one womb.

(3) How many evil men there are in the Church! And one womb carries them until they are separated in the end. And the good shout against the evil, and the evil shout back against the good, and both are wrestling in the bowels of the one. Will they be together always? In the end there is an issuing forth[42] into the light and the birth which is prefigured here in a mystery is made clear and then it will appear: "I loved Jacob, but hated Esau."

11. We have, therefore, brothers, already found the good from the good, Isaac from the free woman; and the evil from the evil, Ismael from the bondwoman; and the evil from the good, Esau from Rebecca. Where shall we find the good from the evil? Jacob remains so that the completion of those four types may be accomplished in the three patriarchs.

(2) Jacob had free women as wives; he also had bondwomen.[43] The free women bore, and the bondwomen bore; and there came to be the twelve sons of Israel. If you reckon from whom all of them were born, not all were born from free women, not all from bondwomen, but yet all from one seed. What then, my brothers? They who were born from the bondwomen, did they not possess the land of promise together with their brothers? We find there that good sons were born

---

40. Cf. Mal 1.2–3; Rom 9.6–13.   41. Cf. Gn 25.22–23.
42. The metaphor of giving birth is continued here; the issuing forth is from the darkness of the internal womb into the light of the external world.
43. Cf. Gn 29; 30.1–24; 35.16–26.

to Jacob from the bondwomen and good sons were born to Jacob from the free women. Their birth from the womb of bondwomen was no obstacle to them when they acknowledged their seed in their father, and consequently they held the kingdom with their brothers. Therefore, as there was no obstacle among the sons of Jacob for those who were born from bondwomen to their holding domain and receiving the land of promise equally with their brothers—birth from bondwomen was not an obstacle for them, but their paternal seed prevailed—so whoever are baptized from evil men seem, as it were, to be born from bondwomen, but still because they are from the seed of the Word of God which is prefigured in Jacob, let them not be saddened; they will possess the inheritance together with their brothers.

(3) Therefore, let him who is born from good seed be untroubled; only let him not imitate the bondwoman, if he is born from a bondwoman. Do not imitate the evil bondwoman who is being proud. For why did the sons of Jacob, born from the bondwomen possess the land of promise with their brothers, but Ismael, born from a bondwoman, was expelled from his inheritance? Why, except that he was proud and they were humble? He acted haughtily and wanted to mislead his brother, playing with him.

12. There is a great mystery there. Ismael and Isaac were playing together. Sara saw them playing and said to Abraham, "Cast out the bondwoman and her son, for the son of the bondwoman shall not be heir with my son Isaac."[44] And when Abraham was saddened, God confirmed for him the word of his wife. Here now the mystery is manifest, because that event was pregnant with some future thing. She saw them playing and says "Cast out the bondwoman and her son."

(2) What does this mean, brothers? For what evil had Ismael done to the boy Isaac because he was playing with him? But that playing was mockery;[45] that playing signified deception.

44. Gn 21.10.
45. There is a word play in the Latin: *illa lusio illusio erat*, "that playing was a playing upon." The common meaning of *illusio*, however, is "mockery"

For, my beloved people, observe a great mystery. The Apostle calls that persecution; he calls that same playing, that same play, persecution. For he says, "But as then he who was born according to the flesh persecuted him who was according to the spirit, so also it is now."[46] That is, they who are born according to the flesh persecute those who are born according to the spirit.

(3) Who are born according to the flesh? The lovers of the world, the devotees of this life. Who are born according to the spirit? The devotees of the kingdom of heaven, the lovers of Christ, longing for eternal life, worshipping God without seeking recompense. They play, and the Apostle says persecution. For after the Apostle said these words, "But as then he who was born according to the flesh persecuted him who was according to the spirit, so also is it now," he continued and showed about what persecution he was speaking: "But what does Scripture say? 'Cast out bondwoman and her son, for the son of the bondwoman shall not be heir with my son Isaac.'"[47]

(4) We ask where Scripture says this so that we may see whether any persecution of Ismael against Isaac preceded, and we find that this was said by Sara when she saw the boys playing together. And the playing, which Scripture says that Sara saw, the Apostle calls this persecution. Therefore they persecute you more who mislead you by deceit: "Come, come be baptized here; here you have true baptism."

---

or "deceit"; hence the translation in the text. For a nearly identical expression and a more extended discussion of this passage from *Genesis*, see Augustine, *Sermones De Scripturis* or *De Vetere Testamento* 3 (PL 38.34–35). This fragment of a sermon, however, may well belong to Bede (see CCL 41.17), and not to Augustine. Nevertheless, it provides a key to understanding the interpretation given in this text since it must reflect a common interpretation of this Old Testament story among the Latin Fathers. This interpretation obviously derived from Paul, Gal 4.29, which Augustine cites here, who saw Ishmael's play as persecution by the worldly of the spiritual; Paul, in turn, probably based his interpretation on Rabbinic tradition which saw an evil intent in the playing (see E. Maly, JBC 1.22). For example, among the Fathers who commented on *Genesis*, Jerome, *Hebraicae Quaestiones in Libro Geneseos* 21.9–10 (CCL 72.24), accepts the pejorative connotation and attributes it to Hebraic exegesis; Origen, *Homilies on Genesis* 7.3 (PG 12.200–201; SC 7bis (1976) 203–205; and FOTC 71.130–131), explains why Paul saw the play as persecution but also indicates that the text allows for a neutral interpretation.

46. Gal 4.29.   47. Cf. Gal 4.30.

(5) Do not play. There is one true [baptism]; that other one is play. You will be misled and this persecution will be grievous for you. It would be better for you that you converted Ismael to the kingdom; but Ismael doesn't wish it because he wishes to play. But you, hold fast the inheritance of your father, and hear: "Cast out the bondwoman and her son; for the son of the bondwoman shall not be heir with my son Isaac."

13. These men, too, dare to say that they are accustomed to suffer persecution from Catholic kings or Catholic rulers. What persecution do they endure? Distress of body; nevertheless if they have sometimes suffered or somehow they have suffered, let them themselves know and let them address their own consciences. Nevertheless they have suffered distress of body; the persecution which they conduct is more serious. Beware when Ismael wants to play with Isaac, when he flatters you; when he offers another baptism, answer, "I already have baptism." For if this baptism is true, he, who wants to give you another, wants to deceive you. Beware of the persecutor of the soul. For if the party of Donatus has, at some time, suffered something from Catholic rulers, it suffered in the body, not in a deceiving of the spirit.

(2) Hear and see in these ancient deeds all the signs and tokens of future things. Sara is found to have harassed Agar, the bondwoman; Sara is a free woman. After the bondwoman began to be haughty, Sara complained to Abraham and said, "Cast out your bondwoman; she has become arrogant toward me."[48] And the woman complained about Abraham as if it had been done by Abraham. But Abraham, who, as regards the bondwoman, was held, not by a lust for abusing her but by the duty of producing children, because Sara had given her to him that he might have an offspring from her, said to her, "Look, [she is] your bondwoman; use her as you wish."[49] And Sara harassed her grievously and she fled from her face.

(3) See, a free woman harassed a bondwoman, and the Apostle does not call that persecution; the servant plays with his master, and he calls it persecution. This harassment is not

48. Cf. Gn 21.10 and 16.5.   49. Cf. Gn 16.6.

called persecution, but that playing is called persecution. What do you think, brothers? You do understand what was meant, don't you? So then, when God wishes to stir up the authorities against heretics, against schismatics, against the disintegrators of the Church, against the rejecters of Christ,[50] against the blasphemers of baptism, let them not be astonished, because God urges that Agar be beaten[51] by Sara.

(4) Let Agar recognize herself, let her bow her neck, because when she departed in humiliation from her mistress, an angel met her and said, "What is the matter, Agar, bondwoman of Sara?" When she complained about her mistress, what did she hear from the angel? "Return to your mistress."[52] For this reason, therefore, is she harassed, that she may return. And would that she return; for her child, like the sons of Jacob, will hold the inheritance with his brothers.

14. But they are amazed because the Christian authorities are stirred up against the detestable disintegrators of the

50. In the Latin *exsufflatores Christi*. The Donatists apparently retained an exorcism rite when rebaptizing converts from both the Catholics and the other Donatist sects; there was a "blowing out" of the devil by breathing upon the face and ears. "Insufflation" or "exsufflation" was a normal part of the baptismal liturgy, but African Catholic Christians, and particularly Augustine, were incensed at this practice as part of rebaptism because it implied that orthodox baptism was the work of the devil. The root word was so often used that it practically lost its literal meaning and simply connoted desecration. See, e.g., in Augustine's writings, *Epistulae* 34.3, 43.8.21 and 24, and 51.5 (PL 33.132, 170, 172, 193; CSEL 34(1).24–25, 102–103, 106, 148); *Contra Epistulam Parmeniani* 2.18.38, 3.4.21, and 3.6.29 (PL 43.80, 91 and 108; CSEL 51.93–94, 125–127, 136–141); *De Baptismo Contra Donatistas* 4.15.22 and 6.20.34–35 (PL 43.168 and 210; CSEL 51.247–249, 317); *Opus Imperfectum Contra Iulianum* 3.182 (PL 45.1323; CSEL 85(1).481–482). See Browne, 177; Blaise, 337; and TLL, s.v. *exsufflatio, exsufflator,* and *exsufflo,* 5.2.1943–1944.

51. In *Sermones De Scripturis* or *De Vetere Testamento* 3, mentioned above in note 45, Augustine writes, *Fugit a facie Sarae illa, et affligebat eam Sara. Quid mirum? Affligebat eam corporaliter:* "She fled from Sara's face, indeed Sara was afflicting her. What wonder? She was afflicting her physically." Even if this sermon is not genuine, it is obviously an accepted interpretation among later Latin Fathers that Sara's abuse of Agar was physical as well as verbal, although the Old Testament text does not necessarily suggest physical abuse. At any rate this *Tractate* clearly interprets the "affliction" since the next sentence applies the lesson of the passage to the *afflictio* suffered by the Donatists who maintained they suffered physical persecution.

52. Cf. Gn 16.7–9.

Church. Should they not, then, be stirred up? And how would they render account of their rule to God? Pay attention, my beloved people, to what I say; for it is the proper role of the Christian kings of the world that they desire that their mother, the Church, from whom they are born spiritually, achieve peace in their times.

(2) We read about the visions and prophetic deeds of Daniel. Three young men in the fire praised the Lord. Nabuchodnosor, the king, was amazed at the youths praising God and at the fire, harmless around them. And when he was amazed, what did Nabuchodnosor, the king, say, neither a Jew nor circumcised, he who had erected a statue of himself and compelled all to adore it, yet moved by the praises of the three youths, when he saw the majesty of God present in the fire, what did he say? "And I shall make a decree for all the tribes and languages in all the land." What kind of decree? "Whoever blaspheme the God of Sidrac, Misac, and Abdenago will be destroyed and their houses ruined."[53] Look, how does a foreign king vent his rage that the God of Israel not be blasphemed because he could free three boys from the fire, and they do not want Christian kings to vent their rage because Christ is rejected, by whom, not three boys, but the world together with the kings themselves is freed from the fire of Gehenna?

(3) For those three boys, my brothers, were freed from temporal fire. Is he not the God of the Maccabees who was also [God] of the three youths? The ones he freed from the fire; the others expired in body amid fiery torments, but remained faithful in spirit in the commands of the Law. The ones were freed openly; the others were crowned secretly.[54] It is a greater thing to be freed from the flame of Gehenna than from the furnace of human authority. Therefore if Nabuchodnosor, the king, praised and acclaimed and gave glory to God because he freed three youths from fire, and gave such great glory that he sent throughout his kingdom a decree, "Whoever blaspheme the God of Sidrac, Misac, and Abdenago will be de-

53. Cf. Dn 3.96.   54. Cf. 2 Mc 7.

stroyed and their houses ruined," how could these kings not be stirred up who behold, not three boys freed from flame, but themselves freed from Gehenna, when they see Christ, by whom they were freed, rejected among Christians, when they hear it said to a Christian, "Say you are not a Christian"?[55] They want to do such things, but of course they don't want to suffer such things.

15. For see what kind of things they do and what kind of things they suffer. They kill souls; they are afflicted in their bodies. They cause eternal deaths; and they complain that they suffer temporal ones.[56] And yet what deaths do they suffer? They tell us about some martyr or other of theirs in a persecution.[57] Look, Marculus[58] was hurled headlong from a rock! Look, Donatus of Bagai[59] was cast into a well! When

55. Cf. Tractate 5.13.   56. Cf. Tractate 5.12.

57. "On conversion the Donatist Christian . . . had the Bible on his lips and martyrdom in his soul." W. Frend, *Martyrdom and Persecution in the Early Church* (Oxford, 1965), 155. Cf. Tractate 6.23; P. Monceaux, *Histoire littéraire de l'Afrique chrétienne* 4 (Paris, 1912) 149–150, 5 (Paris, 1920) 35–47.

58. In 347 A.D. an imperial commission, composed of Macarius and Paulus, was sent to Africa by the Emperor Constans to restore ecclesiastical unity. At Vegesela in central Numidia where Donatism was strongest, they met with ten Donatist bishops who offered such tumultuous resistance that the angered commissioners had them flogged. One bishop, Felicianus, may have died from the flogging; eight others moderated. But Marculus was arrested for continued resistance. At nearby Bagai Donatist armed men fought a bloody battle against the Roman troops and were defeated. To discourage further opposition the commissioners had Marculus marched through Numidia and imprisoned at Nova Petra where on Nov. 29, 347 A.D., he was executed by being thrown from a cliff, according to the *Passio Marculi* which describes this whole event from the Donatist viewpoint (PL 8.758–766). A Catholic interpretation is given by Optatus of Milevis, 3.6 (CSEL 26.86–87). Cf. W. Frend, *The Donatist Church* (Oxford, 1952), 179, 184–185; G. Willis, *Saint Augustine and the Donatist Heresy* (London, 1950), 10, 14; S. Simpson, *St. Augustine and African Church Divisions* (London, 1910), 35–37; Monceaux, 5.69–81; Berrouard, *Homélies sur l'évangile de saint Jean I–XVI*, BA 71 (1969) 925–926.

59. In reaction to the commission mentioned in the previous note, Donatus, bishop of Bagai, summoned a band of Circumcellions to Bagai and a fierce battle ensued. The Donatists were defeated and Donatus apparently arrested. The exact circumstances of his death are unclear, whether he was executed or committed suicide. Monceaux, basing his argument on Optatus' use of the Latin word *occidere*, "to kill by striking down," holds that he was either killed in the battle or afterwards executed as a rebel and that his remains were thrown down the well to prevent fanatical partisans from taking

have Roman authorities decreed such punishments that men be hurled headlong? But what do our people answer? I do not know what was done; nevertheless what do our people hand down? That they hurled themselves headlong and defamed the authorities. Let us remember the normal practice of the Roman authorities, and let us see who is to be believed.

(2) Our people say that they hurled themselves headlong; if they are not the very disciples of those who now hurl themselves headlong from rocks, with no one persecuting them, let us not believe it. What wonder if those men did what they usually do? For the Roman authorities have never used such punishment. For could they not put them to death openly? But those men who wanted themselves to be honored after death did not find a death more likely to bring fame. In short, whatever the fact is, I do not know. And if you have suffered, O party of Donatus, bodily affliction from the Catholic church, you are Agar, having suffered at the hands of Sara. "Return to your mistress."[60]

(3) A vitally important passage has kept us somewhat too long to be in any way able to expound the whole text of the gospel reading. My beloved brothers, let it be enough for now that these things which have been said not be excluded from your hearts, by the utterance of other things. Hold them fast, say such things. Go forth from here, inflamed; enkindle the unresponsive.

relics. Cf. Monceaux, 5.81–82; Frend, *Donatist Church*, 178–179; Berrouard, *Homélies I–XVI*, 925–926; Optatus of Milevis, 3.4, 6 (CSEL 26.81–87); Augustine, *Contra Litteras Petiliani*, 2.20.46 (PL 43.274; CSEL 52.46–47).

60. Cf. Gn 16.9.

TRACTATE 12

On John 3.6–21

E UNDERSTAND THAT it is because we excited your attention yesterday, my beloved people, that you have assembled more eagerly and in greater numbers.[1] But, if it pleases, let us, for the present settle our account with the sermon owed to the gospel reading next in order. Then, my beloved people, you will hear about the peace of the Church, either what we have done or what we hope will still be done.[2]

(2) Therefore, now concentrate the whole attention of your heart on the gospel, and let no one's thoughts be elsewhere. For if he who gives his whole attention scarcely grasps, he who divides himself by diverse thoughts dissipates even what he had grasped, doesn't he? But you remember, my beloved people, that on last Sunday, as far as the Lord deigned to help us, we discussed spiritual rebirth;[3] and we have had this reading read to you again so that, in the name of Christ, with the help of your prayers, we might complete what was not said then.

1. *Tractate* 12 followed *En in Ps* 133 and this is the sermon referred to here. *Tractate* 11 was followed by *En in Ps* 132 and 133. See Le Landais, 26 and 35; La Bonnardière, 50; and Berrouard, *Homélies I–XVI*, 628.
2. This is not done in these *Tractates* and it is not at all clear what Augustine has in mind here. Perhaps, as Berrouard, *Homélies I–XVI*, 628–29, suggests, the actions mentioned in *Epistulae* 86–89 (PL 33.296–313; CSEL 34(1).396–425; and FOTC 18.11–40) are what he refers to here. For example in *Letter* 86, sent to the imperial Prefect of the Province of Africa, Caecilius, he requests intervention in the region; or, in *Letter* 88 he requests that Januarius, the Donatist bishop of Casae Nigrae in Numidia, come personally to witness the cruel violence of the Circumcellions against Catholic Christians, a violence which has compelled them to appeal to the government when they would prefer peaceful resolution of disagreements.
3. I.e., in *Tractate* 11.

2. Spiritual rebirth is one, as physical birth is one. And what Nicodemus said to the Lord, he said truly because a man cannot, when he is old, return again into his mother's womb and be born. He certainly said that a man when he is old cannot do this, as if he could even if he were an infant. For it is not at all possible whether fresh from the womb or already along in years, for a person to return again into his mother's womb and be born. But as the woman's womb in carnal birth is capable of giving birth [to each child] a single time, so the Church's womb is capable of spiritual birth so that each one is baptized a single time. And for this reason that no one, perhaps, may say, "But that one was born in heresy and this one was born in schism." All these arguments have been cut away, if you recall what was discussed with you about our three fathers of whom [God] willed to be called the God, not because they were the only ones, but because in them alone was fulfilled completely the prefiguration of a people yet to come.

(2) For we found one born of a bondwoman who was disinherited and one born of a free woman who was an heir; again we found one born of a free woman who was disinherited and one born of a bondwoman who was an heir. Ismael, born of a bondwoman, was disinherited;[4] Isaac, born of a free woman, was an heir.[5] Esau, born of a free woman, was disinherited;[6] the sons of Jacob, born of bondwomen, were heirs.[7] And so in those three fathers the figure of the whole people yet to come was discerned, and not without reason did God say, "I am the God of Abraham, the God of Isaac, and the God of Jacob. This," he said, "is my name forever."[8]

(3) Let us even more remember what was promised to Abraham himself; for this was promised to Isaac, this was promised also to Jacob.[9] What do we find? "In your seed all the nations will be blessed."[10]

---

4. Cf. Gn 21.9–14.   5. Cf. Gn 25.5.
6. Cf. Gn 27.30–41.   7. Cf. Gn 49.
8. Cf. Ex 3.6 and 15.
9. Cf. Gn 22.18, 26.4, and 28.13–14.
10. Cf. Gn 22.18.

(4) Then one man believed what he did not yet see; men see and are blind. It has been accomplished in the nations what was promised to one man, and they are separated from the communion of the nations who are unwilling to see even what has been fulfilled. But what does it profit them that they are unwilling to see? They see, whether they will or not. The open truth strikes even closed eyes.

3. It was answered to Nicodemus, who was one of those who had believed in Jesus, "and Jesus did not trust himself to them." For he did not trust himself to certain ones although they already had believed in him. So you have it written, "Many believed in his name, seeing the signs which he did. But Jesus himself did not trust himself to them. For he needed not that any should give testimony of man; for he himself knew what was in man."[11] Look, they already believed in Jesus and Jesus himself did not trust himself to them. Why? Because they were not yet born again of water and the Spirit.

(2) From that we have encouraged and do encourage our brothers, the catechumens. For if you should ask them, they have already believed in Jesus; but because they do not yet receive his body and blood, Jesus has not yet trusted himself to them. What are they to do that Jesus may trust himself to them? Let them be born again of water and the Spirit; let the Church which is pregnant with them bring them forth. They have been conceived; let them be brought forth into the light. Let them have breasts whereat they may be nourished. Let them not fear that they may be choked after their birth. Let them not withdraw from their mother's breasts.

4. No man can return into his mother's womb and be born again. But is there someone born from a bondwoman? Were they who were then born from bondwomen returned into the womb of free women that they might be born again? The seed of Abraham was also in Ismael and his wife was the initiator of the idea that Abraham might be able to produce

11. Cf. Jn 2.23–25.

a son from a bondwoman.[12] He was born of the seed of the man, and not from the womb but from the consent only of the wife. Was he disinherited therefore because of the bondwoman? If he were disinherited precisely because he was born from a bondwoman, no sons of bondwomen would be admitted into inheritance. The sons of Jacob were admitted into inheritance; Ismael, however, was disinherited, not because he was born of a bondwoman, but because he was haughty to his mother, haughty toward the son of his mother.

(2) For Sara is more his mother than Agar. The one's womb was lent to be used, the other's will gave assent; Abraham would not do what Sara did not want. Therefore he is more the son of Sara. But because he was haughty toward his brother, haughty in playing because he was making fun of him, what did Sara say? "Cast out the bondwoman and her son, for the son of the bondwoman shall not be heir with my son Isaac."[13] Therefore the womb of the bondwoman did not cast him out, but stiff-neckedness in a servant.

(3) And if a free man should be haughty, he is a slave, and what is worse, the slave of an evil mistress, of haughtiness itself. Therefore, my brothers, answer to the man that a man cannot be born again; answer confidently that a man cannot be born again. Whatever is done over again is mockery; whatever is done over again is play. Ismael plays; let him be sent out. For Sara noticed them playing, Scripture says, and she said to Abraham, "Cast out the bondwoman and her son." The boys' play displeased Sara; she saw the boys playing something strange. Do not women who have sons desire to see their sons playing? She saw and disapproved. She saw something or other in the play; she saw mockery in the play. She noticed the servant's haughtiness; she was displeased, she cast him out. Wicked men born from bondwomen are sent out; and one born from a free woman is sent out, an Esau.

(4) Therefore let no one be presumptuous because he is born from the good; let no one be presumptuous because he

12. Augustine is referring to the fact that Sara, because she was barren, suggested Abraham's relationship with Agar. Cf. Gn 16.1-3 and *Tractate* 11.13.

13. Cf. Gn 21.10.

is baptized through holy men. He who is baptized through holy men, let him still take care lest he be not Jacob but Esau. Therefore I would say this, brothers: it is better to be baptized by men seeking their own interests and loving the world, which is what the name of bondwoman signifies, and to seek spiritually the inheritance of Christ that he may be like the son of Jacob from a bondwoman, rather than to be baptized through holy men and to be haughty so that as an Esau, although born from a free woman, he must be sent out.

(5) Hold these things fast, brothers. We do not coax you; do not place hope in us. We flatter neither ourselves nor you. Each one carries his own pack. It is our task to speak that we may not be adversely judged. It is your task to listen, and to listen with your heart, lest what we give be demanded of you, or rather, when it is demanded, that it be found profit, not loss.

5. The Lord says to Nicodemus and explains to him, "Amen, amen, I say to you, unless a man be born again of water and the Spirit, he cannot enter into the kingdom of God."[14] You, he says, understand carnal birth when you say, "Can a man return into his mother's womb?"[15] It is necessary that he be born again of water and the Spirit for the sake of the kingdom of God. If he is born for the sake of a temporal inheritance of a human father, let him be born from the womb of a carnal mother; if for the sake of the eternal inheritance of God, the Father, let him be born from the Church.

(2) A father, a man who will one day die, begets through his wife a son to succeed him; God begets from the Church sons, not to succeed him, but to remain with him.[16] And [the gospel] continues: "That which is born of the flesh is flesh, and that which is born of the Spirit is spirit." Therefore we are born spiritually, and in the Spirit we are born by word and sacrament. The Spirit is present that we may be born; the Spirit is present invisibly from whom you are born, be-

14. Cf. Jn 3.5.   15. Cf. Jn 3.4.
16. Cf. *Tractate* 7.7 and 11.6.

cause you too are born invisibly. For [the gospel] continues and says, "Do not wonder that I have said to you, 'You must be born again.' The Spirit[17] breathes where he will, and you hear his voice but do not know where he comes from or where he goes."

(3) No one sees the Spirit, and how do we hear the voice of the Spirit? A Psalm sounds forth; it is the Spirit's voice. The gospel sounds forth; it is the Spirit's voice. God's word sounds forth; it is the Spirit's voice. "You hear his voice, but do not know where he comes from or where he goes." But if you too should be born of the Spirit, you will be such that he who is not yet born of the spirit knows not about you where you come from and where you go. For he continues and says this, "So is everyone who is born of the Spirit."

6. "Nicodemus answered and said to him, 'How can these things be done?'" And in truth in their carnal meaning he did not understand. In him was happening what the Lord had said; he was hearing the Spirit's voice and he did not know where he had come from or where he was going.

(2) "Jesus answered and said to him, 'Are you a teacher in Israel and do not know these things?'" What, O brothers? Do we think that the Lord wanted, as it were, to taunt this teacher of the Jews? The Lord knew what he was doing; he wanted him to be born of the Spirit. No one is born of the Spirit unless he be humble, because humility itself causes us to be born of the Spirit, because the Lord is near to those crushed in heart.[18] That man was puffed up by his position as a teacher; and he seemed to himself to be of some importance because he was a scholar of the Jews. The Lord puts down his pride that he may be able to be born of the Spirit;

17. John 3.8 is a difficult verse to translate because the Hebrew, Aramaic, Greek, and Latin words for "spirit" also mean "breath" and "wind." Contemporary translators see the comparison between a physical effect and its unseen cause, and a spiritual effect and its unseen cause, as primary. They translate, "The wind blows where it will, and you hear its sound but do not know where it comes from or where it goes." But it is clear from this commentary that Augustine sees the Latin *spiritus* as the "Holy Spirit," even in verse 8.

18. Cf. Ps 33.19.

he taunts him as one unlearned, not because the Lord wants to seem superior.

(3) What is great, God compared to man, truth compared to falsehood? Christ is greater than Nicodemus: should this statement be made? Can it be made? Ought one think it? If Christ were said to be greater than angels, this would have to be laughed at; for he through whom every creature was made, is incomparably greater than every creature. But he is attacking the man's pride. "Are you a teacher in Israel and do not know these things?" It is as though he is saying, "Look, you know nothing, proud ruler; be born of the Spirit. For if you have been born of the Spirit, you will keep the ways of God that you may follow Christ's humility."

(4) For he is so high above all the angels that "although he was in the form of God, he thought it not robbery to be equal with God; but he emptied himself, taking the form of a servant, being made in the likeness of men, and in habit found as a man. He humbled himself, becoming obedient unto death" (and so that not any kind of death may please you) "even to the death of the cross."[19] He was hanging and he was being taunted. He could descend from the cross, but he deferred that he might arise again from the tomb. The Lord endured proud servants; the physician, the sick. If he [endured] this, what ought they [to endure] who ought to be born of the Spirit?—if he [endured] this, that true teacher in heaven, not only of men but also of angels, [what ought they to endure]?

(5) For if the angels have been taught, they have been taught by the Word of God. If they have been taught by the Word of God, seek by whom they have been taught and you will find, "In the beginning was the Word, and the Word was with God, and the Word was God."[20] Stiffneckedness[21] is taken from the man, but the coarse and hard neck, that the neck may be softened for carrying the yoke of Christ, about which it is said, "My yoke is easy, and my burden light."[22]

---

19. Cf. Phil 2.6–8. 20. Jn 1.1.

21. Augustine plays on the twofold connotation in Christian Latin of *cervix*, "neck" and "arrogant pride"; see Blaise, 145.

22. Cf. Mt 11.30.

7. And [the gospel] continues, "If I have spoken earthly things to you, and you do not believe, how will you believe if I shall speak to you heavenly things?" What earthly things did he speak, brothers? "Unless a man be born again." Is [that] an earthly thing? "The Spirit breathes where he will and you hear his voice but do not know where he comes from and where he goes." Is [that] an earthly thing? Yes, if he was speaking about that wind which you know, as some have understood,[23] when it was asked of them what earthly thing the Lord spoke when he said, "If I have spoken earthly things to you, and you do not believe, how will you believe if I shall speak to you heavenly things?" Therefore when it was asked of some what earthly thing the Lord spoke, experiencing difficulties, they said that in his words, "The Spirit breathes where he will and you hear his voice but do not know where he comes from and where he goes," he spoke about that wind which you know.

(2) For what earthly thing did he name? He was speaking about spiritual birth; he continued and said, "So is everyone who is born of the Spirit." Now, brothers, who of us would not see, for example, the south wind going from south to north, or another wind coming from east to west? How, then, do we not know where it comes from and where it goes? What earthly thing, then, did he speak which men did not believe?

(3) Can it be that which he had said about raising up the temple again?[24] For he had received his body from the earth and he was preparing to raise up the very earth taken from

---

23. The Latin word *spiritus* (or the Greek *tò pneûma*) is interpreted as the "wind," a normal meaning in Latin or Greek, by John Chrysostom, *Homiliae in Ioannem* 26 (PG 59.153–159; and FOTC 33.250–259); Cyrillus of Alexandria, *In Ioannis Evangelium* 2 (PG 73.245; P. E. Pusey, ed., *Sancti Patris Nostri Cyrilli Archiepiscopi Alexandrini in D. Joannis Evangelium* (Brussels, 1965) 1.220–221); Theophylactus, *Ennaratio in Evangelium Ioannis* (PG 123.1205) and Pseudo-Augustine (Ambrosiaster), *Quaestiones Veteris et Novi Testamenti* 59 (PL 35.2254–2256; CSEL 50.105–107). In interpreting it as the Holy Spirit Augustine agrees with Ambrose, *De Fide* 2.47 (PL 16.592; CSEL 78.72), and the greater number of Fathers; see Berrouard, *Homélies I–XVI*, 926–927. Cf. section 5, note 17.

24. Cf. Jn 2.19.

earthly body.[25] For it was not believed that he was going to raise up earth. He said, "If I have spoken earthly things to you, and you do not believe, how will you believe if I shall speak to you heavenly things?" That is, if you do not believe that I can raise up the temple thrown down by you, how will you believe that men can be reborn through the Spirit?

8. And [the gospel] continues: "And no one has ascended into heaven but he who has descended from heaven, the Son of man who is in heaven." Look, he was here, and he was in heaven; he was here by his flesh, he was in heaven in his divinity; no rather, [he was] everywhere in his divinity.

(2) Born of a mother, not withdrawing from the Father. Two births of Christ are understood, one divine, and the other human; one through which we were to be made, the other through which we were to be remade.[26] Both are miraculous; one without a mother, the other without a father.[27] But because he had received his body from Adam, because Mary is from Adam, and [because] he was going to raise up again this very body, he had said something earthly: "Destroy this temple, and in three days I will raise it up."[28] But he said something heavenly: "Unless a man be born again of water and the Holy Spirit, he will not see the kingdom of God."[29]

(3) O brothers, God wanted to be the Son of Man and he wanted men to be the sons of God. He descended for us; let us ascend for him. For he alone descended and ascended, who said this, "No one has ascended into heaven, but he who descended from heaven." Are they not, therefore, going to ascend into heaven whom he makes sons of God? Certainly they are going to ascend; this is the promise to us: "They will be equal to the angels of God."[30] How then has no one as-

---

25. A very puzzling sentence. Earthly is contrasted to heavenly as human to divine, as material to spiritual, as mortal to immortal. Jesus in his human nature had in his human lifetime on this earth a mortal body as do all human beings who live this mortal life; he was about to make his mortal body, possessed of the mortal life of this world, an immortal body, possessed of the immortal life of the other world.

26. Cf. *Tractate* 2.15.
27. Cf. *Tractate* 8.8.
28. Cf. Jn 2.19.
29. Cf. Jn 3.3.
30. Cf. Lk 20.36. Also cf., Mt 22.30, Mk 12.25.

cended but he who descended? Because one descended, one ascended. What about the others? What must be understood but that they will be his members so that one may ascend? Therefore [the gospel] continues, "No one has ascended into heaven, but he who has descended from heaven, the Son of Man who is in heaven."

(4) Are you amazed because he is both here and in heaven? He made his disciples such. Hear Paul the Apostle speaking: "But our conversation is in heaven."[31] If Paul the Apostle, a man, walked in the flesh and on earth, and yet was conversant in heaven, could not the God of heaven and earth be both in heaven and on earth?

9. If, then, no one but he has descended and ascended, what hope is there for the rest? There is for the rest the hope that he descended precisely in order that those, who are going to ascend through, him might be one in him and with him. "He does not," the Apostle says, "say 'And to seeds,' as of many; but as of one, 'to your seed,' who is Christ."[32] And to the faithful he says, "But you are Christ's. But if Christ's, then you are the seed of Abraham."[33] What he said was one, this he said that we all were.

(2) Thus in the Psalms sometimes many sing to show that one comes from many; sometimes one sings to show what comes from many. For that reason one was healed in that well-known pool; and if anyone else descended, he was not healed.[34] Therefore this one manifests the unity of the Church. Woe to those who hate unity and make factions for themselves among men! Let them listen to him who wanted to make them, one and all, one in one. Let them hear him speaking: Do not make yourselves many. "I have planted, Apollo has watered, but God has given the increase but neither he who plants is anything, nor he who waters, but God who gives the increase."[35]

(3) They were saying to him, "I am of Paul, I am of Apollo, I am of Cephas." And he [said], "Has Christ been divided?"[36]

---

31. Cf. Phil 3.20.   32. Cf. Gal 3.16.
33. Cf. Gal 3.29.   34. Cf. Jn 5.4 and *Tractate* 17.
35. Cf. 1 Cor 3.6–7.   36. Cf. 1 Cor 1.12–13.

Be in one, be one thing, be one person. "No one has ascended into heaven but he who descended from heaven." Look, we want to be yours, they said to Paul. And he [said], "I don't want you to be Paul's, but be his whose Paul is together with you."

10. For he descended and died; and by death itself he freed us from death. He was killed by death, he killed death. And you know, brothers, that death itself has entered into the world through the envy of the devil. "God did not make death," Scripture says, "nor does he rejoice," it says, "in the destruction of the living. For he created all things that they might be."[37] But what does it say there? "But by the envy of the devil, death came into the world."[38]

(2) Man would not come, led by force, to death offered by the devil for his drinking; for the devil did not have the power of compulsion, but subtlety of persuasion. Were you not consenting, the devil would have brought in nothing. Your consent, O man, has led you to death. From a mortal mortals are born; from immortals they become mortals. From Adam all men are mortals; but Jesus, the Son of God, the Word of God, through whom all things were made, the only one equal with the Father, became mortal, because the Word was made flesh and dwelt among us.[39]

11. Therefore he accepted death and he suspended death on the cross; and from death itself he set mortals free. What was done symbolically among the ancients, the Lord recalls. He says, "And as Moses lifted up the serpent in the desert, so must the Son of man be lifted up, that everyone who believes in him may not perish, but may have life everlasting." A great mystery, and they who have read it know it.

(2) Then let them hear, either who have not read it or who have forgotten what perhaps they have read or heard. The people of Israel were being struck down in the desert by the bites of serpents; there occurred a great carnage of many dead.[40] For it was the stroke of God, reproaching and flailing

---

37. Cf. Wis 1.13–14.
39. Cf. Jn 1.14.
38. Wis 2.24.
40. Cf. Nm 21.4–9.

[them], that he might instruct [them]. A great symbol of a future event has been shown there; the Lord himself attests in this reading so that no one can interpret other than what the truth itself shows about itself. For it was said to Moses by the Lord that he should make a bronze serpent and lift it up on a piece of wood in the desert, and he should advise the people of Israel that whoever had been bitten by a serpent should set their gaze upon that serpent lifted up on the piece of wood. It was done: men were bitten, they looked upon it, and they were healed.

(3) What are the biting serpents? Sins from the mortality of the flesh. What is the uplifted serpent? The death of the Lord on the cross. For because death was from a serpent, it was represented by the image of the serpent. The bite of the serpent was deadly, the death of the Lord was life-living. They set their gaze upon the serpent that the serpent may have no power. What does this mean? They set their gaze upon death that death may have no power. But whose death? The death of life, if it can be said, the death of life. Rather, because it can be said, it is said wondrously.

(4) But will it not have to be said since it had to be done? Am I to hesitate to say what the Lord has deigned to do for me? Is not Christ life? And yet Christ [dying] on the cross. Is not Christ life? And yet Christ died. But in the death of Christ death died; for life, by having died, killed death; the fullness of life consumed death; death was swallowed up in the body of Christ. So we also shall say in the resurrection when in triumph we shall sing, "Where, death, is your contending? Where, death, is your sting?"[41]

(5) Now, my brothers, in the meantime, that we may be healed of sin, let us look upon the crucified Christ; for he

41. Cf. 1 Cor 15.55. Augustine prefers this reading for this verse; see, e.g., *En in Ps* 148.4.23–31 (CCL 40.2168) and *De Diversis Quaestionibus LXXXIII* 70 (CCL 44A.197–198; and FOTC 70.178–179) where he also interprets this version of the text. He does know the alternative reading; see *Contra Secundam Iuliani Responsionem Imperfectum Opus* 6.40 (PL 45.1604) where he gives both readings. For a good, brief summary of the text problem in 1 Cor 15.55 see T. O'Malley, *Tertullian and the Bible*, Latinitas Christianorum Primaeva 21 (Nijmegen-Utrecht, 1967) 58–59 and 175–176.

said, "As Moses lifted up the serpent in the desert, so must the Son of Man be lifted up, that everyone who believes in him may not perish, but may have life everlasting." As they who looked upon that serpent perished not from the bites of serpents, so they who look with faith upon the death of Christ are healed of the bites of sins. But those men were healed from death for temporal life; but here he says, "that they may have life everlasting." For this is the difference between the symbolically represented image and the thing itself: the symbol offered temporal life; the thing itself, of which that was the symbol, offers eternal life.

12. "For God has not sent his Son into the world to judge the world, but that the world may be saved by him." Therefore, as far as he can, the physician comes to heal the sick man. He kills himself who is unwilling to observe the instructions of the physician. The Savior came to the world. Why has he been called the Savior of the world except that he may save the world, not that he may judge the world? You do not wish to be saved by him; you will be judged of yourself. And why do I say, you will be judged? See what he said: "He who believes in him is not judged; but he who does not believe"— what do you expect him to say, except, is judged?—he says, "has already been judged."

(2) Judgment has not yet appeared, but judgment has already been made. For the Lord knows who are his;[42] he knows who are to persevere to the crown, who are to persevere to the flame. He knows the wheat on his threshing-floor; he knows the chaff. He knows the grain; he knows the cockles. He has already been judged who does not believe. Why has he been judged? "Because he has not believed in the name of the only begotten Son of God."

13. "Now this is the judgment: because the light has come into the world, and men have loved the darkness rather than the light, for their works were evil." My brothers, whose works did the Lord find good? No one's. He found everyone's works

42. Cf. 2 Tm 2.19.

evil. How, then, have some done truth and come to the light? For this, too, follows: "But he who does truth comes to the light that his works may be made manifest, for they have been done in God."

(2) How have some done a good work that they might come to the light, that is, to Christ? And how have some loved darkness? For if he finds all men sinners, and he heals all men from sin, and that serpent, in which the death of the Lord was prefigured, heals those who had been bitten, and on account of the serpent's bite the serpent was erected, that is, the death of the Lord on account of mortal men whom he found unjust, how is this understood, "This is the judgment: because the light has come into the world, and men have loved the darkness rather than the light, for their works were evil"?

(3) What does this mean? Whose, in fact, were the good works? Did you not come to justify the impious? But, he says, "They have loved the darkness rather than the light." He put the real import there. For many have loved their sins, many have confessed their sins. For he who confesses his sins and accuses his sins now acts with God. God accuses your sins; if you, too, accuse them, you are joined to God.

(4) [It is] as if there are two things, man and sinner. What is called man, that God has made; what is called sinner, that man himself has made. Destroy what you have made that God may save what he has made. You must hate your own work in yourself and love God's work in you. Moreover, when what you have made begins to displease you, then your good works begin because you accuse your evil works. The beginning of good works is the confession of evil works. You do truth and you come to the light. What does it mean, you do truth? You do not caress yourself, you do not flatter yourself, you do not fawn upon yourself. You do not say, "I am just," although you are wicked, and you begin to do truth. But you come to the light that your works may be made manifest, because they have been done in God, because also this very thing which displeases you, your sin, would not displease you unless God were shedding his light upon you and his truth showing it to

you. But he, who, even though admonished, loves his own sins, hates the admonishing light and flees it that his evil works which he loves may not be revealed.

(5) But he who does truth accuses his own evils in himself; he does not spare himself, he does not pardon himself that God may pardon, because he himself recognizes what he wishes God to pardon, and he comes to the light to which he gives thanks because it has shown him what he hated in himself. He says to God, "Turn away your face from my sins."[43] And with what countenance does he speak unless he should say again, "For I know my offense, and my sin is before me always"?[44] Let that be before you which you do not want to be before God. But if you put your sin behind you, God will wrench it back at you before your eyes, and he will wrench it back then when there will no longer be any fruit of penance.

14. Hurry, my brothers, that the darkness may not envelop you. Keep watch for your salvation; keep watch while there is time. Let no one be kept back from the temple of God, let no one be kept back from the Lord's work; let no one be called away from constant prayer, let no one be beguiled from his usual devotion. Therefore keep watch while it is day; the day shines, Christ is the day. He is ready to forgive, but those who acknowledge [their sins]; but he is ready to punish those defending themselves, and those boasting that they are just, and those thinking themselves to be something when they are nothing.[45] But he who walks in his love and in his mercy, even though delivered from those deadly and immense sins, such as are crimes, homicides, thefts, adulteries, [still] on account of those [sins] which seem to be minute, sins of the tongue, or of thoughts, or of immoderation in permissible things, he does truth of confession and comes to the light in good works because many minute sins, if they should be neglected, kill.

(2) Minute are the drops which fill rivers; minute are the grains of sand, but if much sand is placed [upon something],

---

43. Cf. Ps 50.11.
44. Cf. Ps 50.5; this reading differs from *En in Ps* 50.8 (CCL 38.603) which is identical with the *Vulgate* reading.
45. Cf. Gal 6.3.

it presses down and crushes. Bilge-water, if ignored, does exactly what a rushing wave does, but it enters little by little through the ship's bilge; but by entering for a long time and not being drawn out, it sinks the ship.

(3) But what is it to draw out except to exert effort by good works that sins may not overwhelm [us], by moaning, fasting, almsgiving, forgiving? Now, the journey of this world is burdensome; it is full of temptations. Let it not puff one up in prosperity; let it not break one in adversity. He who has given you the happiness of the world gave it for your comfort, not for your corruption. Again he who flails you in this world does it for your correction, not for damnation. Endure a father instructing that you may not feel the judge punishing. We say these things to you daily, and they ought to be said often, because they are good and salutary.

TRACTATE 13

On John 3.22–29

HE ORDER OF THE READINGS from the *Gospel According to John*, as you who show concern for your progress can recall,[1] so continues that this [passage] which has just been read is set before us for our discussion today. The discussions [of this gospel], which have been presented earlier, from its very beginning right up to today's reading, have, you recall, already been rendered. And if perhaps you have forgotten many things from them, surely at least the fulfillment of our obligation remains in your memory.

(2) Those things which you heard from here about the baptism of John, even if you do not retain all of them, still I believe that you heard what you may retain. The things which were said also about why the Holy Spirit appeared in the form of a dove, and how that very knotty problem was resolved, namely that there was something which John did not know that he came to know in the Lord by means of the dove, although he already knew him when he said to him, as he was coming to be baptized, "I ought to be baptized by you, and do you come to me?" [And he already knew him] when the Lord answered him, "Let it be so now, that all justice may be fulfilled."[2]

2. Now then the order of the reading compels us to return to the same John. He it is who was prophesied by Isaia, "The

1. The ten *Tractates on the First Epistle of John* were given between *Tractates* 12 and 13. See Augustine, prologue of *In Epistolam Ioannis ad Parthos Tractatus X*, ed. P. Agaësse, SC 75.9–10 and 105; Le Bonnardière, 51 and 55; Le Landais, 34.

2. Cf. Mt 3.14–15 and *Tractates* 4 and 5.

voice of one crying in the desert, 'Prepare the way for the Lord; make straight his paths.'"[3] Such witness he rendered to his Lord and (because he deemed him worthy) to his friend; his Lord and his friend also himself bore witness to John. For he said of John, "among those born of women there has not arisen a greater than John the Baptist."[4] But because he placed himself before him, as regards the fact that he was more than John, he was God. He said, "Yet he who is lesser in the kingdom of heaven is greater than he."[5] Lesser in birth, greater in power, greater in divinity, majesty, splendor, as "In the beginning was the Word, and the Word was with God, and the Word was God."[6]

(2) But so John had borne witness to the Lord in the earlier readings,[7] that he did indeed call him Son of God, but did not call him God, and yet did not deny it. He had kept silent about him being God, he had not denied that he was God; but he did not altogether keep silent about him being God. For perhaps we find this in today's reading. He had called him Son of God,[8] but men, too, were called sons of God. He had said that he was of such excellence that he himself was unworthy to loose the strap of his sandal.[9] Now this greatness presents much to be understood; he—no one greater had arisen among those born of women—was unworthy to loose the straps of his sandal!

(3) For he was greater than all men or angels. For we find that an angel had prevented a man from falling at his feet. For when in the Apocalypse an angel revealed certain things to John who wrote this gospel, very frightened by the greatness of the vision, John fell at the angel's feet. And the angel said, "Arise, see that you do not do this. Adore God, for I am the fellow servant of you and your brothers."[10] Therefore the angel prevented a man from falling at his feet. Is it not clear that he is above all angels to whom a man, such that no one

---

3. Cf. Is 40.3.
5. Ibid.
7. Jn 1.19–34. Cf. *Tractates* 4, 5, and 6.
8. Cf. Jn 1.34 and *Tractate* 7.4.
10. Cf. Apoc (Rv) 22.8–9.

4. Cf. Mt 11.11.
6. Jn 1.1.
9. Cf. Jn 1.27 and *Tractate* 4.9.

greater than he had arisen among those born of women, says that he is unworthy to loose the strap of his sandal?

3. Nevertheless, let John say it somewhat more clearly, that our Lord, Jesus Christ, is God. Let us find this in the present reading, because also, perchance, we have sung about him, "God has reigned over all the earth."[11] Confronted with this they are deaf who think that he reigns in Africa alone.[12] For it was surely said about Christ when it was said, "God has reigned over all the earth." For who else is our king except our Lord, Jesus Christ? He is our king. And what did you hear in the Psalm itself, in the verse sung just a moment ago? "Sing praises to our God, sing praises; sing praises to our king, sing praises."[13] Him whom he has called God, he has called our king. "Sing praises to our God, sing praises; sing praises to our king, sing praises with understanding."[14] That you may not be disposed to understand that he to whom you sing praises [rules] in one area, "For King of all the earth is God."[15]

(2) And how is he king of all the earth who was seen in one area of the earth, in Jerusalem, in Judea, walking among men, born, sucking at the breast, growing up, eating, drinking, being awake, sleeping, sitting wearied at the well, arrested, scourged, smeared with spittle, crowned with thorns, hung upon a tree, pierced with a lance, dead, buried? How then is he king of all the earth? What was seen in [that] place was flesh; to eyes of flesh flesh appeared. In mortal flesh the immortal majesty was hidden.

(3) And with what eyes, if one were to penetrate the structure of flesh, will it be possible for the immortal majesty to be seen? There is another eye; there is an inner eye. For Tobias, too, was not without eyes when, blinded in his bodily eyes, he was giving the precepts of life to his son.[16] The one was holding his father's hand that he might walk on his feet;

11. Cf. Ps 46.3 and 9.
12. The Donatists. See *Tractates* 4.4 and 6.10.
13. Ps 46.7.   14. Cf. Ps 46.7–8.
15. Cf. Ps 46.8.
16. Cf. Tb 2.10–11 (NAB 2.9–10), and 4.

the other was giving counsel to his son that he might keep the way of justice. In the former I see eyes, and in the latter I understand eyes. And the eyes of him who gives the counsel of life are better than the eyes of him who holds the hand. Jesus also was looking for such eyes when he said to Philip, "Have I been so long with you and you have not known me?" He was looking for such eyes when he said, "Philip, he who sees me sees also the Father."[17] Those eyes are in the understanding, those eyes are in the mind. And so when the Psalm had said, "For the king of all the earth is God," it immediately added, "Sing praises with understanding."

(4) For when I say, "Sing praises to our God, sing praises" I say that God is our king. But you have seen our king among men as a man; you have seen him when he suffered, was crucified, and has died. Something was hiding in that flesh which you could see with the eyes of flesh.[18] What was hiding there? "Sing praises with understanding." Do not seek with the eyes what is perceived with the mind. "Sing praises" with the tongue because among you [he is] flesh. But because "the Word was made flesh and dwelt among us,"[19] give the sound to the flesh, give to God the vision of the mind, "Sing praises with understanding." And you see that "the Word was made flesh and dwelt among us."

4. Let John testify too. "After these things Jesus and his disciples came into the land of Judaea, and he stayed there with them and baptized." Having been baptized, he baptized. He did not baptize with that baptism with which he was baptized. The Lord gives baptism, having been baptized by a servant, showing the way of humility and leading to the Lord's baptism, that is, his own baptism, by offering an example of humility, because he himself did not reject the servant's baptism. And in the baptism of the servant a way was prepared for the Lord; and the Lord, having been baptized, made himself the way for those coming.[20] Let us hear him: "I

17. Cf. Jn 14.9.
18. Some editors read, "which you could not see."
19. Cf. Jn 1.14.   20. Cf. *Tractates* 4.12 and 5.15.

am the way, and the truth, and the life."[21] If you seek the truth, hold fast the way; for the way is the same as the truth. (2) This is where you are going; this same is the way by which you are going. You do not go through one thing to something else; you do not come through something else to Christ. You come through Christ to Christ. How through Christ to Christ? Through Christ the man to Christ the God, through the Word made flesh to the Word which in the beginning was God with God, from that which man ate to that which everyday the angels eat. For so it was written, "He gave them the bread of heaven; man ate the bread of the angels."[22] Who is the bread of angels? "In the beginning was the Word, and the Word was with God, and the Word was God."[23] How did man eat the bread of angels? "And the Word was made flesh and dwelt among us."[24]

5. But because we have said that angels eat, do not suppose, brothers, that it is done by bites. For if you understood this, God whom the angels eat is, as it were, being ripped to pieces. Who rips justice to pieces? But again someone says to me, "and who is it who eats justice?" In what way, then, [does Scripture say] "blessed are they who hunger and thirst for justice, for they shall have their fill"?[25] The food which you eat by reason of the flesh, that you may be refreshed, that perishes; it is consumed that it may restore you. Eat justice and you will be refreshed, and it remains whole. In a similar way in seeing this corporeal light these eyes of ours are refreshed, and yet the thing which is seen by corporeal eyes is corporeal. For when many men have been rather long in darkness, their eyesight is enfeebled, as if from a fasting from light. The eyes, deprived of their food (they are nourished, of course, by light) are worn out from fasting and weakened so that they cannot see the very light by which they are refreshed; and if it has been absent too long, they are extinguished and the very sense of sight dies in them, as it were. What then? Since so many eyes are nourished daily by this

21. Cf. Jn 14.6.   22. Cf. Ps 77.24–25.
23. Jn 1.1.   24. Cf. Jn 1.14.
25. Mt 5.6.

light, does it become less? They are both refreshed, and yet it remains whole itself. If God could show this in the case of corporeal light to corporeal eyes, does he not show to pure hearts that indefatigable light, remaining whole, perishing in no part? What light? "In the beginning was the Word, and the Word was with God."[26]

(2) Let us see if [this] is light. "For with you is the fountain of life, and in your light we shall see light."[27] On earth a fountain is one thing, a light is another. Thirsting, you seek a fountain; and that you may reach the fountain, you seek a light; and if it is not day, you light a lamp that you may reach the fountain. That fountain is light itself. To a thirsty man it is a fountain; to a blind man it is a light. Let the eyes be opened that they may see the light; let the jaws of the heart be opened that they may drink the fountain. What you drink, this you see, this you hear. God becomes everything for you, because, of these things which you love, he is everything for you.

(3) If you pay close attention to visible things, neither is God bread nor is God water, nor is God this light, nor is God clothing, nor is God a house. For all these are visible things and are individual. What is bread, this is not water; and what is clothing, this is not house; and what these things are, this is not God, for they are visible things. God is everything for you. If you are hungry, he is bread for you; if you are thirsty, he is water for you. If you are in darkness, he is light for you because he remains incorruptible. If you are naked, he is the clothing of immortality for you, when this corruptible body puts on incorruption and this mortal body puts on immortality.[28]

(4) All things can be said about God, and nothing is said about God worthily. Nothing is more widespread than this deficiency. You seek a suitable name; you do not find it. Whatever way you seek to speak, you find he is all things. What similarity is there between a lamb and a lion? Both were

26. Cf. Jn 1.1.   27. Ps 35.10.
28. Cf. 1 Cor 15.53–54.

said of Christ. "Behold the Lamb of God."[29] How the lion? "The lion of the tribe of Juda has prevailed."[30]

6. Let us hear John: "Jesus was baptizing." We said that Jesus was baptizing. How Jesus? How the Lord? How the Son of God? How the Word? But the Word was made flesh. "Now John was also baptizing in Aenon near Salim." A certain lake [is called] Aenon.[31] How is it understood that it was a lake? "For there was much water there. And they came and were baptized. For John had not yet been put in prison." If you remember (look, I am saying it again), I said why John baptized, because it was necessary for the Lord to be baptized?[32] And why was it necessary for the Lord to be baptized? Because many would despise baptism for the reason that they would think themselves endowed with greater grace than they saw in other believers. For example, a catechumen living chastely would despise a married man and would say that he is better than that believer is. That catechumen would say in his heart, "Why do I need to receive baptism that I might have what this man also has than whom I am already better?"

(2) Therefore that this pride might not destroy some, very much puffed up on account of the merits of their justice, the Lord wanted to be baptized by the servant, as if addressing his excellent children: "Why do you puff yourself up? Why do you build yourselves up because [of what] you have, one man wisdom, another learning, another chastity, another strength of endurance? Can you have as much as I who did the giving? And yet I was baptized by a servant and you disdain [to be baptized] by the Lord." That is, "that all justice may be fulfilled."[33]

7. But someone will say, "It was sufficient, therefore, that John baptized the Lord; what need was there that others be baptized by John?" And we have said this,[34] that if the Lord

29. Cf. Jn 1.29. 30. Cf. Apoc (Rv) 5.5.
31. Some codices read, "Salim is a certain place, Aenon a lake." This alternative reading contains a play on the closeness in vowel sounds between *locus*, 'place' and *lacus*, 'lake'.
32. Cf. *Tractates* 4.13 and 5.3 and 5.
33. Cf. Mt 3.15. 34. Cf. *Tractates* 4.14 and 5.5.

alone were baptized by John, men would not fail to think that John had a better baptism than the Lord. For they would say, "So very great was the baptism that John had, that Christ alone was worthy to be baptized with it." Therefore, that the baptism which the Lord was going to give might be shown to be better, and that the one might be understood as a servant's, the other as the Lord's, the Lord was baptized, that he might provide an example of humility; but he was not baptized alone by John so that the baptism of John might not seem better than the baptism of the Lord.

(2) But our Lord, Jesus Christ, showed the way, as you have heard, brothers, for this reason: that no one, unduly claiming that he has an abundance of some grace, may disdain to be baptized with the baptism of the Lord. For, however far a catechumen may progress, he still carries the burden of his iniquity; it is not forgiven him except when he has come to baptism.[35] Just as the people of Israel were not free from the people of Egypt except when they had come to the Red Sea, so no one is free from the oppressive crush of sins except when he has come to the fountain of baptism.

8. "There arose then a question between John's disciples and the Jews concerning purification." John was baptizing; Christ was baptizing. The disciples of John were perturbed. People were flocking to Christ; people were coming to John. For those who came to John he sent to Jesus to be baptized; they were not sent to John who were baptized by Christ. The disciples of John were distressed and began to discuss the question with the Jews, as usually happens. You should understand that the Jews had said that Christ was greater and the people ought to flock to his baptism. They, not yet understanding, were defending John's baptism. They went to John himself that he might resolve the question.

(2) Understand, my beloved people. Here the very benefit of humility is recognized and it is shown, when men are erring in the question itself, whether John wanted to take glory in himself. For, perhaps, he said, "You speak the truth; you

35. Cf. *Tractates* 4.13 and 11.1.

argue rightly. My baptism is better. For, that you may know that my baptism is better, I baptized Christ himself." John could say that since Christ was baptized. If he wanted to enhance his prestige, what an occasion did he have wherein to enhance his prestige! But he knew better before whom he should humble himself. To him whom he knew that he preceded by birth, he intentionally yielded by confessing him. He understood that his salvation was in Christ. He had already said earlier, "And of his fullness we have all received."[36] And this is to confess [him to be] God.

(3) For how do all men receive of his fullness unless he is God? For if he is a man in such a way that he is not God, even he himself receives of the fullness of God and so is not God. But if all men receive of his fullness, he is the fountain, they the drinkers. They who drink the fountain can both be thirsty and drink. The fountain is never thirsty; the fountain does not need itself. Men need the fountain; with dry innards, with dry mouths they run to the fountain to be refreshed. The fountain flows to refresh; so does the Lord Jesus.

9. Let us see, then, what John answered. "They came to John and said to him, 'Rabbi, he who was with you beyond the Jordan, to whom you gave testimony, behold he baptizes and all men come to him.'" That is, "What do you say? Should they not be prevented, that they may rather come to you?" "He answered and said, 'A man cannot receive anything unless it be given to him from heaven.'" About whom do you think John said this? About himself, "As a man I have received," he said, "from heaven." Pay attention, my beloved people.

(2) "A man cannot receive anything unless it be given to him from heaven. You yourselves do bear me witness that I said, 'I am not the Christ,'" as if saying, "Why do you deceive yourselves? How have you yourselves proposed this question to me? What did you say to me? 'Rabbi, he who was with you beyond the Jordan, to whom you gave testimony.' Therefore,

36. Cf. Jn 1.16.

you know the kind of testimony that I gave for him. Am I now going to say that he was not the one whom I said he was? Therefore, because I have received something from heaven that I might be something, do you wish me to be empty that I should speak against the truth? 'A man cannot receive anything unless it be given to him from heaven. You yourselves do bear me witness that I said, "I am not the Christ." ' "

(3) "You are not the Christ. But what if [you are] greater than he because you baptized him?" " 'I have been sent.' I am the herald; he is the Judge."

10. And now hear a testimony much more forceful, much plainer. See what it is we are dealing with; see what we ought to love; see that to love some human person instead of Christ is adultery. Why do I say this? Let us pay attention to the voice of John.

(2) An error could be made about him; he could be thought to be who he was not. He casts off false honor from himself that he may hold fast the solid truth. See what he calls Christ, what [he calls] himself. "He who has the bride is the bridegroom." Be chaste; love the bridegroom. But what are you who say to us, "He who has the bride is the bridegroom"? "But the friend of the bridegroom, who stands and hears him, rejoices with joy because of the bridegroom's voice."

(3) The Lord, our God, will support me according to the distress of my heart; for it is filled with much moaning to say what sorrow I feel. But I beg you through Christ himself that what I shall be unable to say you may think of; for I know that my sorrow cannot be worthily enough expressed. For I see many adulterers who desire to possess the bride who was bought at so great a price, who, though ugly, was loved that she might become beautiful, with him as the buyer, as the deliverer, as the beautifier. They do this by their words, in order that they be loved instead of the bridegroom.

(4) About him it was said, "He it is who baptizes."[37] Who goes forth from here and says, "I baptize"? Who goes forth from here and says, "This which I shall give is holy"? Who

37. Cf. Jn 1.33.

proceeds from here who says, "It is good for you to be born from me"? Let us listen to the friend of the bridegroom, not the adulterers against the bridegroom. Let us listen to one who is jealous, but not for himself.

11. Brothers, return in heart to your homes. I am speaking of carnal things, I am speaking of earthly things. I speak of a human thing because of the infirmity of your flesh.[38] Many of you have wives; many want to have them. Many, even if you do not want to, have had [wives]; many who do not at all want to have wives have been born of the wives of your fathers. There is no heart which this feeling does not touch. In human affairs no one is isolated from the human race that he does not feel what I am saying.

(2) Suppose that someone, having set out on a trip abroad, had entrusted his bride to his friend: "See to it, I ask you, you are my dear friend, that during my absence no one else be loved in my place." What sort of man, therefore, is he who, protecting the bride or wife of his friend, does indeed take care that no one else be loved. But if he wishes himself to be loved in his friend's place and wishes to take advantage of her who was entrusted to him, how detestable does he appear to the whole human race! Let him see her paying attention a bit saucily [to someone] through a window or joking with someone, he forbids it, as one who is jealous. I see a jealous man, but let me see for whom—his absent friend or his present self.

(3) Suppose that our Lord, Jesus Christ, had done this. He entrusted his bride to his friend; he set out on a trip abroad to take possession of his kingdom, as he himself says in the gospel;[39] and yet he is present in his majesty. Let the friend who has set out across the sea be deceived; and if he is deceived, woe to that man who deceives! Why do they try to deceive God, God, looking into the hearts of all and searching into the secrets of all? There exists some heretic and he says, "I give, I sanctify, I justify. I do not wish you to go to that sect." He is indeed properly jealous, but see for whom. "Do not go to idols." He is properly jealous. "Do not go to fortune-tellers." He is properly jealous.

38. Cf. Rom 6.19.   39. Cf. Lk 19.12.

(4) Let us see for whom he is jealous. "What I give is holy, because I give it; he whom I baptize has been baptized and he whom I do not baptize has not been baptized." Hear the friend of the bridegroom; learn to be jealous for your friend. Hear his voice; "He it is who baptizes."⁴⁰ Why do you want to claim for yourself what is not yours? Is he who has left behind his bride so far away? Do you not know that he who rose again from the dead sits at his Father's right hand? If the Jews despised him hanging on the tree, do you despise him sitting in heaven?

(5) Know you, my beloved people, that I suffer great sorrow over this matter; but, as I have said, I leave the rest for your thoughts. For I am not expressing it, if I should speak all day; if I should lament all day, that is not enough. I am not expressing it, even if I should have, as the prophet says, "a fountain of tears";⁴¹ yet even if I should be changed into tears, and were to become tears, and changed into tongues and were to become tongues, it is too little.

12. Let us go back, let us see what he says: "He who has the bride is the bridegroom." She is not *my* bride. And do you not rejoice in the wedding? Yes, I rejoice, he says. "But the friend of the bridegroom, who stands and hears him, rejoices with joy because of the bridegroom's voice." He says, "I do not rejoice because of my own voice, but I rejoice because of the bridegroom's voice. It is my place to hear; his to speak. For I have need to be enlightened. He is the light; I am as an ear, he is the Word." Therefore the friend of the bridegroom stands and hears him.

(2) Why does he stand? Because he does not fall. Why does he not fall? Because he is humble. See him standing on firm ground: "I am not worthy to loose the strap of his sandal."⁴² Properly you humble yourself, deservedly you do not fall; deservedly you stand, deservedly you hear him, and "you rejoice with joy because of the bridegroom's voice."

(3) So too, the Apostle is the friend of the bridegroom; he

40. Cf. Jn 1.33.   41. Cf. Jer 9.1 (NAB 8.23).
42. Cf. Jn 1.27.

is jealous too, not for himself, but for the bridegroom. Hear the voice of one who is jealous: "With the jealousy of God I am jealous of you,"[43] he said, not with mine, nor for myself, but with the jealousy of God. Why? How? Who is she of whom you are jealous? For whom are you jealous? "For I have espoused you to one husband that I may present you as a chaste virgin to Christ."[44] What therefore do you fear? Why are you jealous? "I fear," he says, "lest, as the serpent seduced Eve by his subtlety, so too, your minds should be corrupted from the chastity which is in Christ."[45]

(4) The whole Church has been called a virgin. You see that the members of the Church are diverse, that they possess and rejoice in diverse gifts. Some are married men, some are married women; some [are] widowers [and] no longer seek wives, some [are] widows [and] no longer seek husbands. Some men preserve their purity from the earliest years; some women have devoted their virginity to God. Diverse are the gifts, but all of them are the one virgin. Where is this virginity? For it is not in the body. Holy chastity even of the body, which belongs to a few women and, if virginity can be spoken of in men, to a few men, is in the Church; and [such a one] is a more honorable member.

(5) But the other members preserve virginity, not in the body but all [of them] in the mind. What is virginity of the mind? Sound faith, firm hope, sincere love. That man who was jealous for the bridegroom was afraid that this virginity be corrupted by the serpent. For as a member of the body is defiled in a certain place, so seduction of the tongue defiles virginity of the heart. Let her not be corrupted in mind who does not wish to keep virginity of body without a good reason.

13. What then shall I say, brothers? Do the heretics, too, have virgins, and are the virgins of the heretics many?[46] Let us see if they love the bridegroom that this virginity may be protected. For whom is it protected? "For Christ," [the Apos-

---

43. Cf. 2 Cor 11.2.   44. Ibid.
45. Cf. 2 Cor 11.3.
46. The Donatists also had virgins; see Berrouard, *Homélies I–XVI*, 701, and P. Monceaux, 4.144–145.

tle] says.[47] Let us see if for Christ, not for Donatus; let us see for whom this virginity is preserved.

(2) You will be able to prove it quickly. Look, I show the bridegroom, because he shows himself. John [the Baptist] gives testimony to him. "He it is who baptizes."[48] O you virgin, if you preserve your virginity for this bridegroom, why do you run to him who says, "I baptize," since the friend of your bridegroom says, "He it is who baptizes"? Then too, your bridegroom holds the whole world [under his sway]; why are you corrupted due to a part of it? Who is the bridegroom? "For king of all the earth is God."[49] Your bridegroom himself holds the whole because he bought the whole. See at what price he bought it that you may understand what he bought. What price did he pay? He gave his blood. Where did he give, where did he pour out his blood? In the passion. Do you not sing to your bridegroom or feign that you sing, when the whole world has been purchased? "They have dug my hands and feet; they have numbered all my bones. Indeed they have looked and stared at me. They have divided my garments among them, and upon my vesture they cast lots."[50]

(3) You are the bride; acknowledge the vesture of your bridegroom. For what vesture were lots cast? Ask the gospel. See to whom you have been espoused; see from whom you receive pledges. Ask the gospel. See what it says to you during the passion of the Lord. "There was a tunic" there; let us see what sort, "woven from the top."[51] What does a tunic woven from the top signify except love? What does a tunic woven from the top signify except unity? Observe this tunic which not even Christ's persecutors divided. For [the gospel] says, "They said to one another, 'Let us not divide it, but let us cast lots for it.'"[52] Look, that which you heard the Psalm tell of. The persecutors did not tear the vesture; Christians divide the Church.

14. But what shall I say, brothers? Let us see clearly what he has bought. For he bought there where he paid the price.

47. Cf. 2 Cor 11.2.
48. Cf. Jn 1.33.
49. Cf. Ps 46.8.
50. Cf. Ps 21.17–19.
51. Cf. Jn 19.23.
52. Cf. Jn 19.24.

For how great [a domain] did he pay it? If he paid it for Africa, let us be Donatists and not be called Donatists but Christians, because Christ bought Africa alone, although even here there are not only Donatists. But in his transaction he did not keep what he bought quiet. He kept accounts; thanks be to God,[53] he did not deceive us. That bride must listen and must therein understand to whom she vowed her virginity.

(2) There in the Psalm where it was said, "They have dug my hands and my feet; they have numbered all my bones,"[54] there the Lord's passion is very clearly declared. And this Psalm is read every year on the last week, when the whole people are especially attentive and the passion of the Lord is close at hand; both among us and among them this Psalm is read.[55] Pay attention, brothers, to what he bought there; let the transaction records be read. Hear what he bought there: "All the ends of the earth shall remember and shall be converted to the Lord; all the kindred of the nations shall adore in his sight; for the kingdom is his and he shall rule the nations."[56]

(3) Look at what he has bought. Look, "for the king of all the earth, God,"[57] is your bridegroom. Why then do you wish one so rich to be reduced to rags? Admit it, he bought the whole; and you say, "Here you have part." Oh, if you were pleasing to the bridegroom! Oh, if only you spoke and were not corrupted, and, what is worse, corrupted in heart, not in the body! You love a man instead of Christ; you love one who says, "I baptize."

(4) You do not hear the friend of the bridegroom saying,

---

53. Cf. *Tractate* 6.10.   54. Cf. Ps 21.17–18.

55. Ps 21 was read during Holy Week in both Catholic and Donatist churches in Africa. See *En in Ps* 21.2.1–2 (CCL 38.121–123; and ACW 29.207–210). This passage provides some support for this statement, albeit no explicit statement, but *Tr In Io Ep* 2.2 (SC 75.154) clearly states that it was read on Wednesday of Holy Week. La Bonnardière, 54–56, maintains that *En in Ps* 21 was part of this series of sermons; she places it on the day after *Tractate* 12 on Wednesday of Holy Week in 407 A.D. with *Tr In Ep Io* 2 on the following Monday, with allusions to Ps 21, and then *Tractate* 13 some weeks later, also with allusions to Ps 21. See also Berrouard, *Homélies I–XVI*, 704.

56. Cf. Ps 21.28–29.   57. Cf. Ps 46.8.

"He it is who baptizes."[58] You do not hear him saying, "He who has the bride is the bridegroom." "I do not have the bride," he said, "but what am I?" "But the friend of the bridegroom, who stands and hears him, rejoices with joy because of the bridegroom's voice."

15. Evidently, therefore, my brothers, it profits these men nothing to preserve virginity, to have continence, to give alms; all those things which are praised in the Church profit them nothing because they tear apart unity, that is, that tunic of love. What do they do? There are many eloquent men among them, great tongues, rivers of tongues. Do they speak like angels?

(2) Let them listen to a friend of the bridegroom who is jealous for the bridegroom, not for himself. "If I should speak with the tongues of men and angels, but have not love, I have become as sounding brass or a tinkling cymbal."[59]

16. But what do they say? "We have baptism." You do, but not your own. It is one thing to have, another to have ownership. You have baptism because you have received that you should be a baptized man; you have received as one enlightened, if however, not benighted by yourself. And when you give, you give as a minister, not as the owner. You shout as a bailiff, not as the judge. The judge speaks through the bailiff, and yet in the official documents it is not written, "The bailiff said," but "The judge said."

(2) Accordingly, see if what you give is yours in authority. But if you have received, confess with the friend of the bridegroom: "A man cannot receive anything unless it be given from heaven." Confess with the friend of the bridegroom: "He who has the bride is the bridegroom, but the friend of the bridegroom stands and hears him." But oh, if only you would stand and hear him and would not fall that you might hear yourself! For, by hearing him, you would stand and hear; for you are speaking and inflating your ego.

(3) I, says the Church, if I am the bride, if I have received the pledges, if I have been redeemed at the price of his blood,

---

58. Cf. Jn 1.33.   59. 1 Cor 13.1.

I hear the voice of the bridegroom; and I hear the voice of the friend of the bridegroom then, if he give glory to my bridegroom, not to himself. Let the friend say, "He who has the bride is the bridegroom; but the friend of the bridegroom stands and hears him, and rejoices with joy because of the bridegroom's voice."

(4) Look, you have sacraments, and I grant it. You have the exterior form, but you are a branch cut off from the vine; you show the exterior form, but I seek the root. Fruit does not come from the exterior form except where there is the root. But where is the root except in love? And hear the exterior form of the branches; let Paul speak. He says, "If I should know all sacraments, and have all prophecy and all faith" (and how great a faith!) "so as to move mountains, yet have not love, I am nothing."[60]

17. Therefore let no one sell you stories. "Pontius too, performed a miracle,[61] and Donatus prayed, and God answered him from heaven." First, either they are deceived or they deceive. Then, grant that he moves mountains. "Yet if I should not have love," [the Apostle] says, "I am nothing." Let us see whether that one had love. I would believe it, had he not divided unity. For against these miracle-workers, so to speak, my God has made me cautious, saying, "In the last days false prophets will arise, working signs and wonders, so as to lead astray, if possible, even the elect. Behold I have told you beforehand."[62]

---

60. 1 Cor 13.2. Augustine here uses *sacramenta* in place of the *mysteria* of the *Vulgate*, and the context clearly requires that it mean "sacraments" rather than its more usual meaning, "mysteries."

61. When Julian the Apostate became Emperor in 361 A.D., Donatism, which had been officially proscribed since 347 A.D., was again tolerated. Those banished by Constantius were recalled, but those banished by Constans were not included. In 362 A.D. the Donatists sent a petition to Julian seeking amnesty for the latter; Pontius was a signatory to this petition. He may also have signed the decree of the Council of Bagai in 394 A.D. Nothing is known about the nature of his miracles. Cf. Augustine, *Ad Catholicos Epistula de Secta Donatistarum* 19.49 (PL 43.428; CSEL 52.295–296); *Contra Litteras Petiliani* 2.97.224 (PL 43.334–335; CSEL 52.141–143); Frend, *Donatist Church*, 185–188, 216; Willis, 16 and 58.

62. Cf. Mk 13.22–23; Mt 24.23–26.

(2) Therefore the bridegroom made us cautious because we ought not to be deceived even by miracles. For sometimes even a deserter frightens a provincial; but [the provincial], who has no desire to be frightened or deceived carefully scrutinizes whether he belongs to the camp and whether that identifying symbol with which he was marked tells something to his advantage. Therefore let us keep our unity, brothers; outside unity, even he who works miracles is nothing.

(3) For the people of Israel were in unity and they did not work miracles; the magicians of the Pharaohs were outside unity and they did works like to those of Moses.[63] The people of Israel, as I said, did not do them. Who were saved before God, they who did or they who did not? Peter the Apostle raised the dead;[64] Simon Magus did many things.[65] There were certain Christians there who were not able to do either what Peter did or what Simon did. But why did they rejoice? Because their names had been written in heaven.[66] For, to be more precise, our Lord, Jesus Christ, said this to the disciples who returned, for the sake of the faith of the nations.

(4) For the disciples themselves, bragging, said, "Behold, Lord, even the devils are subject to us in your name."[67] They confessed well indeed, for they assigned the honor to the name of Christ. And yet what did he say to them? "Do not brag about this, that the devils are subject to you; but rejoice, that your names have been written in heaven."[68]

(5) Peter drove out devils;[69] some little old widow, some layman or other, having love, keeping soundness of the faith, does not do this. Peter is an eye in the body; that one is a finger in the body. Yet he is in the same body as Peter is. And if the finger is less important than the eye, still it has not been cut off from the body. It is better to be a finger and to be in the body than to be an eye and be plucked out of the body.[70]

18. Accordingly, my brothers, let no one fool you, let no

63. Cf. Ex 7.11–12 and 22, 8.7 (NAB 8.3).
64. Cf. Acts 9.40.   65. Cf. Acts 8.9–11.
66. Cf. Lk 10.20.   67. Cf. Lk 10.17.
68. Ibid.   69. Cf. Acts 5.16.
70. Cf. Mt 5.29–30, 18.8–9; Mk 9.43–47.

one deceive you. Love the peace of Christ, who was crucified for us although he was God. Paul says, "Neither he who plants is anything, nor he who waters, but God who gives the increase."[71] And does anyone of us say that he is anything? If we say that we are something and do not give glory to him, we are adulterers; and we want ourselves, not the bridegroom, to be loved. You, love Christ, and us in him in whom you are loved by us. Let the members love each other, but let them all live under the head.

(2) My brothers, I have indeed been impelled by my grief to say much, and I have said little; I could not finish the reading. The Lord will aid me that it be suitably finished. For I did not wish to burden your hearts further; rather I want them to have time for sighs and prayers on behalf of these who are still deaf and do not understand.

71. 1 Cor 3.7.

TRACTATE 14

On John 3.29–36

HIS READING from the holy gospel teaches us the pre-eminence of the divinity of our Lord, Jesus Christ, and the humility of the man who deserved to be called the friend of the bridegroom, that we may distinguish what difference there is between the man who is man, and the man who is God. For the man who is God is our Lord, Jesus Christ, God before all ages and man in our age, God from the Father, man from the virgin, yet one and the same Lord and Savior, Jesus Christ, Son of God, God and man. But John, a man of eminent grace, was sent before him, enlightened by him who is the light. For about John it was said, "He was not the light, but was to give witness concerning the light."[1]

(2) He can indeed be called a light and he himself is accurately called a light, but one that was enlightened, not enlightening. For a light which enlightens is one thing, and a light which is enlightened is another; for our eyes, too, are called lights[2] and yet they are open in darkness and do not see. But the enlightening light is a light in itself and a light for itself; and it does not need another light to be able to give light, but the others need it that they may give light.

2. Therefore John confessed, as you have heard, that, when Jesus was making many disciples it was reported to him as if to provoke him, for they related it to him, as to an envious man: "Look, he is making more disciples than you"—he confessed what he was, and thereby he deserved to belong

1. Jn 1.8.
2. In Latin *lumina* denotes "lights" and connotes "eyes."

to him, because he did not dare to call himself what that one is.

(2) Therefore John said this, "A man cannot receive anything unless it be given him from heaven." Therefore Christ gives, man receives. "You yourselves bear me witness that I said, 'I am not the Christ,' but that I have been sent before him. He who has the bride is the bridegroom; but the friend of the bridegroom, who stands and hears him, rejoices with joy because of the bridegroom's voice." Not for himself did he produce joy in himself. For he who wishes to rejoice in himself will be sad; but he who wishes to rejoice in God will always rejoice because God is eternal.

(3) Do you wish to have eternal joy? Adhere to him who is eternal. John said that he was such a man. The friend of the bridegroom, he says, rejoices because of the bridegroom's voice, not because of his own voice; and "he stands and hears him." Therefore, if he falls he does not hear him; for about that certain one who did fall it was said, "and he stood not in the truth."[3] It was said about the devil. Therefore the friend of the bridegroom ought to stand and hear. What is "to stand"? To remain in his grace which he has received. And he hears the voice at which he may rejoice. Such was John; he knew the source of his rejoicing, he did not claim for himself what he was not. He knew that he was one enlightened, not the enlightener. "But it was the true light," says the Evangelist, "which enlightens every man who comes into this world."[4] Therefore, if every man, also John himself, because he, too, is of men.

(4) For although among those born of women no one has arisen greater than John,[5] still he, too, is one of those who were born of women. Ought he to be compared to him who was born because he wanted to be, and therefore by an unheard-of delivery because it was an unheard-of birth? For both begettings of the Lord are extraordinary, both the divine and the human; the divine has no mother, the human

---

3. Cf. Jn 8.44.   4. Cf. Jn 1.9.
5. Cf. Mt 11.11.

has no father.[6] Therefore, John, one of the rest of us, but still of greater grace so that among those born of women no one arose greater than he, gave so great a witnessing to our Lord, Jesus Christ, that he calls him the bridegroom, himself the friend of the bridegroom, yet not worthy to loose the strap of his sandal.[7]

(5) You have already heard much about this, my beloved people; let us see what follows, for it is somewhat hard to understand. But as John himself says that "A man cannot receive anything unless it be given him from heaven," whatever we shall not understand, let us ask him who gives from heaven, because we are men and we cannot receive anything unless he who is not a man give it.

3. This, then, follows and John says, "This my joy, therefore, is fulfilled." What is his joy? I have my grace. I assume no more for myself that I may not lose also what I have received. What is this joy? "I rejoice with joy because of the bridegroom's voice." Therefore let a man understand that he ought not to rejoice in his own wisdom but in the wisdom he has received from God. Let him seek nothing more and he does not lose what he has found. For many have become fools for the very reason that they have said that they are wise. The Apostle finds fault with such and says of them, "Because that which is known of God," he says, "is manifest to them; for God has manifested it to them."[8]

(2) Hear what he says about certain ungrateful, impious persons. "For God has manifested it to them. For the invisible things of him, from the creation of the world, are clearly seen, being understood by the things that are made; his eternal power and divinity, so that they are inexcusable." Why inexcusable? "Because, knowing God,"—he did not say that they did not know—"knowing God, they have not glorified him as God or given thanks; but they became vain in their thoughts, and their foolish heart was darkened. For, professing to be wise, they became fools." For if they had known

6. Cf. *Tractates* 8.8 and 12.8.   7. Cf. Jn 1.27.
8. Cf. Rom 1.19–21.

God, at the same time they had known that no one except God had made them wise. They would not therefore attribute to themselves what they did not have from themselves, but to him from whom they had received it. But by not giving thanks they became fools.

(3) Therefore what God had given to the grateful[9] he took away from the ungrateful. John did not want to be this; he wanted to be grateful. He confessed that he had received; and he said that he rejoiced because of the bridegroom's voice, and he said, "This my joy, therefore, is fulfilled."

4. "He must increase, but I must decrease." What does this mean? He must be exalted, but I must be humbled. How does Jesus increase? How does God increase? The perfect does not increase. God, moreover, neither increases nor decreases. For if he increases, he is not perfect; if he decreases, he is not God. But Jesus is God; how does he increase? If in age, because he deigned to be a man and was a boy; and although he was the Word of God, he lay an infant in the manger, and although he had created his mother, he sucked the milk of infancy from his mother. Because, therefore, Jesus increased with the age of flesh, therefore, perhaps, it was said, "He must increase, but I must decrease."

(2) But why also this? John and Jesus, as far as pertains to the flesh, were of the same age; for there was a difference of six months between them;[10] they had grown up at the same time. And if our Lord, Jesus Christ, wanted to be here for a longer time before his death, and [wanted] John to be here with him, then, as they had grown up at the same time, so they could have grown old at the same time. Why then [would he say], "He must increase, but I must decrease"?

(3) First of all, because the Lord was also now thirty years old;[11] does a young man, if he is already thirty years old, still increase? Already from this age men begin to go downhill and to decline to a senior age, and from that to old age. But even if they were both boys, he would not say, "He must in-

---

9. Or, *gratis*, i.e., "freely." 10. Cf. Lk 1.36.
11. Cf. Lk 3.23.

crease, but I must decrease." But he would say, "We must increase together." Now, however, the one is thirty years old; the other also is thirty years old. The six months which separated them distinguish no age. One finds the distinction more from the reading than from actually looking at them.

5. What, then, does this mean, "He must increase, but I must decrease"? This is a great mystery. Understand it, my beloved people. Before the Lord Jesus came, men bragged about themselves; he came so that the glory of man might decrease and the glory of God be increased. For he came without sin, and he found all men with sin. If he came so that he might forgive sins, let God bestow, let man confess. For the confession of man is the lowliness of man; the compassion of God is the loftiness of God. If, therefore, he came to forgive man his sins, let man acknowledge his lowliness and let God exercise his mercy.

(2) "He must increase, but I must decrease." That is, he must give, but I must receive; he must be glorified, but I must confess. Let man understand his status and let him confess to God, and let him hear the Apostle speaking to a proud and puffed up man who wished to exalt himself: "For what have you that you have not received? But if you have received, why do you glory as if you have not received?"[12] Therefore let man understand that he has received, [man] who wanted to call his own what is not his, and let him decrease; for it is good for him that God be glorified in him. Let him decrease in himself that he may be increased in God.

(3) Christ and John signified these witnesses and this truth, even by their passions. For John decreased by being beheaded. Christ was lifted up on the cross, that there also it might be clear what it means, "He must increase but I must decrease." Then too, Christ was born when the days were already beginning to grow longer; John was born when the days were beginning to grow shorter. Thus creation itself and their very passions bore witness to the words of John saying, "He must increase, but I must decrease." Therefore let the

12. Cf. 1 Cor 4.7.

glory of God increase in us and let our glory decrease that our glory, too, may increase in God.

(4) For the Apostle says this; Holy Scripture says it. "Let him who glories, glory in the Lord."[13] Do you wish to glory in yourself? You wish to increase, but you increase harmfully and bring harm to yourself. For he who increases harmfully justly decreases. Therefore let God increase, who is always perfect, let him increase in you. For the more you understand God, and the more you grasp him, God seems to increase in you; but he does not increase in himself, but is always perfect.

(5) Yesterday you understood a little; today you understand more; tomorrow you will understand much more. The very light of God increases in you just as though God increases who remains always perfect. Just as if someone's eyes were healed of a long-time blindness, and began to see a little bit of light, and on another day to see more, and on the third day even more, so light would seem to him to increase, yet light is perfect whether he should see it or should not see it. So also is the interior man. He advances toward perfection in God and God seems to increase in him; yet he decreases that he may fall from his own glory and rise into the glory of God.

6. And now what we have just heard appears distinctly and clearly. "He who comes from above is over all." See what he says about Christ. What about himself? "He who is of the earth, of the earth he is, and of the earth he speaks. He who comes from above is over all." Christ is. But "he who is of the earth, of the earth he is, and of the earth he speaks." John is. And is this the whole? Is John of the earth and of the earth does he speak? The whole witness which he bears about Christ, of the earth does he speak? Are not the voices of God heard by John where he bears witness about Christ? How then of the earth does he speak? But he said it about man. As far as pertains to man himself, he is of the earth, and of the earth he speaks; but if he speaks any divine things, he has been enlightened by God. For if he were not enlightened, earth would be speaking earth. And so the grace of God stands to one side, the nature of man stands to another.

13. Cf. 1 Cor 1.31; Jer 9.24 (NAB 9.23).

(2) Now examine the nature of man: it is born and increases, it learns these customs of men. What does [this nature] know except earth, of the earth? It speaks human things, it knows human things, it understands human things. Carnal itself, [this nature] judges carnally, it surmises carnally. Look, it is complete man. Let the grace of God come, let it enlighten man's darkness as [the Psalmist] says, "You, O Lord, will light my lamp; O my God, enlighten my darkness."[14] Let grace take possession of the mind of man and turn it to its own light; immediately [man] begins to say what the Apostle says, "Yet not I, but the grace of God with me"[15] and "And it is no longer I that live, but Christ lives in me."[16] That is, "He must increase, but I must decrease."

(3) Therefore, John, as far as pertains to John, is of the earth, and of the earth he speaks; if you heard anything divine from John, it is of the one enlightening, not of the one receiving.[17]

7. "He who comes from heaven is over all. And what he has seen and heard, this he testifies, and his testimony no one receives." "He comes from heaven, he is over all," our Lord, Jesus Christ, about whom it was said earlier, "No one has ascended into heaven but he who has descended from heaven, the Son of man who is in heaven."[18] But he is over all; "and what he has seen and heard, this he speaks."

(2) For the Son of God himself also has a Father; he also has a Father and hears from the Father. And what is it that he hears from the Father? Who unravels this? When can my tongue, when can my heart suffice, either my heart for understanding, or my tongue for expressing what it is that the Son heard from the Father? Perhaps the Son heard the Word of the Father? No, no, the Son is the Word of the Father. You see how every human attempt is worn out here; you see how every conjecture of our hearts, every effort of the mind, shrouded in darkness, fails here. I hear Scripture saying that the Son speaks this which he hears from the Father; again I

14. Cf. Ps 17.29.
16. Cf. Gal 2.20.
18. Jn 3.13; *Tractate* 12.8.

15. Cf. 1 Cor 15.10.
17. Cf. *Tractate* 5.1.

hear Scripture saying that the Son himself is the Word of the Father: "In the beginning was the Word, and the Word was with God, and the Word was God."[19]

(3) We speak fleeting and transient words; as soon as your word has sounded in your mouth, it passes; it produces its noise and passes into silence. Can you pursue your sound and hold it fast so that it may stay? Yet your thought remains, and about that thought which remains you say many words which pass away. What are we saying, brothers? When God spoke, did he use a voice, did he use sounds, did he use syllables? If he did, in what language did he speak? Hebrew? or Greek? or Latin? Languages are necessary in that place where there is a separation of nations. But there no one can say that God spoke this language or that. Observe your own heart. When you conceive a word which you are to say—for I shall say, if I shall be able, what we observe in ourselves, not in what way we may comprehend that—when, therefore, you conceive a word which you are to express, you wish to say a thing, and the very conception of the thing in your heart is already a word; it has not yet gone forth but has already been born in your heart and waits that it may go forth.

(4) But you notice the person to whom it is to go forth, with whom you are to speak. If he is Latin, you look for a Latin word; if he is Greek, you think of the Greek word; if he is a Punic, you consider if you know the Punic language. According to the diversity of listeners, you use different languages that you might express the conceived word. But that which you had conceived in your heart was contained in no language. Therefore when God in speaking sought no language and adopted no kind of speech, how was he heard by the Son since God spoke the Son himself? For just as you have in your heart the word which you speak and it is with you and the very conception is spiritual (for just as your soul is spirit, so, too, the word which you have conceived is spirit; for it has not yet received sound to be divided into syllables, but it re-

19. Jn 1.1.

mains in the conception of the heart and in the mirror of the intellect), so God put forth the Word, that is, he begot the Son. And you, indeed, beget in time the word even in your heart; God begot without time the Son through whom he created all times. Therefore, since the Son is the Word of God, but the Son spoke to us, not his own word but the Word of the Father, he who was speaking the Word of the Father wanted to speak himself to us.

(5) Therefore, as it was fitting and necessary, John said this; as we could, we explained it. For him for whom understanding worthy of so great a thing has not yet come to his heart, he has a place to which he may turn himself; he has a place at which he may knock; he has one from whom he may seek, he has one from whom he may ask, he has one from whom he may receive.

8. "He who comes from heaven is over all. And what he has seen and heard, this he attests,[20] and his testimony no one receives." If no one, why did he come? Therefore no one of certain ones. There is a certain people, prepared for the wrath of God, to be damned with the devil; no one of these receives the witness of Christ. For if no one at all, no man, what does that which follows mean, "He who has received his testimony has certified that God is truthful"?

(2) Certainly, therefore, not "no one," if you yourself say, "He who has received his testimony has certified that God is truthful." Therefore, perhaps John, if asked, would answer and say, I know why I said, "no one." For there is a certain people, born for the wrath of God and predestined[21] for this. For God knows who will believe and who will not believe; God knows who will persevere in that which they have believed and who will lapse, and all who are to be for eternal life have

---

20. At the beginning of section 7, in citing this sentence, Augustine uses the Latin verb *testificatur,* but here he has *testatur* which is the *Vulgate* reading.

21. The Latin word is *praecognitus* which may also be translated "fore-known." For the meaning "predestined," see Blaise, 642. For a thorough discussion of Augustine's views on predestination see J. Saint-Martin, "La prédestination d'après les pères latins, particulièrement d'après saint Augustin," DThC 12.1.2832–2896.

been numbered by God.[22] And he already knows that separated people. And if he himself knows, and granted to the prophets to know through his Spirit, he granted it also to John. Therefore John was observing, but not with his own eye; for as far as pertains to him, he is earth and of the earth he speaks. But in that grace of the Spirit which he received from God, he saw a certain people, ungodly, unbelieving; observing that people in its unbelief, he said, "The testimony of him who comes from heaven no one receives."

(3) No one of whom? Of those who will be on the left hand, of those to whom it will be said, "Go into the everlasting fire which has been prepared for the devil and his angels."[23] Who, then, receives? Those who will be on the right hand, those to whom it will be said, "Come, blessed of my Father, possess the kingdom which has been prepared for you from the beginning of the world."[24] Therefore he observed a division in the Spirit; but a mingling in the human race; and what was not yet separated in place, he separated in understanding, he separated in the sight of his heart. And he saw two multitudes, the believers and the unbelievers. He observed the unbelievers and said, "He who comes from heaven is over all. And what he has seen and heard, this he attests, and his testimony no one receives." Then he moved away from the left hand and looked at the right hand; and continuing, he said, "He who has received his testimony has certified that God is truthful."

(4) What does it mean "has certified that God is truthful" except that man is prone to lie and God is truthful? For no one of men can say what truth there is unless he be enlightened by him who cannot lie.[25] Therefore God is truthful, but Christ is God. Do you want to prove it? Receive his testimony, and you find, "For he who has received his testimony has certified that God is truthful." Who? He who comes from

22. I take *Deo* here to be a dative of agent; this might also be translated, "have been allocated to God." On God's foreknowledge see also *Tractates* 7.14, 8.9, and 12.12. That there are a specific number of the elect, see *De Correptione et Gratia* 13.39 (PL 44.940; BA 24(1).358; and FOTC 5.293).

23. Cf. Mt 25.41.   24. Cf. Mt 25.34.

25. Cf. *Tractate* 5.1.

heaven and is over all, is truthful God. But if you do not yet understand that he is God, you have not yet received his testimony; receive, and you certify, you understand with confidence, you acknowledge with certitude that God is truthful.

9. "For he whom God has sent speaks the words of God." He is the truthful God, and God sent him. God sent God. Unite both; one God, the truthful God sent by God. Ask about each one, there is God; ask about both, there is God. They are not as individuals, God, and both together, gods; but each single one is God and both together are God. For so great is the love of the Holy Spirit there, so great the peace of unity that when it is asked about each one, let your answer be, God; when it is asked about the Trinity, let your answer be, God. For if the spirit of man is one spirit when it cleaves to God, since the Apostle clearly says, "He who cleaves to the Lord is one spirit,"[26] how much more is the Son, an equal, cleaving to the Father, one God together with him!

(2) Hear a second testimony: You know how many believed when they sold all that they had and laid [the money from] the sale at the feet of the apostles, that distribution might be made to each according to his need.[27] And what does Scripture say about that congregation of holy people? "They had one soul and one heart toward the Lord." If the love from so many souls made one soul and from so many hearts made one heart, how great is the love between Father and Son? It can, of course, be greater than among those men who were of one heart. Therefore if of many brothers there is one heart because of love, and of many brothers there is one soul because of love, are you going to say that God the Father and God the Son are two? If they are two gods, there is not the greatest love there. For if the love here is so great that it makes your soul and the soul of your friend one soul, how is there not one God there, Father and Son? Far be it that a faith not false think this.

(3) In short, understand from this the excellence of that love. There are many souls of many men; and if they love one

26. 1 Cor 6.17.   27. Cf. Acts 4.32–37.

another, there is one soul. But they can also be called many souls, they can, in the case of men, because there is not so great a union. There, however, you may say one God, but you may not say two or three gods. From this the supereminence and supreme grandeur of love, so great that it cannot be greater, is shown to you.

10. "For he whom God has sent speaks the words of God." He said this, of course, about Christ that he might distinguish himself from him. Why so? Did not God send John himself? And didn't he say himself, "I have been sent before him" and "He who sent me to baptize with water";[28] and about him it was said, "Behold, I send my messenger before you, and he will prepare your way"?[29] Does not he, too, speak the words of God, about whom it was said that he is more than a prophet?[30] Therefore if God also sent him and he speaks the words of God, how, in regard to the distinction [between himself and Christ], do we know that he said about Christ, "For he whom God has sent speaks the words of God"?

(2) But see what he adds: "For not by measure does God give the Spirit." What does this mean, "For not by measure does God give the Spirit"? We find that God does give the Spirit by measure. Hear the Apostle saying, "according to the measure of the giving of Christ."[31] He gives to men by measure; he does not give to the only Son by measure. How does he give to men by measure? "To one indeed by the Spirit is given the word of wisdom; to another, the word of knowledge according to the same Spirit; to another, faith in the same Spirit; to another prophecy; to another the discerning of spirits; to another [diverse] kinds of tongues; to another the gift of healings."

(3) "Are all apostles? Are all prophets? Are all teachers? Are all [the workers of] miracles? Do all have the gifts of healings? Do all speak with tongues? Do all interpret?"[32] This man has one thing; that man, another; and what that one

---

28. Cf. Jn 1.33.   29. Cf. Mt 11.10, quoting Mal 3.1.
30. Cf. Mt 11.9.   31. Eph 4.7.
32. Cf. 1 Cor 12.8–10 and 29–30.

has, this one does not have. There is a measure, a certain division of gifts. Therefore it is given to men by measure and there harmony makes one body. Just as the hand receives one thing to do its work, the eye another to see, the ear another to hear, the foot another to walk, and yet there is one soul which effects everything,[33] in the hand that it work, in the foot that it walk, in the ear that it hear, in the eye that it see, so, too, there are various gifts of the faithful, distributed [to them] as to members according to the measure proper to each. But Christ, who gives, does not receive according to measure.

11. For hear further what follows, because he had said about the Son, "For not according to measure does God give the Spirit. The Father loves the Son and has handed over all things to him." He added "has handed over all things to him" that also here you might know with what distinction it was said, "The Father loves the Son."

(2) For why? Does the Father not love John? And yet he has not handed over all things to him. Does the Father not love Paul? And yet he has not handed over all things to him. "The Father loves the Son," but as the Father loves the Son, not as a lord loves a servant; as the only [Son], not as an adopted [son]. And so "He has handed over all things to him."

(3) What does "all things" mean? That the Son be as great as the Father is. For he begot him for equality with himself for whom it were not robbery to be equal to God, in the form of God.[34] "The Father loves the Son and has handed over all things to him." Therefore, when he deigned to send the Son to us, let us not think that anything was sent to us less than the Father is. The Father in sending the Son sent his other self.

12. For indeed his disciples, still thinking that the Father was something greater than the Son, seeing the flesh and not understanding the divinity, said to him, "Lord, show us the Father and it is enough for us."[35] As though they were saying,

33. Cf. *Tractate* 8.2.   34. Cf. Phil 2.6.
35. Cf. Jn 14.8.

"We already know you and we bless you because we know you; for we thank you because you have shown yourself to us. But we do not yet know the Father; for this reason our heart is afire and is astir with a certain holy longing for seeing your Father who sent you; show him to us and we shall desire nothing more from you. For it is enough for us when he has been shown than whom no one can be greater."

(2) A good longing, a good desire, but little understanding! For the Lord Jesus himself, observing that they were little ones seeking great things, and that he was himself a great one among little ones and yet a little one among little ones, said to Philip, one of the disciples, who has said this, "Have I been so long a time with you, and have you not known me, Philip?"[36] Here Philip could have answered, "We know you; but did we say to you, 'Show us yourself'? You we know, but we are looking for the Father." [Jesus] immediately added, "He who sees me sees also the Father." Therefore if he was sent, equal to the Father, let us not judge him by the weakness of the flesh, but let us reflect upon his majesty, clothed with flesh, not submerged by flesh. For as God remaining with the Father, among men he became a man so that, through him who became a man for you, you might become such as grasps God.

(3) For man could not grasp God; man could see the man but could not grasp God. Why could he not grasp God? Because he did not have the eye of the heart by which he could grasp. Therefore there was a thing within, wounded, and a thing without, healthy; he had healthy eyes of the body, he had wounded eyes of the heart. He became man for the body's eye so that, believing in him who could be seen bodily, you would be cured to see him himself whom you could not see spiritually.[37] "Have I been so long a time with you, and have you not known me, Philip? He who sees me sees also the Father."

(4) Why did they not see him? Look, they saw him, and they did not see the Father; they saw his flesh, but the majesty

---

36. Cf. Jn 14.9.   37. Cf. *Tractate* 2.16.

was hidden. What the disciples who loved him saw, the Jews who crucified him saw also. Therefore within he was the whole, and within in the flesh in such a way that he remained with the Father; for he did not forsake the Father when he came to the flesh.

13. Human thought does not grasp what I am saying; let it defer understanding and begin from faith. Let it hear what follows: "He who believes in the Son has life everlasting, but he who is unbelieving towards the Son shall not see life, but the wrath of God rests upon him." He did not say, "The wrath of God comes to him" but "The wrath of God rests upon him." All who are born mortals have the wrath of God with them. What wrath of God? That which Adam first received. For if the first man sinned and heard "you will die the death,"[38] he became mortal and we began to be born mortals; with the wrath of God we are born.

(2) The Son has come from there, not having sin; and he was clothed with flesh, he was clothed with mortality. If he has shared the wrath of God with us, are we reluctant to share the grace of God with him? Therefore he who is unwilling to believe in the Son, "the wrath of God rests upon him." What wrath of God? That about which the Apostle says, "we also were by nature children of wrath, even as the rest."[39] Therefore we are all children of wrath, because coming from the curse of death.

(3) Believe in Christ made mortal for you, that you may grasp him immortal; for when you grasp his immortality, neither will you be mortal. He lived; you died. He died that you may live. He brought the grace of God; he took away the wrath of God. God conquered death, that death might not conquer man.

38. Cf. Gn 2.17.   39. Cf. Eph 2.3.

TRACTATE 15

On John 4.1–42

T IS NOT STRANGE to your ears, my beloved people, that the evangelist John soars to greater heights like an eagle, that he transcends the murky darkness of earth, and that he looks upon the light of truth with steadier gaze. For through our ministry, with God's help, many things have already been discussed from his gospel; this reading which was proclaimed today follows next in order. The things which I am going to say, by the gift of the Lord, many of you are going to hear more for review than for learning.[1] Nevertheless your attention ought not to be lax simply because there is not learning but review.

(2) This was read, and we take this reading in hand to discuss it, as to what the Lord Jesus talked about with the Samaritan woman at Jacob's well. For great mysteries were stated there, and analogies of great matters, feeding the hungering soul, refreshing the faint one.

2. For "when" the Lord "had heard" these things, "that the Pharisees had learned that he was making more disciples

---

1. There is no other sermon of Augustine that deals in detail with the Samaritan woman; see Berrouard, *Homélies I–XVI*, 756, 947–948, 951–952. Augustine does discuss Jn 4.6–29 at some length, but in less detail than here, in the *De Diversis Quaestionibus LXXXIII* 64 (CCL 44A.137–146; and FOTC 70.127–135). He interprets there the well, the sixth hour, the Lord's tiredness, sitting, thirst, the living water, the woman's husbands, and the leaving behind of the water jar; what he says is the same or very similar to what is said in this *Tractate*. He briefly discusses the passage in *Sermo* 101.2 (PL 38.606–607; *SPM* 1 [1950]) in connection with Lk 10.2; there he says that the Samaritan woman is grain, sown by the prophets and now ripe for harvesting by the Lord's laborers, the apostles, though she, too, in proclaiming Christ to her countrymen, is a harvester. The same interpretation will be found here in section 32.

than John and was baptizing more (although Jesus did not baptize, but his disciples), he left the country of Judea and went again into Galilee." There is no need for a lengthy discourse on this lest, by delaying on the obvious, we experience a shortness of time for investigating and clarifying obscurities. Of course, if the Lord knew that the Pharisees had learned thus about him, that he was making more disciples and that he was baptizing more, so that this would effect salvation for them if they followed him, so that they themselves, too, would be disciples and would themselves wish to be baptized by him, he would rather not have left the country of Judea, but would have remained there for their sakes; but because he knew their knowledge, [and because], at the same time, he also knew their envy, that they did not learn this for the purpose of following but of persecuting, he went away from there. Indeed, he had the power not to be detained by them, even if he were present, if he were unwilling; he had the power not to be killed, if he were unwilling; for he had the power even not to be born, if he were unwilling.[2]

(2) But because in everything he did as a man he provided an example for the men who would believe in him (for each servant of God does not sin if he departs to another place when perhaps he sees the fury of those persecuting him or seeking his soul for evil; but the servant of God might seem to himself to sin if he were to do this, had not the Lord preceded him in doing it), that good teacher did this to teach, not because he was afraid.

3. Perhaps it may also disturb you why it was said, "Jesus was baptizing more than John," and after it was said "He was baptizing," it was added, "although Jesus was not baptizing but his disciples." What is this? Had a falsehood been told and then corrected by the addition, "although Jesus was not baptizing, but his disciples"? Or is each statement true, that Jesus was baptizing and was not baptizing?

(2) For he was baptizing because he himself was cleansing; he was not baptizing because he himself was not doing the

---

2. Cf. *Tractate* 11.2.

immersion.[3] His disciples provided the ministry of the body; he provided the aid of his majesty.[4] For when would he cease from baptizing as long as he does not cease from cleansing? And about him it was said by the same John, speaking through the person of John the Baptist, "He it is who baptizes."[5] Therefore Jesus still baptizes; and as long as we must be baptized, Jesus baptizes. Let a man approach confidently to a lesser minister; for he has a superior teacher.

4. But perhaps someone says, "Christ does indeed baptize in spirit, but not in body." As if, in fact, each one is initiated even with the sacrament of bodily and visible baptism by the gift of another than him.

(2) Do you wish to know that he baptizes not only with the spirit but also with the water? Hear the Apostle. He says, "As Christ loved the Church, and delivered himself up for it, cleansing it by the bath of water in the Word, that he might present it to himself, a glorious Church, not having spot or wrinkle or any such thing."[6] Cleansing it. By what? "By the bath of water in the Word." What is the baptism of Christ? The bath of water in the Word. Take away the water; there is no baptism. Take away the Word; there is no baptism.

5. Now then, after these preliminaries, through which he came to the conversation with that woman, let us see what remains, full of mysteries and pregnant with symbols. [The gospel] says, "Now he had to pass through Samaria. He came therefore to a city of Samaria which is called Sichar, near the land which Jacob gave to his son Joseph. Now Jacob's spring was there."

(2) It was a well; now every well is a spring, but not every spring is a well. For where the water flows out of the ground and is provided to those who draw [from it] for their use, it is named a spring. But let it be ready at hand and on the surface, it is named only a spring; but let it be at a depth below the surfaces, it is then called a well but not so that the name of spring is lost.

---

3. For the meaning of the Latin verb *tingere*, see Blaise, 818.
4. Cf. *Tractates* 5.18 and 6.7–8.
5. Cf. Jn 1.33.   6. Cf. Eph 5.25–27.

6. "Jesus, therefore, wearied from the journey, was sitting thus at the spring. It was about the sixth hour." Now the mysteries begin. For Jesus is not wearied without a reason; for the power of God is not wearied without a reason. For he through whom the wearied are refreshed is not wearied without a reason. For he—at whose departure we are wearied and by whose presence we are strengthened—is not wearied without a purpose. Yet Jesus is wearied, and he is wearied from the journey; and he is sitting, and sitting next to the well, and wearied, he is sitting at the sixth hour. All of these things hint at something; they want to reveal something. They make us keenly attentive, they encourage us to knock. Therefore may he himself open both to us and to you, he who thought it good so to encourage us that he said, "Knock, and it shall be opened to you."[7]

(2) It was for you that Jesus was wearied from the journey. We find a strong Jesus[8] and we find a weak Jesus, strong because "In the beginning was the Word, and the Word was with God, and the Word was God. He was in the beginning with God."[9] Do you wish to see how this Son of God is strong? "All things were made through him and without him was made nothing,"[10] and they were made without effort. What, then, is stronger than he through whom all things were made without effort? Do you wish to know how he was weak? "The Word was made flesh and dwelt among us."[11] The strength of Christ created you; the weakness of Christ recreated you. The strength of Christ caused what-was-not to be; the weakness of Christ caused what-was to perish not. He produced us in his strength; he sought us in his weakness.[12]

7. Therefore, he, weak himself, nourishes the weak as a hen [nourishes] her chicks; in fact, he even applied this simile to himself. He said to Jerusalem, "How often would I have

7. Cf. Mt. 7.7.
8. Some codices read, "We find Jesus [who is] power."
9. Jn 1.1–2.   10. Cf. Jn 1.3.
11. Cf. Jn 1.14.
12. This is a theme frequently repeated in these early *Tractates;* see 1.12, 2.15, 10.1, and 12.8.

gathered together your children under my wings, as a hen
her chicks, and you would not."[13] But you see, brothers, how
the hen is weakened with her chicks. No other bird is [in-
stantly] identified as being a mother. We see some sparrows
make a nest before our eyes; we see swallows, storks, doves
make a nest every day. Only when we see them in their nests
do we realize that they are parents. But the hen is so weakened over her chicks that even if the chicks themselves were
not following her, [if] you did not see the young, you would
still identify her as a mother. With drooping wings, rough
plumage, a raucous voice, she becomes so dispirited and
downcast in all her limbs, that, as I said, even if you should
not see the young, you would still recognize her as a mother.

(2) So therefore Jesus was weak, wearied from the journey.
His journey is his flesh, assumed for us. For how does he who
is everywhere and is absent nowhere take a journey? Where
is he going to, or where is he going from, except that he could
not come to us unless he assumed the form of visible flesh?
Therefore, because he deigned to come to us in this manner,
that he appeared in the form of a servant by assuming flesh,
the very assumption of flesh is his journey. Therefore what
else does "wearied from the journey" mean than wearied in
the flesh?

(3) Jesus was weak in the flesh. But you, be not weakened;
in his weakness be strong, "because the weakness of God is
stronger than men."[14]

8. Under this image of things Adam who was "a figure of
him who was to come"[15] provided for us a great disclosure of
the mystery; rather God provided it in him. For while he was
sleeping, he was both judged worthy of receiving a wife and
a wife was made for him from his rib;[16] for, from Christ,
while he was sleeping on the cross, the Church was going to
come into being—from his side, from his side, obviously,
while he was sleeping, because from the lance-pierced side of

13. Cf. Mt 23.37.   14. Cf. 1 Cor 1.25.
15. Cf. Rom 5.14.   16. Cf. Gn 2.21–22.

Christ hanging on the cross the sacraments of the Church flowed forth.[17]

(2) But why did I want to say this, brothers? Because the weakness of Christ makes us strong. A great image preceded there. God could have taken flesh from the man with which to make the woman, and that, it seems, would have been more appropriate, as it were. For the weaker sex was being made, and weakness ought to have come more from flesh than from bone, since bones are the stronger parts in the flesh. He did not take flesh with which to make the woman, but he took bone; and the woman was fashioned from the bone that was taken and flesh was filled up in the place of the bone. He could have returned bone for bone; he could have taken, not a rib, but flesh for making the woman. What then did he signify? The woman was made, in respect of the rib, as one strong; Adam was made, in respect of the flesh, as one weak. It is Christ and the Church; his weakness is our strength.

9. Why, then, at the sixth hour? Because in the sixth age of the world.[18] In the gospel, count as one hour the one age from Adam to Noe, the second from Noe to Abraham, the third from Abraham to David, the fourth from David to the banishment to Babylon, the fifth from the banishment to Babylon to the baptism of John; the sixth is in progress from then on. Why are you amazed? Jesus came; and, humbling himself, he came to the well. He came wearied, because he carried weak flesh. At the sixth hour, because in the sixth age of the world. To the well, because to the depth of this dwelling-place[19] of ours. Wherefore it is said in the Psalm, "Out of the depths I have cried to you, O Lord."[20] He sat, as I said, because he was humbled.

---

17. Cf. *Tractate* 9.10.   18. Cf. *Tractate* 9, passim.

19. He means the world, not a person's body; cf. *De Diversibus Quaestionibus LXXXIII* 64.2 (PL 40.55; CCL 44A.137–138; and FOTC 70.128–129). Also in section 16 he takes the water in the well as the pleasure of the world in its dark depths.

20. Ps 129.1.

10. "And there came a woman." A figure of the Church, not yet justified, but now about to be justified; for the discourse deals with this topic. She comes unknowing, she finds him, and there is a conversation with her. Let us see what, let us see why. "There came a woman of Samaria to draw water." The Samaritans did not belong to the nation of the Jews. They were foreigners although they inhabited neighboring lands. It is too long a story to recount the origin of the Samaritans, lest too many things detain us, and we should not speak about what is necessary. Therefore it is enough for us to classify the Samaritans as foreigners. And that you may not think that I have said this more rashly than truly, hear the Lord himself, what he said about that Samaritan, one of the ten lepers whom he had cleansed, who alone returned to give thanks: "Were not ten made clean? And where are the nine? There was no other to give glory to God except this foreigner!"[21]

(2) It is relevant to the image of the reality that this woman, who mystically signified the Church, comes from foreigners. For the Church was to come from the nations alien to the race of the Jews. Therefore let us hear ourselves in that woman, let us recognize ourselves in that woman, and let us give thanks to God in that woman for ourselves. For she was a symbol, not the truth; for she both exhibited the symbol and became the truth. For she believed in him who was extending from that woman a symbol to us. Therefore, "she comes to draw water." She had come simply to draw water as either men or women usually do.

11. "Jesus says to her, 'Give me to drink.' For his disciples had gone away into the city to buy food. Then that Samaritan woman says to him, 'How do you, although you are a Jew, ask of me to drink, who am a Samaritan woman?' For the Jews do not communicate with the Samaritans."

(2) You see the foreigners; the Jews did not at all use their vessels. And because the woman was carrying a vessel with her with which to draw water, she was astounded, for this

21. Cf. Lk 17.17–18.

reason, because a Jew was asking for a drink from it, something which Jews do not usually do. But he who was seeking a drink was thirsting for that woman's faith.

12. Next hear who asks for a drink. "Jesus answered and said to her, 'If you knew the gift of God, and who he is who says to you, "Give me to drink," you perhaps would have asked of him, and he would have given you living water.'" He asks for a drink, and he promises a drink. He is in need as one who is going to receive; and he is rich as one who is going to satisfy. "If you knew," he says, "the gift of God."

(2) The gift of God is the Holy Spirit. But he is still speaking obscurely to the woman and entering little by little into her heart. Perhaps he is already teaching. For what is sweeter and kinder than this exhortation? "If you knew the gift of God and knew who he is who says to you, 'Give me to drink,' you perhaps would ask, and he would give you living water."

(3) Thus far he keeps her in suspense. That water which comes out of a spring is commonly called living water. For that which is collected from the rain in pools or cisterns is not called living water. Even if it has flowed from a spring and has been collected in some place, and has been standing and has not admitted to itself that from which it was flowing, but with its course interrupted, separated, as it were, from the path of the spring—that is not called living water. But that is called living water which is taken flowing. Such was the water in that spring. Why, then, did he promise her what he was asking for?

13. Yet the woman, left in suspense, says, "Sir, you have nothing to draw with, and the well is deep." See how she understood living water, namely the water that was in that spring. You want to give me living water, and I am carrying the means to draw and you are not. Here is living water; how are you going to give it to me?

(2) Although understanding something else and knowing carnally, she is knocking in a way, that the teacher may open what was closed. She was knocking with ignorance, not with zeal; she is still to be pitied, not yet to be instructed.

14. The Lord says something clearer about that living

water. For the woman had said, "Are you greater than our
father Jacob who gave us the well, and drank[22] from it himself, and his sons, and his cattle?" You cannot give me from
this living water because you do not have a bucket. Perhaps
you are promising another spring? Can you be better than
our father who dug this well and used it himself with his
family. Let the Lord, then, say what he meant by living water.

(2) "Jesus answered and said to her, 'Whosoever drinks of
this water will thirst again. But he, who drinks of the water
that I will give him shall not thirst, forever; but the water that
I will give him shall become in him a fountain of water,
springing up into life everlasting.'" The Lord spoke more
clearly [when he said], "shall become in him a fountain of
water, springing up into life everlasting. He who drinks of
that water shall not thirst, forever."

(3) What is clearer, that he promised not visible water, but
invisible? What is clearer, that he spoke, not in a physical
sense, but in a spiritual one?

15. Yet that woman still understands the physical sense;
she was delighted not to thirst and thought that this was
promised her by the Lord according to the flesh. And, indeed, this will happen, but at the resurrection of the dead.
She wanted this right now. For God had once granted his
servant Elias that he neither hunger nor thirst for forty
days.[23] Could he who could grant this for forty days not grant
it forever?

(2) Yet she sighed, not wanting to be in need, not wanting
to work. She was forced to come continually to that spring, to
be burdened with the weight by which her need might be
fulfilled and, when what she had drawn was used up, to come
back again. And this was her daily work, because that need
was repeated and not extinguished. Therefore, delighted by
such a gift, she asks that he give her living water.

16. But, indeed, let us not pass over the fact that the Lord
was promising something spiritual. What does it mean, "He

22. The CCL reading *bibet*, "will drink," is clearly a misprint.
23. Cf. 3 Kgs 19.8.

who drinks of this water will thirst again"? It is true both according to this water, and according to what that water signified. For the water in the well is the pleasure of the world in its dark depths; here men drink it from the water jar of desires. To be sure, they, bending down, let down their desire that they might reach the pleasure drawn from the deep; and they enjoy the pleasure, for which desire was first sent out, and anticipates. For he who has not first sent out desire cannot reach the pleasure.

(2) Therefore understand the water jar to be desire, and the water from the deep to be pleasure. When each one attains the pleasure of this world, it is food, it is drink, it is the bath, it is the theater, it is sexual intercourse. Will he not thirst again? Therefore, he says, "He who drinks of this water will thirst again." But if he receives water from me, "he will not thirst forever." "We will be filled," [the Psalm] says, "with the good things of your house."[24] Therefore of what water will he give except that of which it was said, "With you is the fountain of life"?[25] For how will they thirst who "will be inebriated with the richness of your house"?[26]

17. He was promising, therefore, a certain abundant nourishment of the Holy Spirit, and she did not yet understand. And, not understanding, what did she respond? "The woman says to him, 'Sir, give me this water that I may not thirst nor come here to draw.'" Her need forced her to work, and her weakness objected to the work. Would that she had heard, "Come to me, all you who labor and are burdened, and I shall refesh you."[27] For Jesus was saying this to her, that she might labor no longer but she did not yet understand.

18. Then, wishing her to understand, "Jesus says to her, 'Go, call your husband and come here.'" What is this "Call your husband"? Did he want to give her that water through her husband? Or was it that, because she did not understand, he wanted to teach her through her husband? Perhaps as the Apostle says about women, "But if they want to learn any-

24. Cf. Ps 64.5.
26. Cf. Ps 35.9.
25. Cf. Ps 35.10.
27. Cf. Mt 11.28.

thing, let them ask their husbands at home."[28] But there it is said, "Let them ask their husbands at home," where Jesus is not the one who would teach; and it is said to women whom the Apostle was prohibiting from speaking in church. But when the Lord himself was there and, being present, was speaking to one who was present, what need was there that he speak to her through her husband? Was it through her husband that he spoke to Mary, sitting at his feet and receiving his word, when Martha, very busy with much serving, was grumbling even about her sister's good fortune?[29] Therefore, my brothers, let us hear and understand what the Lord says to the woman, "Call your husband."

(2) For perhaps he is also saying to our soul, "Call your husband." Let us ask also about the husband of the soul. Why is not Jesus himself now the true husband of the soul? Let your understanding be present because what we are about to say is scarcely grasped except by the attentive. Therefore let your understanding be present and perchance the understanding itself will be the husband of the soul.

19. Therefore Jesus, seeing that the woman didn't understand and wishing her to understand, said, "Call your husband." For you do not know what I am saying precisely because your understanding is not present; I am speaking according to the spirit, you are hearing according to the flesh. What I am saying pertains neither to the pleasure of the ears, nor to the eyes, nor to smell, nor to taste, nor to touch; my words are grasped by the mind alone, they are drawn by the understanding alone. Your understanding is not present; how do you grasp what I am saying? "Call your husband," that is, bring forth your understanding.

(2) For what advantage is it to you to have a soul? It is no great thing, for even a brute animal has one. How are you better? Because you have an understanding which the brute animal does not have.[30] What then does it mean, "Call your husband"? You do not grasp me, you do not understand me.

28. Cf. 1 Cor 14.35. 29. Cf. Lk 10.39–40.
30. Cf. *Tractates* 3.4 and 8.2.

I am speaking to you about a gift of God, but you are thinking about the flesh. According to the flesh you do not want to be thirsty; I am speaking to the spirit. Your understanding is absent; "Call your husband." "Do not be like the horse and the mule which have no understanding."[31] Therefore, my brothers, to have a soul and not to have an understanding, that is, not to use it nor to live according to it, is a beast's life. For there is in us something bestial by which we live in the flesh; but it must be ruled by the understanding. For the understanding rules from above the impulses of the soul when it moves itself according to the flesh and desires to pour itself out immoderately into carnal delights.

(3) Who ought to be called a husband? He who rules, or he who is ruled? Without a doubt when life has been well ordered, the understanding rules the soul, while belonging to the soul itself.[32] For it is not something other than the soul, but understanding is something of the soul, just as the eye is not something other than the flesh, but the eye is something of the flesh. But although the eye is something of the flesh, nevertheless it alone fully enjoys the light; but the remaining members of the flesh can be flooded with light; they cannot perceive the light. The eye alone is both flooded by it and enjoys it fully. So in our souls there is something which is called understanding. This very part of the soul, which is called understanding and the mind, is enlightened by a higher light. Now that higher light by which the human mind is enlightened is God. For "there was the true light which enlightens every man who comes into this world."[33] Such a light was Christ; such a light was speaking with the woman. And she was not present with her understanding which would be enlightened by that light, and not only be flooded by it, but also enjoy it. Therefore the Lord, as if he were saying, "I wish to enlighten, and the one whom [I wish to enlighten] is not here," said, "Call your husband."

(4) Use understanding as that through which you may be

---

31. Cf. Ps 31.9.   32. Cf. *Tractate* 2.14.
33. Jn 1.9.

taught, by which you may be ruled. Therefore, put the soul, apart from understanding, as the woman, and, furthermore, that "she" has understanding, as her husband. But this husband does not rule his woman well except when he is ruled by one above him. For the husband is the head of the wife, but Christ is the head of the husband.[34] The head of the husband was speaking with the woman and the husband was not present. And as if the Lord said, "Bring your head here that he might receive his head," therefore, "call your husband and come here," that is, be at hand, be present. For you are, so to speak, absent as long as you do not understand the voice of the truth who is present; be present, but not alone, be here with your husband.

20. And still she does not understand, as her husband was not yet summoned; she still savors the flesh, for her husband is absent. "I have," she said, "no husband." And the Lord continues and speaks mysteries. You are to understand that this woman truly did not have a husband then; but she was cohabiting with some man in an illicit relationship, an adulterer rather than a husband. "And the Lord [said] to her, 'You have said well, "I have no husband."'" Why then did you say, "Call your husband"? And hear that the Lord well knew that she had no husband: "He said to her, etc." And that the woman might not perhaps think that the Lord had said, "You have said well, 'I have no husband,'" for this reason, namely that he learned this from the woman, not because he himself knew it because of his divinity, hear something which you did not say, "For you have had five husbands. And this one whom you have is not your husband. This you have said truly."

21. Again he compels us to search out something more subtle in these five husbands. To be sure, many have understood, and, indeed, it is not absurd nor entirely improbable, the five husbands of this woman to be the five books of Moses.[35] For the Samaritans used them and were under the

---

34. Cf. 1 Cor 11.3.
35. This was the interpretation of Ambrose, *Expositio Evangelii Secundum Lucam* 7.199, 9.38 (CCL 14.283 and 344). Origen, *Commentaria In Evangelium*

same Law; for from it they, too, had circumcision. But because what follows restricts us—"And he whom you now have is not your husband"[36]—it seems to me that we could more easily take the five earlier husbands of the soul to be the five senses of the body. For when each man is born, before he can use his mind and reason, he is ruled only by the senses of the flesh. In the small child the soul seeks after, or flees from, what is heard, what is seen, what gives off a smell, what has taste, what is perceived by touch. It seeks after whatever soothes, flees from whatever offends these five senses. For pleasure soothes these five senses; pain offends them. The soul lives first according to these five senses, like five husbands, because it is ruled by them.

(2) But why are they called husbands? Because they are licit, made by God, of course, and given by God to the soul. It is still a weak soul which is ruled by these five senses and lives under these five husbands; but when the soul comes to the years of exercising reason, if excellent training and instruction in wisdom have taken it under their protection, there succeeds to those five husbands for ruling only a true and licit husband, both better than they, and who may rule better, and who may rule for eternity, cultivate for eternity, instruct for eternity. For these five senses do not rule us for eternity, but for these temporal things which are to be sought after or fled from. But when the understanding, imbued with wisdom, begins to rule the soul, the soul now knows not only how to flee from a ditch and to walk on the level ground which the eyes show to the weak soul, but to hear only sweetly harmonious sounds and to reject the dissonant, to be delighted by pleasant odors and to repel stenches, to be captivated by sweetness and offended by bitterness, and to be soothed by soft things and

---

Ioannis 13.9 (PG 14.412–413; SC 222.58–62), holds the same view as Augustine. In the *De Diversis Quaestionibus LXXXIII* 64.6–7 (CCL 44A.142–145; and FOTC 70.132), he expounds both views, but he rejects the interpretation of the five books of Moses on the ground that the woman no longer has the five husbands whereas the Christian "embraces those five books all the more avidly in order to understand them spiritually."

36. Observe that this version of this sentence is different from the one at the end of section 20 and in section 22.

vexed by hard ones. For all these things are necessary for the weak soul.

(3) Therefore, what guidance is furnished through that understanding? It will not distinguish white and black, but just and unjust, good and evil, useful and useless, chastity and impurity, to love the one, to avoid the other, love and hate, to abide in the one, not to abide in the other.

22. This husband had not succeeded those five husbands in this woman. For where he does not succeed, error dominates. For when the soul begins to be capable of reason, it is either ruled by a wise mind or by error; but error does not rule; it destroys. Therefore after these five senses, that woman was still erring and error was bandying her about. But this error was not a licit husband, but an adulterer. Therefore the Lord said to her, "You have said well, 'I have no husband.' For you have had five husbands." The five senses of the flesh first ruled you; you have come to the age of using reason but you have not attained wisdom but have fallen into error. Therefore after these five husbands, "this one whom you have is not your husband." And what was he, if not a husband, but an adulterer? "Call" therefore, not the adulterer, but "your husband," that you comprehend me with your understanding and not perceive something false about me by error.

(2) For the woman who was thinking about that water was still in error since the Lord was now speaking about the Holy Spirit. Why was she in error except that she had an adulterer, not a husband? Therefore, remove from here that adulterer who corrupts you, and "Go, call your husband." Call, and come, that you may understand me.

23. "The woman says to him, 'Sir, I see that you are a prophet.'" The husband has begun to come; he has not yet fully come. She thought the Lord a prophet. He was, indeed, a prophet too; for he said of himself, "A prophet is not without honor, except in his own country."[37] Likewise it was said to Moses about him, "I will raise up for them a prophet from among their brothers like to you."[38] Like, namely, according

37. Cf. Mt 13.57; Mk 6.4; Lk 4.24; and Jn 4.44.
38. Cf. Dt 18.18.

to the form of the flesh, not to the eminence of majesty. Therefore, we find the Lord Jesus called a prophet. Accordingly
that woman is no longer greatly in error. "I see," she says,
"that you are a prophet." She begins to call her husband, to
exclude the adulterer. "I see that you are a prophet." And she
begins to ask about a thing that constantly disturbs her.

(2) For there has been a dispute between the Samaritans
and the Jews because the Jews worshipped God in the temple
built by Solomon. The Samaritans, located far from it, did not
worship in it. Therefore the Jews boasted that they were better
because they worshipped God in the temple. "For the Jews do
not communicate with the Samaritans," because [the Samar-
itans] said to them, "How do you boast and assert that you
are therefore better than we are because you have a temple
which we do not have? Did our fathers who pleased God worship in that temple? Did they not worship on this mountain
where we are? We therefore," they say, "pray to God better
on this mountain where our fathers prayed." They were both
contending in ignorance, not having a husband; the ones over
a temple, the others over a mountain, were full of conceit
toward one another.

24. At any rate, what does the Lord now teach the woman,
as if her husband began to be present? "The woman says to
him, 'Sir, I see you are a prophet. Our fathers worshiped on
this mountain, and you say that at Jerusalem is the place where
men ought to worship.' Jesus says to her, 'Woman, believe
me.'" For the Church will come, as was said in the Song of
Songs, "She will come and will pass through from the beginning of faith."[39] She will come that she might pass through
and she cannot pass through except "from the beginning of
faith." Rightly, with her husband now present, she hears,
"Woman, believe me." For now there is in you one who may
believe because your husband is present.

(2) You have begun to be present with your understanding,
when you called me a prophet. "Woman, believe me," because
if you do not believe, you will not understand.[40] Therefore,

39. Cf. Cant (Song) 4.8 (LXX).   40. Cf. Is 7.9 (LXX).

"Woman, believe me, that the hour will come when neither on this mountain nor in Jerusalem will you worship the Father. You worship what you do not know; we worship what we know, for salvation is from the Jews. But the hour will come." When? "And it is now." What hour, then? "When the true worshippers will worship the Father in spirit and in truth." Not on this mountain, not in the temple, but in spirit and in truth. "For the Father also seeks such to worship him." Why does the Father seek such to worship him, not on the mountain, not in the temple, but in spirit and in truth?

(3) "God is a spirit." If God were a body, he ought to be worshipped on the mountain, for the mountain is a bodily thing; he ought to be worshipped in the temple, for the temple is a bodily thing. "God is a spirit, and they who worship him must worship in spirit and in truth."

25. We have heard, and it is clear; we had gone outside, we have been sent within. "Oh would that I had found," you said, "some high and lonely mountain![41] For, I believe, because God is on high, he hears me from a high place." Because you are on a mountain, do you think that you are near God and that you are heard quickly, as if shouting from nearby? He dwells on high, but "He looks on the low."[42] "The Lord is near." To whom? Perhaps to the high? "To those who are contrite of heart."[43] It is a wondrous thing: He both lives on high and draws near to the low. "He looks on the low, but the high he knows from afar."[44] He sees the proud from afar; the higher they seem to themselves, so much of the less does he approach them.

(2) Did you therefore seek the mountain? Come down that you may reach it. But do you want to ascend? Ascend; do not seek the mountain. "Ascendings," it says, "are in his heart," a Psalm says this, "in a valley of weeping."[45] A valley has lowness. Therefore act wholly within. And if, perhaps, you seek some high place, some holy place, present yourself within as

---

41. Cf. *Tractate* 10.1.   42. Ps 137.6.
43. Cf. Ps 33.19.   44. Cf. Ps 137.6.
45. Cf. Ps 83.6–7 (LXX). For "ascendings" Augustine here reads *adscensiones* with the *Vulgate*; in *En in Ps* 83.10 (CCL 39.1155–57) he has *adscensus*.

a temple for God. "For the temple of God is holy, which you are."[46] Do you want to pray in a temple? Pray in yourself. But first be a temple of God, because he will hear you praying in his temple.

26. "The hour then is coming, and it is now, when the true worshippers will worship the Father in spirit and in truth. We worship what we know; you worship what you do not know. For salvation is from the Jews." He gave much to the Jews; but do not take it to be these renegades. Understand that wall to which another has been joined in order that, abiding in peace upon the cornerstone which is Christ, they may be joined together. For one wall is from the Jews; one, from the Gentiles. Those walls are distant from each other, but only until they are joined in the corner.[47]

(2) But foreigners are sojourners and strangers to the testaments of God.[48] Therefore, according to this, it was said, "We worship what we know." It was said, about the role of the Jews but not of all the Jews, not of the renegade Jews, but about such as the apostles were, such as the prophets were, such as were all those holy people who sold their possessions and laid the price for their possessions at the feet of the apostles.[49] For God has not cast off his people whom he foreknew.[50]

27. That woman heard this and added [more]. She already called him a prophet; she saw that he with whom she was speaking said such things which now even more pertained to a prophet. And see what she answered: "The woman says to him, 'I know the Messias will come (who is called Christ); therefore, when he has come, he will show us all things.'" What does this mean? "Now," she says, "the Jews contend for the temple and we contend for the mountain; when he has come, he will both scorn the mountain and overturn the temple. This one will teach us all things that we may know how to worship in spirit and in truth."

(2) She knew who could teach her, but still did not yet recognize him already teaching. She was now, therefore, wor-

46. Cf. 1 Cor 3.17.   47. Cf. *Tractate* 9.17.
48. Cf. Eph 2.11–22.   49. Cf. Acts 4.34–35.
50. Cf. Rom 11.2.

thy that he be made manifest to her. Now *Messias* is "the Anointed." In Greek "the Anointed" is *Christus*. In Hebrew it is *Messias*, whence also in Punic *Messe* means "anoint"! These languages, Hebrew, Punic, and Syrian,[51] are relatives and neighbors.

28. Therefore "the woman says to him, 'I know the Messias will come (who is called Christ), and when he has come, He will tell[52] all things to us.' Jesus says to her, 'I, who am speaking with you, am he.'" She called her husband; her husband was made head of the woman, Christ was made head of the husband.[53] Now the woman is established in faith and is ruled, one who will live a good life. After she hears, "I, who am speaking with you, am he," what would she now say further, since Christ the Lord willed to manifest himself to the woman to whom he had said, "Believe me"?

29. "And immediately his disciples came; and they wondered that he was speaking with the woman." That he was seeking a lost woman, he who had come to seek what had been lost,[54] at this they wondered. For they were wondering at a good thing; they were not suspecting evil. "Yet no one said, 'What do you seek?' or 'Why do you speak with her?'"

30. "The woman therefore left her water jar." When she had heard the words, "I, who am speaking with you, am he," and had received the Lord Christ in her heart, what should she do except now leave her water jar and run to proclaim the good news? She cast out her desire and hastened to announce the truth. Let them who want to preach the gospel learn; let them cast aside the water jar at the well. Remember

51. Both Gibb and Browne take this to be Syriac, an eastern dialect of Aramaic that developed in the area of Upper Mesopotamia and Syria about the fourth century B.C. and became the predominant Christian language in the area of Edessa, an important Christian center after about 200 A.D. It is probably Syriac that Augustine has in mind. See P. Auvroy, et al., *Sacred Languages*, tr. J. Tester (New York, 1960), 69–71; A. Jones, *The Later Roman Empire 284–602* (Oxford, 1964) 2.994; H. Katzner, *The Languages of the World* (New York, 1975), 164–165; and B. Metzger, *The Early Versions of the New Testament* (Oxford, 1977), 4–8.

52. Observe a difference in this text from its quotation in the previous section.

53. Cf. 1 Cor 11.3.   54. Cf. Lk 19.10.

what I said earlier about the water jar.[55] It is a vessel with which water was drawn; in its Greek name it is called *hydría* because in Greek water is called *hýdor,* just as if *aquarium* (a container for water) were used. Therefore she cast aside the water jar which was no longer useful, but a burden; for she was eagerly longing to be satiated with that water.

(2) That she might announce the Christ, her burden thrown away, "she ran to the city and says to the men there, 'Come and see a man who has told me all that I have done.'" Step by step, that they might not be, as it were, angered and indignant and persecute her: "'Come and see a man who has told me all that I have done. Is not he the Christ?' They went out of the city and came to him."

31. "Meanwhile, his disciples implored him, saying, 'Rabbi, eat.'" For they had gone to buy food and they had come back. "But he said, 'I have food to eat which you do not know.' The disciples therefore said to one another, 'Has someone brought him [something] to eat?'"

(2) What wonder if that woman did not understand the water? Look, the disciples do not yet understand the food. But he has heard their thoughts, and he now instructs them as their teacher, not in a roundabout way as that woman whose husband he was seeking, but now openly, he says, "My food is to do the will of him who sent me." Therefore, it was also his drink, in the case of that woman, to do the will of him who had sent him. For this reason he said, "I thirst, give me to drink,"[56] namely that he might produce faith in her, drink her faith, and transport her into his body; for his body is the Church. Therefore he said, it is "my food to do the will of him who sent me."

32. "Do you not say, 'There are yet four months, and the harvest comes'?" He was burning with excitement for the work; he was making arrangements to send the laborers. You reckon four months to the harvest; I am showing you another harvest, white and ready. "Look, I say to you, lift up your eyes

55. See section 16 and cf. *Tractate* 9.6.
56. A conflation of Jn 19.28 and 4.7.

and see that the countrysides are already white for the harvest." Therefore he will send the reapers. "For in this is the saying true, that it is one man who reaps, another who sows, so that both he who sows and he who reaps may rejoice together."
(2) "I have sent you to reap that in which you have not labored. Others have labored, and you have entered into their labor." What then? Did he send the reapers and not the sowers? Where [did he send] the reapers? Where others had already labored. For where the labor had already been done, of course, the sowing had been done; and what had been sown had now become ripe and needed the scythe and threshing. Where, therefore, were reapers to be sent? Where the prophets had already preached; for they were the sowers. For if they were not the sowers, how had it come to that woman [to say], "I know the Messias will come"? Already that woman was ripe fruit, and there were white harvests, and they required the scythe. "I have sent you" therefore; where? "To reap what you have not sown; others have sown, and you have entered into their labors."

(3) Who labored? Abraham, Isaac, and Jacob. Read their labors! In all their labors [there was] prophecy of Christ; and thus [they were] the sowers. Moses and the rest of the patriarchs and all the prophets, how much did they endure in that cold when they were sowing! Therefore in Judea the harvest was now ready. Rightly there the crop was, so to speak, ripe, when so many thousands of men were bringing the price of their possessions; and laying it at the feet of the apostles, their shoulders freed of worldly baggage, they were following Christ, the Lord.[57] Truly a ripe harvest. What came of it? From that harvest a few grains were cast out, and they sowed the world, and there arises another harvest which is to be reaped at the end of the world. About this harvest it is said, "They who sow in tears shall reap in joy."[58] To this harvest,

57. Cf. Acts 4.34–35 and section 26.
58. Ps 125.5.

therefore, not apostles, but angels will be sent; he says, "The reapers are the angels."[59]

(4) Therefore, this harvest grows amid tares and waits to be purged in the end. That harvest was truly ripe already, to which the disciples were first sent, where the prophets labored. But still, brothers, see what was said: "Both he who sows and he who reaps may rejoice together." They had labors dissimilar in time; but they will enjoy rejoicing together; they will together receive as their pay eternal life.

33. "Now many of the Samaritans of that city believed in him because of the word of the woman giving testimony, 'He told me all that I have done.' Now when the Samaritans had come to him, they asked him to stay with them; and he stayed there two days. And many more believed because of his word. And they said to the woman, 'We now believe, not because of your saying, for we ourselves heard and know that this is indeed the Savior of the world.'"

(2) And this must be considered but briefly because the reading has ended. The woman first proclaimed, and the Samaritans believed on the woman's testimony. They asked him to stay with them, and he stayed there two days; and more believed. And when they had believed, they said to the woman, "Now we do not believe because of your word, but we ourselves have learned and know that this is, indeed, the Savior of the world," first through her report, then through his presence.

(3) So is it done today with those who are outside and not yet Christians. Christ is announced through Christian friends; and, as if with that woman, that is, the Church, announcing, they come to Christ; they believe through this report. He stays with them for two days, that is, he gives them two precepts of love;[60] and many more believe in him even more strongly, that he is, indeed, the Savior of the world.

59. Cf. Mt 13.39.
60. Cf. Mt 22.34–40; Mk 12.28–31; Lk 10.25–28.

TRACTATE 16

On John 4.43–53

ODAY'S GOSPEL READING, which is to be the subject of our sermon, continues yesterday's reading. Indeed, the meanings in it are not difficult to investigate, but they are worthy of our preaching, worthy of our admiration and praise. Accordingly, let us recount this passage of the gospel with commendation, rather than examine it with rigor. For, after the two days which he had spent in Samaria, Jesus "went away into Galilee" where he had been raised. Moreover, the Evangelist continues and says, "For Jesus himself gave testimony that a prophet has no honor in his own country." Therefore Jesus did not depart from Samaria after two days because he had no honor in Samaria; for Samaria was not his country, but Galilee. Since, therefore, he had departed from this place so quickly and had come to Galilee where he had been raised, how does he attest "that a prophet has no honor in his own country"? It seems rather that he could have attested that a prophet does not have honor in his own country if he had remained in Samaria and disdained to go to Galilee.

2. Pay attention, then, my beloved people, to the not small mystery which has been conveyed to us as the Lord suggests and gives what I should say. You know the proposed question; seek out its solution. But let us repeat the proposition that we may make the solution desirable. It concerns us why the Evangelist said, "For Jesus himself gave testimony that a prophet has no honor in his own country." Perturbed by this, we retrace the earlier words to find why the Evangelist wanted to say this; and we find the earlier words of [the Evangelist] who tells us thus, that after two days he set out from Samaria to Galilee. Was it for this reason, then, O Evangelist, that you

said that Jesus gave testimony that a prophet has no honor in his own country, because after two days he left Samaria and hastened to come to Galilee? No, rather, I seem to understand it as more appropriate that, if Jesus did not have honor in his own country, he would not have left Samaria and hurried to this same country.

(2) But if I am not mistaken—no, rather, because it is true and I am not mistaken, for the Evangelist said what he was saying better than I—he who drank it from the breast of the Lord[1] saw the truth better than I. For he is John the Evangelist who among all the disciples was reclining on the breast of the Lord and whom the Lord, although owing love to all, nevertheless loved above the others. Therefore would he be mistaken and I perceive the right? No, rather, if I am devout and sensible, I shall listen obediently to what he said that I might deserve to perceive what he perceived.

3. And so, my dearest people, what I think on this point, accept without prejudice if you think something better. For we all have one teacher, and we are fellow students in one school. Therefore I think this; and see if what I think is not true or approaches the truth. He spent two days in Samaria and the Samaritans believed in him; he spent so very many days in Galilee, and the Galileans did not believe in him. Go back over or recall in your memory both yesterday's reading and sermon. He came into Samaria where first that woman, with whom he spoke great mysteries at Jacob's well, had proclaimed him; when he had been seen and heard, the Samaritans believed in him on account of the woman's word, and they believed more strongly on account of his word, and more believed. So it was written.

(2) After he spent two days there (and by this number of days there is mystically revealed the number of the two commandments on which two commandments the whole Law and the prophets depend, as you remember we mentioned yesterday),[2] he went to Galilee and came into the city of Cana in

---

1. Cf. Jn 13.23 and 25, 21.20.
2. Cf. Mt 22.34–40 and *Tractate* 15.33.

Galilee where he made the water into wine. And there, when he turned water into wine, as John himself writes, his disciples believed in him; and certainly the house was filled with crowds of guests.[3] So great a miracle was performed and only his disciples believed in him.

(3) Now he sought this city of Galilee again. "And behold, a certain royal official, whose son was sick, came to him, and began to ask him to come down" (to that city or house) "and heal his son, for he was at the point of death." He who asked, did he not believe? What are you expecting to hear from me? Ask the Lord what he perceived about that man. For when he was asked, he answered as follows: "Unless you see signs and wonders, you do not believe." He charged the man with being lukewarm in faith, or even cold, or even of no faith at all, but with a desire to try to find out, for the sake of his son's health, what sort of person Christ was, who he was, how much he could do. For we heard the words of a man asking; we do not see the heart of a man lacking faith; but he who both heard his words and looked into his heart declared it. Then too, the Evangelist, by himself the witness of his narrative, showed that he had not yet believed who desired the Lord to come to his house to heal his son. For after it was reported to him that his son was well, and he found that he had become well at the very hour at which the Lord had said, "Go, your son lives," the Evangelist says, "And he himself believed and his whole house." Therefore if he himself and his whole house believed for the reason that his son was reported to him to be well, and [if] he compared the hour of the reporters with the hour at which he foretold, when he was asking, he was not yet believing.

(4) The Samaritans had waited for no sign; they believed from his word only. His own fellow citizens, however, deserved to hear, "Unless you see signs and wonders, you do not believe." And yet when so great a miracle was performed there, only [this man] himself and his household believed. More Samaritans believed in light of his word alone; that one

3. Cf. Jn 2.1–11.

household where the miracle was performed believed in light of that miracle. What, therefore, brothers, is it that the Lord is showing us. At that time Galilee of Judea was the country of the Lord, because he was reared there. Now, however, because that fact portends something—not without reason have prodigies been mentioned except that they portend something; for a prodigy (*prodigium*) gets its name as an announcement (*porrodicium*)[4] because it tells in advance, signifies [something] in the time ahead, and portends something that will be—therefore, because all those things were portending something, all those things were predicting something, let us now make the country of our Lord Jesus Christ according to the flesh (for he had no country on earth except according to the flesh which he received on earth), let us, therefore, make the Jewish people the Lord's country. Look, he does not have honor in his own country.

(5) Observe the masses of the Jews right now; observe that nation now scattered in the whole world and uprooted; observe the branches, broken, cut away, scattered, withered, broken branches on which the wild olive deserved to be grafted.[5] Look at the crowd of Jews; what does it say now? He whom you adore, whom you worship was our brother. And let us answer: "A prophet has no honor in his own country." In point of fact they saw the Lord Jesus walking on earth and performing miracles, making the blind see, opening the ears of the deaf, loosening the mouths of the dumb, strengthening the limbs of paralytics, walking on the sea, giving orders to winds and waves, raising the dead, working such great signs; and even from this scarcely a few believed.

(6) I say to the people of God, "So many of us have be-

---

4. This etymology for *prodigium* appears here, in *De Civitate Dei* 21.8 (CCL 48.773), and in Paulus Diaconus, *Homilia* CXC (PL 95.1439) where he is commenting on the same verse; Isidore of Seville gives the same etymology in *Etymologicarum Libri* 11.3.3 (Oxford Classical Texts, ed. W. Lindsay [Oxford, 1911]). See Blaise, 635. Neither A. Ernout and A. Meillet, in *Dictionnaire étymologique de la langue latine*, 4th ed. (Paris, 1959), nor A. Walde and J. B. Hofmann, in *Lateinisches etymologisches Wörterbuch*, 4th ed. (Heidelberg, 1965), accept or even mention this etymology.

5. Cf. Rom 11.17.

lieved. What signs have we seen? Therefore that which was done then portends this which is happening now. The Jews were or are like the Galileans; we are like to those Samaritans. We have heard the gospel; we have given assent to the gospel; we have believed in Christ through the gospel. We have seen no signs, we demand none."

4. For, that Thomas, who desired to put his finger into the places of the wounds, even though one of the Twelve chosen and holy ones, was an Israelite, from the race of the Lord, of course. The Lord accused him exactly as this royal official. To the latter he said, "Unless you see signs and wonders, you do not believe."[6] But to the former he said, "Because you have seen, you have believed." He had come to the Galileans, after the Samaritans who had believed his word, among whom he had performed no miracles, whom he had left, without anxiety, at an early moment, since by the presence of his divinity he had not left. Therefore, when the Lord was saying to Thomas, "Come, put in your hand; and be not faithless, but believing," and when he exclaimed, after touching the places of the wounds, and said, "My Lord and my God!" he is reproached and it is said to him, "Because you have seen, you have believed."[7] Why, except that "a prophet has no honor in his own country"? But because this prophet has honor among foreigners, what follows?

(2) "Blessed are they who do not see and believe."[8] We have been foretold; and what the Lord praised before, he has deigned to fulfill even in us. They who crucified him saw him, touched him, and so a few believed. We have not seen him, have not handled him; we have heard, we have believed. Let the happiness which he promised come to be in us, let it be accomplished in us, both here because we have been preferred to his own country, and in the world to come because we have been grafted in place of the broken branches.

5. For he was showing that he would break these branches and graft this wild-olive when moved by the faith of the cen-

6. Cf. Jn 20.29.   7. Cf. Jn 20.27–29.
8. Cf. Jn 20.29.

turion who said to him, "'I am not worthy that you should enter under my roof, but only say the word, and my serving boy will be healed. For I also am a man subject to authority, having under me soldiers; and I say to this one, "Go," and he goes; and to this one, "Come," and he comes; and to my slave, "Do this," and he does it.' Jesus turned to them who were following him and said, 'Amen, I say to you, I have not found so great faith in Israel.' "9 Why did he not find so great faith in Israel? Because "a prophet has no honor in his own country."

(2) Could not the Lord have also said to that centurion what he said to this royal official, "Go, your serving boy lives"? See the difference. This royal official wanted the Lord to go down to his house; that centurion said that he was unworthy. To the one there it was said, "I am coming and I shall heal him."10 To the one here it has been said, "Go, your son lives." To the one there he promised his presence; this one he cured with a word. Yet the one here was coercing his presence; the one there was saying that he was unworthy of his presence. Here there is a ceding to loftiness; there there is a conceding to lowliness. As if he were to say to the one here, "Go, your son lives," don't be a nuisance to me; "unless you see signs and wonders, you do not believe." You want my presence in your home; I can command even with a word. Do not believe from signs. A foreign centurion believed that I could do [the deed] by word and he believed before I did [it]. But you, "unless you see signs and wonders, you do not believe."

(3) Therefore if it is so, let the proud branches be broken; let the lowly wild-olive be engrafted. Yet let the root remain, with some branches cut off and the others accepted. Where does the root remain? In the patriarchs. For the country of Christ is the people of Israel, because he came from them according to the flesh; but the root of this tree is Abraham, Isaac, and Jacob, the holy patriarchs. And where are they? In rest with God, in great honor; so that, having obtained re-

9. Cf. Mt 8.8–10; Lk 7.6–9.   10. Cf. Mt 8.7.

lief,[11] that poor man, after the death of his body, was lifted up into the bosom of Abraham and was seen from afar in the bosom of Abraham by the proud rich man.[12] Therefore the root remains; the root is praised; but the proud branches deserved both to be cut off and to wither. But the lowly wild-olive has found a place by their cutting.

6. Therefore, hear how the natural branches are cut off, how the wild-olive is engrafted, from this very centurion whom I have thought ought to be mentioned in comparison with this royal official. He said, "Amen I say to you, I have not found so great faith in Israel. Therefore I say to you that many will come from the east and from the west."[13] How widely the wild-olive had taken possession of the earth! This earth was a bitter forest, but because of humility, because "I am not worthy that you should come under my roof," "many will come from the east and from the west."[14]

(2) And suppose that they will come; what will become of them? For if they will come, now they are cut from the forest. Where are they to be grafted that they may not wither? He says, "And they will take their place at the table with Abraham and Isaac and Jacob." At what banquet, lest perhaps you invite not to living forever but to drinking much? "They will take their place at the table with Abraham and Isaac and Jacob." Where? He says, "in the kingdom of heaven."[15] And what will be the case with those who have come from the stock of Abraham? What will become of the branches with which the tree was filled? What, except that they will be cut off so that these may be engrafted? Show that they will be cut off. "But the children of the kingdom will go into the darkness outside."[16]

---

11. Berrouard, *Homélies I–XVI*, 828–829, sees the adjective *adiutus* as an etymological reference to the name Lazarus, the Greek form of the Hebrew Eleazer, which in Hebrew means "God has helped." Hence he translates, "helped by God." He refers to *Quaestiones Evangeliorum* 2.38.1 (CCL 44B.88), *En in Ps* 69.7 (CCL 39.938), and Jerome, *Liber de Nominibus Hebraicis* (PL 23.844; CCL 72.140).

12. Cf. Lk 16.22–23.   13. Cf. Mt 8.10–11.
14. Cf. Mt 8.8 and 11.   15. Cf. Mt 8.11.
16. Cf. Mt 8.12.

7. Therefore, let the prophet have honor among us because he did not have honor in his own country. He did not have honor in the country in which he was made; let him have honor in the country which he made. For the maker of all things was made in that country; he was made in that country according to the form of a servant. For the city itself in which he was made, Sion itself, the nation of the Jews itself, Jerusalem itself, he himself made when he was the Word of God with the Father; for "all things were made through him and without him was made nothing."[17]

(2) Therefore about that man about whom we heard today, "there is one mediator between God and men, the man Christ Jesus";[18] a Psalm also foretold, saying, "Mother Sion, a man will say."[19] A certain man, the mediator between God and man, a man, says, "Mother Sion." Why does he say "Mother Sion"? Because he received his flesh from her, from her was the Virgin Mary from whose womb the form of a servant was taken, in which he deigned to appear most humble. A man says, "Mother Sion," and that man who says, "Mother Sion," was made in her, "The man was made in her."[20] For he was God before her and was made man in her. He who was made man in her, "The highest himself has founded her,"[21] not the most humble. "He was made man in her," most humble, because "the Word was made flesh and dwelt among us."[22] "The highest himself has founded her"; because "in the beginning was the Word, and the Word was with God, and the Word was God," "all things were made through him."[23]

(3) But because he made this country, let him have honor here. The country in which he was begotten drove him out; let the country which he begot anew receive him.

17. Cf. Jn 1.3.   18. Cf. 1 Tm 2.5.
19. Cf. Ps 86.5 (LXX); the same text occurs in *En in Ps* 86.7–8 (CCL 39.1204–1205).
20. Ibid.   21. Ibid.
22. Cf. Jn 1.14.   23. Cf. Jn 1.1 and 3.

TRACTATE 17

On John 5.1–18

T HE PERFORMANCE of an amazing deed[1] by God ought not to be a source of amazement; for it would be an amazing thing if a human being had performed it. We ought to rejoice more than be amazed that our Lord and Savior, Jesus Christ, became man than that God performed divine acts among men. For what he became for men is more valuable for our salvation than what he did among men; and that he healed the vices of souls is more valuable than that he healed the maladies of bodies which were going to die. But because the soul itself did not know him by whom it had to be healed and had eyes in the flesh with which it might see physical acts but did not yet have healthy eyes in the heart with which it might recognize the God lying hidden [there], he did what [the soul] could see so that that might be healed with which it could not see. He entered a place where there was lying a great multitude of the sick, blind, lame, and those with shrivelled limbs. And since he was the physician of both souls and bodies and one who had come to heal all the souls of those who would believe, he chose one of those sick men whom he might heal in order to signify unity.

(2) If with common good sense, and as [one would] with his human capability and mental power, we should reflect upon him doing this, both as far as pertains to power, he did nothing great, and as pertains to kindness, he did too little. So many were lying there and only one was cured when with

1. I.e., a "miracle," *miraculum;* the translation reflects a word play in the Latin. Throughout this section Augustine uses the Latin verb *facere* in several connotations, "perform," "become," "do," "make"; no single English verb can serve the same function.

108

one word he could have made all of them rise up. What, then, ought to be understood except that that power and that goodness were rather doing what souls might understand in his deeds for their eternal salvation than what bodies might gain for their temporal health? For the true health of bodies which is awaited from the Lord will be in the end at the resurrection of the dead. Then what will live will not die; then what will be healed will not become ill; then what will be filled will not hunger or thirst; then what will be renewed will not grow old. But now in those deeds of our Lord and Savior, Jesus Christ, the opened eyes of the blind were closed by death, the strengthened limbs of the paralytics were loosened by death, and whatever healed temporally in mortal limbs succumbed in the end; but the soul which believed made the passage to eternal life. Therefore from the healing of this sick man he gave a great sign to the soul which would believe, whose sins he had come to forgive, to heal whose maladies he had humbled himself.

(3) As far as God deigns to bestow, if you give your attention and assist our weakness by prayer, I shall discuss, as well as I can, the profound mystery of this event and this sign. But whatever I cannot do, he, with whose help I do what I can, will supply for you.

2. Concerning this pool which was circled by five porticoes in which the great multitude of the sick was lying, I recall that we have discussed it quite often;[2] and I am going to say something which many of you may relearn with me rather than learn. But, in fact, it is not at all unsuitable to repeat even what is known so that both they who did not learn may be instructed and they who did learn may be strengthened. Accordingly, as these things are known, they must be touched on briefly, and not instilled at a leisurely pace. That pool and that water, in my opinion, signified the people of the Jews; for the Apocalypse of John clearly indicates to us that peoples are signified by the name of waters, where, when many waters

2. Cf., e.g., *Tractate* 12.9 and *En in Ps* 132.6 (CCL 40.1931). Berrouard, *Homélies XVII–XXXIII*, 717, gives a list of other sermons relevant to this passage which does not include the two mentioned here.

were shown to him and he asked what they were, he received the answer that they were peoples.[3] Therefore that water, that is, that people, was shut in by the five books of Moses as by five porticoes.

(2) But those books brought forth sick men; they did not heal. For the Law convicted sinners; it did not absolve them.[4] Therefore, the letter without grace made them guilty; but when they confessed, grace freed them. For the Apostle says this: "For if a law had been given which could give life, justice would be altogether from the law." Why, then, was the Law given? He continues and says, "But the Scripture has concluded all things under sin that the promise, by the faith of Jesus Christ, might be given to those that believe."[5]

(3) What is clearer? Have not these words explained to us both the five porticoes and the multitude of the sick? The five porticoes are the Law. Why did the five porticoes not heal the sick? Because "if a law had been given which could give life, justice would be altogether from the law." Why then did [the porticoes] continue to hold those whom they were not healing? Because "the Scripture has concluded all things under sin that the promise, by the faith of Jesus Christ, might be given to those that believe."

3. What happened, then, that they, who could not be healed in the porticoes, were healed in that agitated water? For, suddenly, the water was seen to be agitated, but he by whom it was agitated was not seen. You may believe that this used to happen by an angel's power,[6] but still not without

3. Cf. Apoc (Rv) 17.15. Water in Scripture had various significations; see *Tr In Io Ep* 6.11.
4. Cf. *Tractate* 3.2, 11–12 and 14.
5. Cf. Gal 3.21–22.
6. Some codices of John's Gospel have an additional verse, 5.4, which relates how an angel came down and stirred up the water of the pool, a probable interpolation as the verse has a non-Johannine style and is not found in the earliest manuscripts. Augustine's words here do not require that he read the verse, but strongly suggest it. Cf. Sermones 125.3 (PL 38.690) where he specifically mentions the angel but does not quote the verse. See NAB, Jn 5.4, note; Berrouard, *Homélies XVII–XXXIII*, 717–719; Comeau, 70–71; B. Vawter, JBC 433; and R. Brown, *The Gospel According to John I–XII, The Anchor Bible* 29 (New York, 1966) 207.

some significant symbolic meaning. After the agitation of the water the one who was able to, thrust himself in, and he alone was healed; whoever thrust himself in after him did it without effect.

(2) What, then, does this mean, except that one came, Christ, to the Jewish people, and by doing great things, by teaching useful things, he agitated sinners, he agitated the water by his presence and stirred it up in preparation for his passion? But he agitated it, while being hidden.

(3) "For if they had known, they would never have crucified the Lord of glory."[7] Therefore to descend into the agitated water is to believe humbly in the Lord's passion. One was healed there signifying unity; afterwards, whoever came was not healed because whoever is outside unity will not be able to be healed.

4. Let us, therefore, see what he intended to signify in that one whom alone from so many of the sick he, preserving the mystery of unity, as I said before, deigned to heal. He found in the years of the man a number, so to speak, of the sickness: "He was thirty–eight years under his infirmity." How this number pertains more to the sickness than the cure, must be explained a little more carefully. I want you to be attentive; the Lord will give aid that I may speak aptly and you may hear sufficiently.

(2) The sacred number forty is recommended to us as hallowed in reference to a certain perfection. I think, my beloved people, this is well known to you. The divine Scriptures very often attest it. Fasting was consecrated by this number, you well know. For Moses fasted for forty days; and Elias, the same number.[8] And our Lord and Savior, Jesus Christ, himself completed this number of fasting.[9] Through Moses the Law is signified, through Elias the prophets are signified, through the Lord the gospel is signified. And so the three

---

7. Cf. 1 Cor 2.8.
8. Cf. Ex 34.28; 3 Kgs 19.8. On the significance of the numbers 10, 40, and 50 in Augustine's writings see Berrouard, *Homélies XVII–XXXIII*, 719–722.
9. Cf. Mt 4.2, Lk 4.2.

appeared on that mountain where he showed himself to his disciples in the brightness of his face and garments.[10] For he appeared between Moses and Elias, as though the gospel should have witness from the Law and the prophets.[11] Therefore whether in the Law or in the prophets or in the gospel the number forty is recommended to us in fasting.

(3) But there is a great and general fasting, which is perfect fasting, to abstain from the iniquities and illicit pleasures of the world: "that, denying ungodliness and worldly desires, we may live soberly and justly and godly in this world." What reward does the Apostle add to this fasting? He continues and says, "looking for that blessed hope and the manifestation of the glory of the blessed God and our Savior, Jesus Christ."[12] Therefore, in this world we celebrate, so to speak, a Lent of abstinence when we live well, when we abstain from iniquities and illicit pleasures. But because this abstinence will not be without a wage, we look for "that blessed hope and revelation of the glory of the great God and our Savior, Jesus Christ."[13] In that hope, when reality shall have come to pass from hope, we shall receive a *denarius* as a wage. For this wage was paid to the laborers toiling in the vineyard, according to the gospel,[14] which I believe you remember; for not everything has to be related, as to beginners and the unlearned.

(4) Therefore a *denarius,* which has received its name from the number ten,[15] is paid; and when joined to forty, it becomes fifty. Wherefore we celebrate with toil the forty-day period before easter; but with joy, as if having received our pay, the fifty-day period after Easter. For, as it were, to this healthful toil of good work which belongs to the number forty is added the *denarius* of rest and happiness that it may become fifty.

10. Cf. Mt 17.1–3; Mk 9.1–3; Lk 9.28–30.
11. Cf. Rom 3.21.   12. Cf. Ti 2.12–13.
13. Note that Augustine has altered the reading of Ti 2.13 from above; there he has *illam beatam spem et manifestationem gloriae beati Dei,* but here *beatam illam spem et revelationem gloriae magni Dei.* See Berrouard, *Homélies XVII–XXXIII, 82–83.*
14. Cf. Mt 20.2 and 9–10.
15. That is, from *deni,* "ten apiece," not directly from *decem,* "ten."

5. The Lord Jesus himself also signified this much more clearly when he spent forty days after his resurrection on earth with his disciples;[16] moreover, when he had ascended into heaven on the fortieth day and ten days had passed, he sent the "wage" [consisting] of the Holy Spirit.[17] These things were made known by signs and by certain outward signs the events themselves were anticipated. We are nourished by outward signs that we might be able to come to the enduring realities themselves. For we are workmen and we still labor in the vineyard; when the day is ended, when the work is ended, the wage will be paid.

(2) But what workman endures to receive the wage unless he is nourished while he is working? For even you will not give only a wage to your workman, will you? Will you not also present to him that with which he may restore his strength during his toil? Of course, you feed him to whom you will give the wage. Accordingly, the Lord feeds us too, while we toil with these signs of the Scriptures. For if this joy of understanding mysteries is withdrawn from us, we faint in our toil and there will be no one to come to the wage.

6. How, therefore, is work perfected in the number forty? Perhaps for this reason, because the Law was given in the Ten Commandments and the Law had to be preached through the whole world, and this whole world is made known [to us] in its four parts, east, west, south, and north: whence the number ten multiplied by four gives forty. Or because through the gospel which has four books the Law is fulfilled, because it was said in the gospel, "I have not come to destroy the Law but to fulfill."[18] Therefore, whether for the former reason or the latter, or some more likely one which escapes us and does not escape more learned men, still it is definite that a certain perfection in good works is signified by the number forty; and these good works are especially practiced in an abstention from the illicit desires of the world, that is, by a general fasting.

16. Cf. Acts 1.3.   17. Cf. Acts 2.1–4.
18. Cf. Mt 5.17.

(2) Hear also the Apostle speaking, "Love is the fulfillment of the Law."[19] Where is love from? Through the grace of God, through the Holy Spirit. For we would not have that from ourselves, as if making that for ourselves. It is a gift of God, and a great gift. "Because the love of God," he says, "is poured forth in our hearts by the Holy Spirit who has been given to us."[20] Love, therefore, fulfills the Law, and it was very truly said, "Love is the fulfillment of the Law." Let us seek after this love, in the manner in which it is made known by the Lord. Remember what I have proposed: I intend to explain the number of the thirty–eight years in that sick man, why that number thirty–eight belongs to the sickness rather than the cure. Therefore, as I was saying, love fulfills the Law. The number forty pertains to the fulfillment of the Law in all works; but in love two commandments are recommended to us.

(3) Look at [it], I beg of you, and fix what I am saying in your memory; be not despisers of the word, that your soul may not become the wayside where the tossed grains cannot germinate: "And the birds of the sky," [the gospel] says, "will come and gather it."[21] Collect it and lay it up in your hearts. Two commandments of love were recommended by the Lord: "You shall love the Lord, your God, with your whole heart, and with your whole soul, and with your whole mind" and "You shall love your neighbor as yourself. On these two commandments depend the whole Law and the prophets."[22]

(4) Rightly, too, did the widow place all her means, two mites, among the gifts for God;[23] rightly, too, did that innkeeper receive two pieces of money[24] for that ailing man wounded by the robbers, that he might be healed;[25] rightly

---

19. Cf. Rom 13.10.   20. Cf. Rom 5.5.
21. Cf. Mt 13.4; Mk 4.4; Lk 8.5.
22. Cf. Mt 22.37–40; Mk 12.30–31; Lk 10.27.
23. Cf. Mk 12.42–44; Lk 21.2–4.
24. Augustine uses the Latin word *nummus* which by itself does not usually designate a coin of precise value, though it can be used especially in combination with other words to designate the *sesterce* or the *denarius*. Both the Greek and the *Vulgate* use the *denarius* as the coin paid by the Samaritan in this story from Luke.
25. Cf. Lk 10.30–35.

did Jesus spend two days among the Samaritans that he might strengthen them in love.[26] Therefore in circumstances when something good is being signified by that number two, the twofold love is especially recommended. If therefore the number forty holds the perfection of the Law and the Law is not fulfilled except in the double commandment of love, why do you wonder that he was sick who had two less than forty?

7. Accordingly, let us now see with what mystery this sick man is cured by the Lord. For there came the Lord himself, the teacher of love, full of love, "making short," as it was predicted about him, "his word upon the earth";[27] and he showed that the Law and the prophets depend on the two commandments of love. Therefore Moses depended on them in his [number] forty; Elias [depended] on them with his; and the Lord brought in this number in his witness. This sick man is cured by the Lord when he is present; but what does he say to him first? "Do you want to be healed?" That man answered that he had no one by whom he might be put into the pool. Truly a man was necessary to him for his healing, but that man who is also God. "For there is one God, and one mediator of God and man, the man, Christ Jesus."[28] Therefore the man who was necessary came; why should the healing be put off?

(2) "Arise," he says, "take up your bed and walk." He said three things: "Arise," "Take up your bed," "and walk." But "Arise" was not a command of work, but the working of a cure. But he commanded the cured man two things, "Take up your bed and walk." I ask you, why would not "walk" suffice? Or at any rate why would not "Arise" suffice? For when that man arose healed, he would not have remained in that place. Would he not have arisen to go away? Therefore, it also strikes me that he, who found him lying there, lacking two things, ordered two things, as in fact, by ordering two certain things, he fulfilled what he was lacking.

8. How, then, may we find, in these two commands of the

26. Cf. Jn 4.40 and *Tractates* 15.33 and 16.3.
27. Cf. Rom 9.28, quoting Is 10.23 (LXX).
28. 1 Tm 2.5.

Lord, those two commandments of love signified? He said, "Take up your bed and walk." Recall with me, my brothers, what those two commandments are. For they ought to be very well known and they ought not to come into your mind only when they are mentioned by us, but ought never to be erased from your hearts. Indeed, always consider that God and neighbor must be loved, "God with all the heart, with all the soul, with all the mind," and "the neighbor as the self."[29] These must always be reflected upon, these must be pondered, these must be adhered to, these must be acted upon, these must be fulfilled. The love of God is first in the order of commandment, but the love of neighbor is first in the order of action. For one who would enjoin this love on you in two commandments would not recommend to you the neighbor first and God afterwards, but God first and the neighbor afterwards. But because you do not yet see God, by loving your neighbor you merit seeing him; by loving your neighbor you cleanse your eye for seeing God, as John clearly says, "If you do not love your brother whom you see, how will you be able to love God whom you do not see?"[30]

(2) Look, it is said to you, "Love God." If you should say to me, "Show me him whom I am to love," what shall I answer except what John himself says, "No one has seen God at any time"?[31] And that you may not suppose that you are altogether unsuited for seeing God, he says, "God is love, and he who abides in love abides in God."[32] Therefore, love your neighbor and look upon the source in you from which you love your neighbor; there you will see, as far as you can, God. Therefore, begin to love your neighbor. "Break your bread with the hungry; bring the needy without shelter into your house; if you see a naked man, clothe him, and despise not the household of your seed."

(3) But doing this, what will you achieve? "Then your light shall break forth as the morning."[33] Your light is your God; he is the morning to you because he will come to you after

29. Cf. Mt 22.37–39.   30. Cf. 1 Jn 4.20.
31. Cf. Jn 1.18.   32. Cf. 1 Jn 4.16.
33. Cf. Is 58.7–8.

the night of the world; for he neither rises nor sets because he remains forever. He who had set for you when you were lost will be morning for you when you return. Therefore, I think "Take up your bed" meant, "Love your neighbor."

9. But it is still closed and requires explanation, as I think, why love of neighbor is represented through the taking up of the bed—if it does not upset us that a neighbor is represented by a bed, an inert and insensate thing. Let the neighbor be not angered if he is represented to us by a thing which is without soul and without sensation. Our Lord and Savior, Jesus Christ, himself was called a cornerstone that he might build two peoples in himself.[34] He was also called a rock from which water flowed forth: "And the rock was Christ."[35] What wonder, then, is there, if Christ is a rock, for a neighbor to be wood? Yet not any kind of wood, as that was not any kind of rock but one from which water flowed forth for the thirsty, nor was that any kind of stone but a cornerstone which joined in itself two walls coming from different directions. So neither should you understand the neighbor to be any kind of wood, but a bed.

(2) What significance is there, then, in the bed, I ask you? What, except that that sick man was carried on the bed, but when healed, carries the bed? What was said by the Apostle? "Bear your burdens, each for the other, and so you will fulfill the law of Christ."[36] Now the law of Christ is love, and love is not fulfilled unless we bear our burdens, each for the other. "Bearing with one another," he says, "in love, eager to preserve the unity of the Spirit in the bond of peace."[37] When you were sick, your neighbor was carrying you. You have been healed; carry your neighbor. "Bear your burdens, each for the other, and so you will fulfill the law of Christ." So you will fulfill, O man, what was lacking to you.

(3) "Take up," therefore, "your bed." But when you have taken it up, do not stay; "walk." In loving your neighbor, in being concerned about your neighbor, you are taking a trip.

---

34. Cf. Eph 2.19–22; see *Tractates* 9.17 and 15.26.
35. Cf. 1 Cor 10.4.   36. Cf. Gal 6.2.
37. Cf. Eph 4.2–3.

Where are you taking a trip to, except to the Lord God, to him whom we ought to love with all our heart, with all our soul, with all our mind? For we have not yet reached the Lord, but we have our neighbor with us. Therefore carry him with whom you are walking that you may reach him with whom you long to stay. Therefore "Take up your bed and walk."

10. He did this, and the Jews were scandalized. For they saw the man carrying his bed on the Sabbath. They did not slander the Lord because he had healed the man on the Sabbath so that he could answer them that if the mule of any one of them had fallen into a well, he would, of course, draw out this mule on the Sabbath and save it.[38] Accordingly, they were not reproaching him now because the man was healed on the Sabbath, but because he was carrying his bed. If his healing did not have to be delayed, it wasn't necessary also to order work, was it? "It is not lawful," they said, "to do what you are doing, to take up your bed." And he opposed his calumniators with the author of his healing. "He who healed me, he said to me, 'Take up your bed and walk.'" Would I not accept an order from him from whom I recovered my health? And they said, "Who is that man who said to you, 'Take up your bed and walk'?"

11. "But the man who had been healed did not know who it was" from whom he had heard this. "But Jesus" when he had done this and had ordered it, "had turned aside" from him "in the crowd." See how this, too, is fulfilled. We carry our neighbor, and we walk, to God; but we do not yet see him to whom we walk. So, too, that man did not yet know Jesus. This profound doctrine,[39] that we believe in him whom we do not yet see, has been made known; and that he may not be seen, he turns aside in the crowd.

(2) It is difficult to see Christ in the crowd; a certain solitude is necessary for our minds. God is seen by a certain solitude of contemplation. A crowd has noisy talking; this seeing requires seclusion. "Take up your bed": you have been carried, now you carry your neighbor. "And walk": that you may come.

38. Cf. Lk 14.5.   39. *sacramentum*.

Do not seek Jesus in the crowd; he is not as one of the crowd, he precedes the whole crowd. That great fish first ascended from the sea[40] and sits in heaven, interceding for us.[41] As the high priest, he alone entered the inner temple; the crowd stands outside.[42] Walk, you who carry your neighbor, if you who were used to being carried have learned to carry. Even now, in fact, you do not yet know Jesus, you do not yet see Jesus. What comes afterwards?

(3) Because he did not desist from taking up his bed and walking, "Afterwards Jesus saw him in the temple." He did not see him in the crowd; he saw him in the temple. In fact, the Lord Jesus saw him both in the crowd and in the temple; but that sick man did not recognize Jesus in the crowd, he did recognize him in the temple. Therefore that man came to the Lord; he saw him in the temple, he saw him in a sacred place, in a holy place. And what did he hear from him? "Behold, you have been healed. Do not sin, lest some worse thing happen to you."

12. Then, after he saw Jesus and recognized Jesus as the author of his healing, that man was not slothful in proclaiming him whom he had seen: "He went away and told the Jews that it was Jesus who had healed him." He brought the news and they raged. He made known his salvation;[43] they did not seek their own salvation.

13. "The Jews kept persecuting the Lord Jesus because he did these things on the Sabbath." Let us hear then what the Lord now answered to the Jews. As for men healed on the Sabbath, I have said what he usually answered, that they did not disregard their animals on the Sabbath, either by freeing them or feeding them. As for carrying the bed, what did he answer? An obvious physical work was done before the eyes of the Jews, not the healing of a body, but the working of a

---

40. Berrouard, *Homélies XVII–XXXIII*, 727–728, sees here the early Christian Greek word for "fish," *ichthús*, which stood for Jesus Christ, God's Son, the Savior.

41. Cf. Rom 8.34.

42. Cf. Heb 6.19–20 and Lk 1.8–10.

43. There is an untranslatable play on connotations of *salus* here, "health" and "salvation."

body; and this did not seem as necessary as the healing. Therefore let the Lord clearly state that the mystery of the Sabbath and the sign of observing one day was given to the Jews on a temporary basis, and indeed that the very fulfillment of the mystery had come in him.

(2) He said, "My Father works even until now, and I work." He has sent a great disturbance upon them; the water is agitated by the coming of the Lord, but he who agitates it is hidden. Nevertheless when the water has been agitated, there must be healed one great sick one—the whole world, by the Lord's suffering.

14. Therefore let us see truth's answer: "My Father works even until now, and I work." Was Scripture therefore wrong in saying, "On the seventh day God rested from all his works"?[44] And does the Lord Jesus speak against this Scripture which had been furnished through Moses, when he himself says to the Jews, "If you would believe Moses, you would believe me also, for he wrote of me"?[45] See, therefore, whether Moses did not mean to signify something because "God rested on the seventh day." For God had not grown weak in working at his creation and did not need rest like a man. How had he, who created with a word, grown weak? Nevertheless, it is true that "on the seventh day God rested from his works," and what Jesus said is true, "My Father works even until now."

(2) But who can explain in words—a man to men, a weak man to weak men, an unlearned man to those desiring to learn, even if, perchance, he understands something, not having the ability to set forth and explain to men who perhaps

44. Cf. Gn 2.2.
45. Cf. Jn 5.46. Berrouard, *Homélies XVII–XXXIII*, 105, points out that Augustine has in mind here a contradiction alleged by the Manichaeans between Gn 2.2 and Jn 5.17. In *Contra Faustum* 16.6 and 28–29 (PL 42.318–319 and 334–335; CSEL 25(1).444–445 and 738–747) Faustus raises the supposed contradiction and Augustine responds. In *De Genesi contra Manichaeos* 1.22.33–34 (PL 34.189–190; BAC 15 [1957]) and *Contra Adimantum* 2 (PL 42.131–132; CSEL 25(1).116–118) he offers two other resolutions. The fertile character of Augustine's allegorical method is well illustrated by these four passages where God's rest is explained in four different ways. See also Berrouard, *Homélies XVII–XXXIII*, 728–729, for further discussion and other references.

grasp with difficulty even if what is being grasped can be explained—who, I say, my brothers, can explain in words how God both works even when at rest and is at rest even when working? I beg you that you put this off while you are advancing on the way. For this seeing requires the temple of God, it requires a holy place. Carry your neighbor and walk; you will see him there where you do not require the words of men.

15. Perhaps we can rather say this: Even in that statement, "God rested on the seventh day," [Moses] signified, by a great mystery, the Lord himself and our Savior, Jesus Christ, who was speaking these words and saying, "My Father works even until now, and I work." Because, of course, the Lord Jesus also is God. For he is the Word of God and you heard that "In the beginning was the Word," not any kind of word, but "the Word was God" and "all things were made through him."[46] Perhaps he was signified, that he would rest from all his works on the seventh day. For read the gospel and see what great things Jesus worked.

(2) He worked our salvation on the cross, that all the predictions of the prophets might be fulfilled in him. He was crowned with thorns, he was suspended on the wood; he said, "I thirst." He received vinegar on a sponge[47] that what was said might be fulfilled, "and in my thirst they gave me vinegar to drink."[48] But when all his works were fulfilled, on the sixth day of the week, with his head bowed, he gave up his spirit.[49] And in the tomb, on the Sabbath, he rested from all his works. Therefore, as if he were saying to the Jews, "Why do you expect me not to work on the Sabbath? The Sabbath day has been enjoined upon you as a sign of me. You observe the works of God; I was there when they were made; through me all things were made. I know: 'My Father works even until now.'"

(3) "My Father worked to make the light, but he spoke that the light might be made; if he spoke, he worked by the Word.

46. Cf. Jn 1.1 and 3.   47. Cf. Jn 19.2, 18 and 28–29.
48. Cf. Ps 68.22.   49. Cf. Jn 19.30.

I was, I am his Word. Through me the world was made in those works; through me it is governed in these works. My Father both worked then, when he made the world, and he works even until now, when he governs the world. Therefore he both made it through me when he made it; and he governs it through me when he governs it." He said these things, but to whom? To the deaf, the blind, the lame, the sick who did not acknowledge the physician and who wished to kill him as if with minds destroyed by madness.

16. Accordingly, what did the Evangelist continue and say? "This, then, is why the Jews sought the more to kill him, because he not only broke the Sabbath, but also said God was his Father." Not in any way whatsoever, but how? "Making himself equal to God." For we all say to God: "Our Father who art in heaven";[50] we read that the Jews, too, said, "Since you are our Father."[51] Therefore they were not angered at this, that he said God was his Father, but because [he did so] in a way far different from men.

(2) Look, the Jews understand what the Arians do not understand. For the Arians say that the Son is unequal to the Father, and for that reason the heresy was expelled from the Church.[52] Look, these blind fellows, these killers of Christ, still understood Christ's words. They did not understand that he was the Christ; they did not understand that he was the Son of God, but they still understood in those words that he was being revealed as the Son of God such as would be equal to God. They did not know who he was; nevertheless they realized that he was being proclaimed as such a one, because "He said God was his Father, making himself equal to God." Was he not, then, equal to God? He did not make himself equal, but he [God] had begotten him equal. If he were to make himself an equal to God, he would fall by robbery. For he who meant to make himself equal to God when he was not, fell,[53]

50. Cf. Mt 6.9.   51. Cf. Is 63.16.
52. There is a variant reading: "and for that reason the heresy assails the Church." Berrouard, *Homélies XVII–XXXIII*, 112, argues in favor of this variant.
53. Cf. Is 14.12–15.

and he became a devil from being an angel, and he handed over to the man for his drinking [the cup of] this pride by which he was himself cast down. For he said to the man whom he, because he had fallen, envied because the man still stood firm: "Taste, and you will be like gods."[54] That is, rob by usurpation what you were not made, because I, too, was cast down for robbing. This he did not disclose, but this he did suggest. But Christ was born equal to the Father, not made. He was born of the substance of the Father. Whence the Apostle thus represents him, "who, although he was in the form of God, thought it not robbery to be equal with God."[55]

(3) What does it mean, "thought it not robbery"? He did not usurp the equality of God, but existed in it in which he had been born. And how might we come to the equal God? "He emptied himself, taking the form of a servant."[56] Therefore he did not empty himself, losing what he was, but receiving what he was not. The Jews, despising the form of the servant, could not understand the Lord Christ as an equal with the Father, although they did not at all doubt that he said this about himself. And therefore they raged. And yet he still endured them and sought for the health of the ones raging.

54. Cf. Gn 3.5.   55. Phil 2.6.
56. Cf. Phil 2.7.

TRACTATE 18

On John 5.19–20

OHN THE EVANGELIST, among his colleagues and partners, the other evangelists, has received from the Lord (upon whose breast he reclined at the supper[1] that he might signify thereby that he drank the deeper secrets from depths of his heart) this special and particular gift, that he should say about the Son of God those things which can stir, perhaps, the attentive minds of the little ones, but cannot fill them, not yet able to understand. But to all minds somewhat more matured and attaining a certain age of inner manhood, he gives in his words something by which they may be exercised and fed. You heard it when it was read and you recall how this discourse came about. For yesterday it was read, "This is why the Jews wanted to kill Jesus, because he not only broke the Sabbath, but also said God was his Father, making himself equal to God."[2] This which displeased the Jews pleased the Father himself. Without a doubt this also pleases those who do honor to the Son as they do to the Father, because if it should not please them, they will be displeasing.[3] For God will not be greater because he pleases you; but you will be lesser if he displeases you.[4] But against this calumny of theirs, coming either from ignorance or from malice, the Lord does not at all say something which they may grasp but [something] by which they may be disturbed and troubled and perhaps, when troubled, may even seek the physician. Moreover, he said things which were to be written

---

1. Cf. Jn 13.23–25. For a similar interpretation of this event cf. *Tractates* 1.7, 16.2, 20.1, 36.1, 61.5–6, 119.2, and 124.7.
2. Cf. Jn 5.18.   3. Cf. Jn 5.23.
4. Cf. *Tractate* 11.5.

down that they might also be read by us afterwards. Therefore, granted we have seen what happened in the hearts of
the Jews when they heard these words, let us consider more
fully what happens in us when we hear these words.

(2) For heresies and certain dogmas of perversity, which
ensnare souls and hurl them down into the abyss, have been
born only when good Scriptures are not well understood; and
what is not well understood in them is asserted brashly and
boldly. And so, my dearest people, very cautiously ought we
to hear these words for whose understanding we are little
ones, keeping with both devout heart and trembling, as it was
written, this rule of soundness:[5] that, as far as we can understand according to the faith with which we have been imbued,
we rejoice as at food; but, as far as we cannot yet understand
according to the sound rule of faith, we lay aside doubt and
defer understanding, that is, that even if we do not know what
it is, nevertheless we not at all doubt that it is good and true.[6]

(3) And, my brothers, you must ponder who I am who have
undertaken to speak to you and what I have undertaken. For
I, a man, have undertaken to discuss the divine; a creature
of flesh, [to discuss] the spiritual; a mortal, [to discuss] the
eternal. My dearest people, may vain presumption be far
from me, if I wish to dwell in good health in the house of
God, which is the Church of the living God, the pillar and
foundation of the truth.[7] In keeping with my limitations, I
take what I set before you. Where it is opened, I feed with
you; where it is closed, I knock with you.[8]

2. Therefore the Jews were distressed and became indignant, rightly, indeed, because a man dared to make himself
equal to God, but wrongly, for the reason that they did not
understand God in the man. They saw the flesh; they did not
know God. They looked upon the dwelling-place, they did
not know the dweller. That flesh was a temple; God dwelt

5. The scriptural text which Augustine has in mind here remains un-
identified; see Berrouard, *Homélies XVII–XXXIII*, 119.

6. Persistence in belief leads eventually to understanding; see *Tractate* 8.6.

7. Cf. 1 Tm 3.15.   8. Cf. Mt 7.7–8; Lk 11.9–10.

within.[9] Therefore Jesus did not equate his flesh to the Father; he did not regard the form of the servant as comparable to the Lord: not what was made for us, but what he was when he made us. For, because you have believed rightly, you know—I am speaking to Catholics—who Christ is: not the Word only nor the flesh only, but the Word was made flesh that he might dwell among us.

(2) I am reviewing what you know about the Word. "In the beginning was the Word, and the Word was with God, and the Word was God."[10] Here is equality with the Father. But "the Word was made flesh and dwelt among us";[11] the Father is greater than this flesh. Thus the Father is both equal and greater, equal to the Word, greater than the flesh, equal to him through whom he made us, greater than him who was made for us. In accordance with this sound Catholic rule[12] which you particularly ought to know—and hold it fast, you who do know it—from which your faith certainly ought not to stray, which must by no arguments of men be wrenched from your hearts, let us turn our attention to what we understand; and what, perchance, we do not understand, let us defer, to be attended to in accordance with this rule some day when we shall be qualified.

(3) Therefore we know [him], equal to the Father, the Son of God, because we know [him] in the beginning [as] God the Word. Why then "did the Jews want to kill him"? "Because he not only broke the Sabbath, but also said God was his Father, making himself equal to God."[13] They saw the flesh; they did not see the Word. Therefore let the Word also speak against them through the flesh, and let the inner dweller re-

9. Berrouard, *Homélies XVII–XXXIII*, 122, suggests Col 2.9 as the source of this statement.

10. Jn 1.1.   11. Cf. Jn 1.14.

12. This sound Catholic rule is a principle of exegesis which is spelled out in *De Diversis Quaestionibus LXXXIII* 69.1 (CCL 44A.184–185; and FOTC 70.166–167) and *De Trinitate* 1.11.22 (CCL 50.60–61; and FOTC 45.33–34). When Christ is spoken of in Scripture as equal to the Father, his divine nature is referred to; when he is spoken of as inferior to the Father, his human nature is referred to. See Berrouard, *Homélies XVII–XXXIII*, 731–732.

13. Cf. Jn 5.18.

sound through his dwelling-place, that whoever can may know who dwells within.

3. What, then, does he say to them? "Then Jesus answered and said to them," who had been disturbed because he made himself equal to God, "'Amen, amen, I say to you, the Son cannot do anything of himself, but only what he sees the Father doing.'" What the Jews answered to this was not written, and perhaps they kept quiet. Yet, certain men, who wish themselves to be considered Christians, do not keep quiet, and in some way from these words they conceive certain arguments against us which must not be taken lightly, both for their sakes and ours. Indeed the Arian heretics, in saying that the Son himself who assumed flesh is less than the Father is, not as a result of the flesh, but before the flesh, and that he [the Son] is not of the same substance as the Father is, take from these words an occasion for calumny and answer to us, "you see that the Lord Jesus, when he noticed that the Jews were aroused by the fact that he made himself equal to God the Father, added such words to show that he was not equal. For it aroused the Jews," they say, "against Christ that he made himself equal to God. And Christ, wishing to restore them then from this distress and to show them that the Son is not equal to the Father, that is, equal to God, spoke, as if saying, 'Why are you indignant? I am not equal, for "The Son cannot do anything of himself, but only what he sees the Father doing."' For," they say, "He who 'cannot do anything of himself, but only what he sees the Father doing' is, of course, less and not equal."

4. In this twisted and perverse rule of his heart, let the heretic hear us, not yet rebuking, but still as if seeking; and let him explain to us what he perceives. For I think, O whoever you are (for let us pretend that he is present here), you hold with us that "in the beginning was the Word." "I do hold it," he says. And that "the Word was with God"? "And I do hold this," he says. Continue, therefore, and hold this more boldly, that "the Word was God."[14]

14. Jn 1.1.

(2) "And I hold this," he says, "but the one God is greater, the other God is lesser." Now I detect a somewhat pagan odor; I thought I was talking with a Christian. If there is a greater God and there is a lesser God, we worship two gods, not one God. "Why," he says, "and do you not say that two gods are equal to one another?" This I do not say; for I so understand this equality that I understand also undivided love there, and if undivided love, perfect unity. For if the love which God sent to men makes one heart from many hearts of men, and makes many souls of men to be one soul, as it was written in the Acts of the Apostles about those who believed and loved one another ("They had one soul and one heart toward God"),[15] if therefore, my soul and your soul, when we know the same thing and love each other, become one soul, how much more are God the Father and God the Son one God in the source of love?[16]

5. But concentrate on these words by which your heart has been stirred, and recollect with me what we were looking for about the Word. We now hold, "The Word was God."[17] I add another thing, because when he said, "the same in the beginning was with God," immediately the Evangelist added, "All things were made through him."[18] Now I agitate you by my inquiry, now I rouse you up against yourself, and I summon you to give witness against yourself. Only with good memory hold on to these statements about the Word: "The Word was God" and "All things were made through him." Listen now to the words by which you were stirred so that you said the Son was lesser, of course because he said, "The Son cannot do anything of himself, but only what he sees the Father doing." "Yes," he says.

15. Cf. Acts 4.32 and *Tractate* 14.9. The words "toward God" are an addition to the text by Augustine; see Berrouard, *Homélies XVII–XXXIII*, 128.
16. Cf. *Tractate* 9.8 where "the source of love" is shown to be Holy Spirit.
17. Cf. Jn 1.1.
18. Cf. Jn 1.2–3. Throughout this discussion there is a practical translation problem with the Latin verb *facere* which means both "to make" and "to do." I here have used "make" as much as English idiom allows; but some of the argument's effectiveness is lost by the need sometimes to use "do" in English.

(2) Explain this to me a little; you understand, I think, that the Father does certain things, but the Son observes how the Father does them that he himself may also be able to do what he saw the Father doing. You have established, as it were, two craftsmen: the Father and the Son, in the same way as a master and an apprentice, as father craftsmen are accustomed to teach their sons their skill.[19] Look, I come down to your carnal meaning; for a time I think in the same way as you; let us see if this thought of ours may find a result according to those ideas which we have already spoken together and thought together about the Word, that "The Word is God" and "All things were made through him." Suppose, therefore, the Father to be, as it were, a craftsman, doing certain works, and the Son to be, as it were, an apprentice who "cannot do anything, but only what he sees the Father doing." For he concentrates on the hands of the Father, in some way, so that, as he sees him fashioning, so also he may himself fashion in his own works. But all those things which this Father makes and which he also wishes that the Son observe and also himself make such like, through whom does he make them? Ah ha! Now this is the point where you should support your earlier opinion which you reviewed with me and held with me, that "In the beginning was the Word" and "The Word was with God" and "The Word was God" and "All things were made through him." Therefore although you have held with me that through the Word all things were made, you again make in your mind, with carnal judgment and childish sentiment, God making and the Word observing, so that when God has made, the Word also may make.

(3) For what does God make independently of the Word? For if he makes anything, not all things would have been made through the Word. You have destroyed what you held; but if all things have been made through the Word, correct what you wrongly understand. The Father made, and he did not make except through the Word; how does the Word observe that he may see the Father making without the Word

19. The same comparison occurs in *Tractates* 19.1, 20.9, 21.2, and 23.8.

what he may make in like manner? Whatever the Father made, he made through the Word or it is false that "all things were made through him." But it is true. "All things were made through him." Was this, perhaps, insufficient for you? "And without him was made nothing."[20]

6. Therefore, withdraw from this wisdom of the flesh, and let us seek how it was said, "The Son cannot do anything of himself, but only what he sees the Father doing." Let us seek, if we are worthy to comprehend. For I admit; it is a great thing, utterly difficult, to see the Father doing through the Son, not the Father and the Son doing individual works, but the Father [doing] every work whatsoever through the Son so that no works are done either by the Father without the Son or by the Son without the Father, because "all things were made through him, and without him was made nothing." With these things very firmly established on the foundation of faith, now what kind of thing is the "seeing," since "The Son can do nothing of himself but only what he sees the Father doing"? You seek, I think, to know the Son doing; seek first to know the Son seeing.

(2) For what exactly does he say? "The Son cannot do anything of himself, but only what he sees the Father doing." Concentrate on what he said, "but only what he sees the Father doing." Vision precedes, performance follows; for he sees what he may do. Why are you seeking to know how he *does* while you do not yet know how he *sees*? Why do you hurry to what is later, leaving behind what is earlier? He spoke of himself seeing and doing, not doing and seeing; for "He cannot do anything of himself, but only what he sees the Father doing." Do you want me to explain to you how he does? You explain to me how he sees. If you cannot explain this, neither [can] I [explain] that; if you are not yet capable of perceiving this, neither [can] I [perceive] that. Let both of us, therefore, seek; let both knock, that both may deserve to receive. Why do you, as if you were learned, find fault with an unlearned man? I as to doing, you as to seeing, let both of us unlearned

20. Cf. Jn 1.3.

men seek from the teacher, and let us not quarrel childishly in his school. Yet we have already learned together that "all things were made through him." Therefore it is clear that the Father does not do some works which the Son may see that he may do similar ones, but the Father does the same works through the Son because all things were made through the Word.

(3) Now who knows how God makes? I do not say, how did he make the world, but how did he make your eye, cleaving carnally to which you compare visible things to invisible? For you think such things about God as you have been accustomed to see with these eyes. But if God could be seen with these eyes, he would not say, "Blessed are the clean of heart, for they shall see God."[21] Therefore you have the body's eyes for seeing the craftsman, but you do not yet have the heart's eye for seeing God. Thus, what you are used to seeing in a craftsman you want to transfer to God. Put earthly things on earth. Lift up your heart.

7. Well now, my dearest people, shall we explain what we have asked, how the Word sees, how the Father is seen by the Word, what the "seeing" of the Word is? I am not so rash, so imprudent that I promise both myself and you to explain this. Whatever I suspect your limitation [to be], I nevertheless know my own. Therefore, if it please, let us delay no longer, let us run through the reading, and let us see that carnal hearts are disturbed by the words of the Lord, disturbed for this purpose, that they not remain in that which they hold. Let [this tenet] be wrested [from them] as from children some toy is taken away with which they amuse themselves to their harm, so that more useful things may be implanted in them, as more mature persons, and so that they who crawl on the ground may be able to develop. Rise, seek, sigh, gasp with longing, and knock at the closed doors. But if we do not yet long, do not yet eagerly desire, do not yet sigh, we shall cast down our pearls to all sorts of persons, or we ourselves shall find pearls of varied quality.[22]

21. Mt 5.8.
22. Cf. Mt 7.6 and 13.45–46.

(2) I would, therefore, arouse, my dearest people, longing in your heart. Virtuous habits lead to sound understanding; the way of life leads to a way of life.[23] Earthly life is one thing; heavenly life, another. The life of cattle is one thing; the life of humans, another; the life of angels, yet another. The life of cattle seethes with earthly pleasures; it seeks earthly things alone, and is inclined and addicted to them. The life of angels is solely heavenly. The life of humans is midway between that of angels and that of cattle. If man lives according to the flesh, he is put in the same class with cattle; if he lives according to the spirit, he is associated with angels. When you live according to the spirit, seek also in this angelic life whether you are a little one or a grown-up. For if you are still a little one, the angels say to you, "Grow up. We eat bread, but you are still nourished by milk, by the milk of faith, that you may attain the food of vision."[24]

(3) But if sordid pleasures are still coveted, if deceptions are still being planned, if lies are not avoided, if perjuries are heaped upon lies, so unclean a heart dares to say, "Explain to me how the Word sees," even if I were able to do it, even if I should now see. Furthermore, if I perhaps am not of this character and still am far from this vision, how far is that man who is not yet seized with this heavenly longing and is weighted down by earthly longings? There is much difference between one who loathes and one who desires. And again, there is much difference between one who desires and one who enjoys. You live like cattle; you loathe. The angels totally enjoy. But if you do not live like cattle, now you do not loathe; you desire something but do not obtain it. By the very desire you have entered upon the life of the angels. Let it grow in you, and be perfected in you, and may you obtain this, not from me, but from him who made both me and you.

8. Nevertheless the Lord, too, has not in any way forsaken us; for he wanted it to be understood in that statement, "The Son cannot do anything of himself, but only what he sees the

23. On the Neoplatonic characteristic of this concept see Berrouard, *Homélies XVII–XXXIII*, 732–733.
24. Cf. *Tractate* 13.4.

Father doing," that the Father does not do some works which the Son may see, and the Son does others when he has seen the Father doing, but both the Father himself and the Son himself do the same works. For he continued and said, "For whatsoever things he does, these the Son also does in like manner." Not when he *has* done, the Son does *other* things in like manner, but "whatsoever things he does, *these* the Son also does in like manner." If the Son does *these things* which the Father has done, the Father does them through the Son; if the Father does what he does through the Son, the Father does not do some things, the Son others, but the same works belong to Father and Son.

(2) And how does the Son also do the same works? He does both the same works and "in like manner." That you might not think, perhaps, the same works but in dissimilar manner, he says, "the same" and "in like manner." And how could he do the same works not in like manner? Take an example which I believe will be no big problem for you: When we write letters, our heart first makes them, and then our hand. Indeed, why have you all shouted your approval, except that you know this? What I said is certain and clear to all of us. The letters are made first from our heart, then from our body; the hand serves the commanding heart, both heart and hand make the same letters. Does the heart make some and the hand others? The hand does, indeed, make the same letters, but not in like manner; for our heart makes them conceptually, but the hand visibly. See how the same things happen in a dissimilar manner.

(3) Wherefore it was not enough for the Lord to say, "Whatsoever things the Father does, these the Son also does," unless he were to add, "and in like manner." For what if you were to understand it in this way, as whatever things the heart does, these the hand also does, but not in like manner? But here he added, "these the Son also does in like manner." If he both does these and does in like manner, bestir yourself. Let the Jew be constrained, let the Christian believe, let the heretic be convicted. The Son is equal to the Father.

9. "For the Father loves the Son and shows him all that he

himself does." Look, it is "shows." "Shows" as if to whom? Of course, as if to one seeing. We return to that which we cannot explain, how the Word sees. Look, man was made through the Word; but man has eyes, he has ears, he has hands, various members in his body. By the eyes he can see; by the ears he can hear; by the hands, work: diverse members, diverse functions of the members. That member cannot do what another member can; nevertheless, because of the unity of the body, the eye sees both for itself and for the ear, and the ear hears for itself and for the eyes. Must some such phenomenon be thought to exist in the Word because all things are through him? And Scripture said in a Psalm, "Understand, you who are senseless ones among the people; and you fools, be wise at last. Shall he who shaped the ear not hear, or he who formed the eye not consider?"[25] Therefore if the Word formed the eye, because all things are through the Word, if the Word shaped the ear, because all things are through the Word, we cannot say, "The Word does not hear, The Word does not see," or the Psalm may rebuke us and say, "you fools, be wise at last."

(2) Therefore if the Word hears and the Word sees, the Son hears and the Son sees. And yet are we to seek for eyes and ears in him in different places? Does he hear from one place, does he see from another? And cannot his ear do what his eye does; cannot his eye do what his ear does? Or is it that he is totally sight, and totally hearing? Perhaps so; rather, not perhaps, but truly so provided that both this "seeing" of his, and this "hearing" of his, is in a far different manner than for us. Both to see and to hear are together in the Word; and to see is not one thing, to hear another, but hearing is sight and sight is hearing.

10. And we who hear in one way, see in another, how do we know this? Perhaps we turn back to ourselves, if we are not the transgressors to whom it was said, "Return, you transgressors, to the heart."[26] Return to the heart! Why do you go

25. Cf. Ps 93.8–9.
26. Cf. Is 46.8 (LXX).

away from yourselves, and perish from yourselves? Why do
you go the ways of solitude? You go astray by wandering
about. Return. Where? To the Lord. It is quickly done! First,
return to your heart. You are wandering without, an exile
from yourself; you do not know yourself, and you ask by
whom you were made! Return, return to the heart; remove
yourself from the body. Your body is your dwelling-place;
your heart perceives even through your body, but your body
is not what your heart is. Forsake even your body, return to
your heart. In your body you found eyes in one place, ears
in another; do you find this in your heart? Or is it that in
your heart you do not have ears? About what [ears] therefore
was the Lord speaking, "He who has ears to hear, let him
hear"?[27] Or is it that you do not have eyes in the heart? Of
what [eyes] does the Apostle say, "the eyes of your heart enlightened"?[28] Return to your heart! See there what perhaps
you perceive about God because the image of God is there.

(2) In the inner man Christ dwells; in the inner man you
are renewed according to the image of God.[29] In his image
recognize its author. See how all the senses of the body report
to the heart within what they have perceived outside; see how
many assistants the inner ruler has, and what he may do on
his own even without these assistants. The eyes report black
and white to the heart. The ears report the harmonious and
the discordant to the same heart; the nostrils report odors
and stenches to the same heart; the taste reports bitter and
sweet to the same heart; the touch reports soft and hard to
the same heart. The heart itself reports just and unjust to
itself. Your heart both sees and hears, and passes judgment
on the other sensible objects. And where the senses of the
body have no approach, it discerns between just and unjust,

27. Cf. Lk 8.8. In ascribing bodily senses to the soul, the *habitatrix corporis*
("the inhabitant of the body"), as he refers to it in *Tractate* 8.2, Augustine
uses metaphorical language that is not only natural and scriptural but also
may have been influenced by Origen. See Berrouard, *Homélies XVII–XXXIII*,
736–738.
28. Cf. Eph 1.18 and *Tractate* 13.3.
29. Cf. Eph 3.16–17 and Col 3.10.

good and evil.³⁰ Show me the eyes, ears, nostrils of your heart. The things which are referred to your heart are diverse, and diverse members are not found there. (3) In your flesh you hear in one place, you see in another; in your heart you hear there where you see. If the image [does] this, how much more powerfully [does] he [do it] whose image it is? Therefore the Son both hears and the Son sees; and the Son is the very seeing and hearing. And for him hearing is the same as being, and for him seeing is the same as being. But for you seeing is not the same as being, because even if you should lose your sight, you can still be, and if you should lose your hearing, you can still be.

11. Do you think we have knocked? Has anything been aroused in us by which we suspect even slightly whence light may come to us? I think, brothers, that when we speak about these things, when we reflect upon them, we are training ourselves. And when we train ourselves in ourselves and are again, so to speak, bent back by our weight to these ordinary ideas, we are such as are the weak-eyed, when they are led out to see light, if, perhaps, they did not at all have sight before and they begin in some way or other through the diligence of the doctors to recover their sight. And when the physician wishes to test how much healing has come to them, he tries to show them what they desired to see and could not when they were blind. And when the sight of the eyes is now returning to some extent, they are led out to the light; and when they have seen, they are, to a certain extent, repulsed by the very brightness, and they reply to the physician who is showing [the light], "Just now I saw, but I cannot see." What, then, does the physician do? He resumes the usual treatment, and he adds a salve, so that he may nourish the desire for that which was seen and could not be seen and from this very desire a cure may be effected more fully; and if any stinging medication is applied to restore health, let the sick man bear it bravely, so that he, inflamed by a love for that light, may say to himself, "When will it be that I see with strong eyes

30. Cf. *Tractate* 15.21.

that which I could not see with sore and weak eyes?" He urges the physician and asks him to cure him.

(2) Therefore, brothers, if perhaps, some such thing has happened in your hearts, if at any time you have stirred up your heart to see the Word, and, repulsed by his light, you have withdrawn to the usual way, ask the physician to apply stinging salves, the commandments of justice. There is something to see, but there is not the means to see. You did not believe me before that there is something to see; you trembled, you fled away. You surely know that there is something to see, but that you are not capable of seeing. Therefore be healed.[31] What are the salves? Do not lie, do not commit perjury, do not commit adultery, do not steal, do not cheat. But you have grown accustomed; and when you are called away from the usual way by some pain, this is what stings, but heals.

(3) For I am speaking rather freely to you, out of fear for myself and for you. If you stop from being cured and neglect to be capable of enjoying this light, by the sickness of your eyes you will love the darkness; and by loving the darkness, you will remain in darkness; and by remaining in darkness, you will be cast forth into the darkness outside; "there will be weeping and gnashing of teeth."[32] If love of light had no effect on you, let fear of pain have some.

12. I think that I have spoken enough, and yet have not finished the gospel reading. If I should say the rest, I shall burden you and I fear that even the water already drawn may be spilled out. Therefore let these things be sufficient for you, my beloved people. We are debtors, not now, but always as long as we live, because we live for you. But nevertheless by living well you comfort this life of ours in this world, a weak, laborious, hazardous [life].

(2) Do not sadden and exhaust us by any bad habits of yours. For when we are offended by your evil life, if we should flee from you and separate ourselves from you, and

31. Cf. *Tractate* 1.19.
32. Cf. Mt 22.13.

not approach you, will you not complain and say, "And if we were sick, you would take care of us; and if we were infirm, you would visit us"? Look, we do take care; look, we do visit. But let it not happen to us as you have heard from the Apostle, "I fear lest I have labored among you in vain."[33]

33. Cf. Gal 4.11.

TRACTATE 19

On John 5.19–30

I N THE PREVIOUS SERMON, as far as [the matter] excited our enthusiasm and impelled our poor understanding, we spoke, taking occasion from the gospel's words, where it was written, "The Son cannot do anything of himself, but only what he sees the Father doing." And we said what the Son's "seeing" is, that is, the Word's "seeing," because the Son is the Word. And [we also said], because all things were made through the Word, how it can be understood that the Son first sees the Father doing, and only then he himself does what he has seen done, although the Father does nothing except through the Son. For, "all things were made through him and without him was made nothing."[1] Yet we did not offer any explanation, but because we did not understand any explanation. Sometimes, to be sure, speech is defective even where the understanding advances toward perfection, how much more does speech suffer defectiveness when the understanding does not have an advancing toward perfection.

(2) So now, as far as the Lord grants it, let us briefly run through the reading, and today at least let us complete the task which is owed. If, perchance, any time or strength remains, we shall reexamine, if we can (as far as it is possible both by us and with you), what the "seeing" of the Word is, what "to be shown to the Word" is. To be sure, if all these things which were said here are understood carnally according to human meaning, a soul, full of imagined appearances, makes nothing else for us except certain images as of two

1. Cf. Jn 1.3.

men, the Father and the Son, the one showing, the other seeing; the one speaking, the other hearing. And all these things are idols of the heart; and if these [idols] have been already thrown out of their temples, how much more ought they be thrown out of Christian hearts?

2. He said, "The Son cannot do anything of himself, but only what he sees the Father doing." This is true; hold this fast, yet provided that you do not lose what you held in the beginning of this same gospel, that "in the beginning was the Word, and the Word was with God, and the Word was God" and especially that "all things were made through him."[2] For join what you have heard now to that already heard, and let both be united in your hearts. And so "the Son cannot do anything of himself, but only what he sees the Father doing"—yet so that the Father does not do the things which he does except through the Son because the Son is his Word and "in the beginning was the Word, and the Word was with God, and the Word was God" and "all things were made through him." "For whatsoever things he does, these the Son also does in like manner." Not some other things, but these; not in dissimilar manner, but in like manner.

3. "For the Father loves the Son, and shows him all things which he himself does." That "He shows him all things which he himself does" seems also to pertain to what he said earlier, "but only what he sees the Father doing." But if the Father shows the things which he does, and the Son cannot do unless the Father has shown, and the Father cannot show unless he has done, it will logically follow that the Father does not do all things through the Son; furthermore, if we hold it as definite and unshaken that the Father does all things through the Son, he shows to the Son before he does. For, if the Father shows to the Son when he has [already] done, so that the Son might do the things shown, but the things shown have already been done, without a doubt the Father does something without the Son. But the Father does not do anything without the

2. Cf. Jn 1.1 and 3. On the necessary inconsistency in translating *facere* both "make" and "do" see *Tractate* 18.5, note 18.

Son because the Son of God is the Word of God and all things were made through him. It remains, therefore, perhaps, that the things which the Father is going to do, he shows as going to be done, that they may be done through the Son. For if the Son does those things which the Father shows already done, then, of course, the Father did not do through the Son those things which he shows already done. For they would not be able to be shown to the Son unless done; the Son would not be able to do them unless shown; therefore they [would be able to be] without the Son.

(2) But it is true, "All things were made through him"; therefore, before they were done they were shown. But we have said that this must be deferred, to which we must return after the reading has been run through in sequence if, as we said, any time or strength remains for us for those things which we have deferred to be reexamined.

4. Hear further, and more difficult, words: He says, "and greater works than these he will show him, that you may wonder." "Greater than these." Greater than which? [The answer] presents itself ready at hand: [Greater] than these which you have just heard, cures of sick bodies. For from this man who was in his infirmity for thirty-eight years and was healed by the Word of Christ, the whole occasion of this discourse arose; and because of this the Lord could say, "greater works than these he will show him, that you may wonder." For there are greater works than these, and the Father will show them to the Son. It is not "He has shown," as about a thing past, but "He will show," as about a thing future, that is, "He is going to show."[3]

(2) Again a difficult question arises. For is there anything in the Father which has not yet been shown to the Son? Is there anything in the Father which was still hidden from the

3. It is perhaps necessary for Augustine to say this because his congregation, or many in it, in their African dialect, confused the sound of *v* with *b* so that *demonstravit*, "has shown," sounded the same as *demonstrabit*, "will show." See W. Baehrens, *Sprachlicher Kommentar zur Vulgärlateinischen Appendix Probi* (Halle, 1922), 79–82, for a discussion of this phenomenon in general and 81 for Africa in particular.

Son when the Son spoke these words? For if "He will show,"
that is, he is going to show, he has not yet shown, and he is
going to show it to the Son when he also shows it to these
men. For he continues, "that you may wonder." And it is difficult to see how the eternal Father shows anything, as if in
time, to the coeternal Son who knows all things which are in
the Father.

5. Nevertheless, what are those greater [works]? For this
is, perhaps, easy to understand. He says, "For as the Father
raises the dead and gives life, so also the Son gives life to
whom he wishes." Therefore, "greater works" are to raise the
dead, than to heal the sick. But "as the Father raises the dead
and gives life, so also the Son gives life to whom he wishes."
Does the Father, therefore, [raise] some, and the Son others?
But all things through him; and so the Son [raises] the same
ones as also the Father, because not other things, nor in another manner, but "these the Son also does in like manner."
So it must be clearly understood and so held; but remember
that "The Son gives life to whom he wishes." Therefore grasp
herein not only the Son's power but also his will. Both the
Son gives life to whom he wishes and the Father gives life to
whom he wishes; and the Son to the very same ones as also
the Father, and through this both the same power and will
belong to the Father and the Son.

(2) What is it, then, that follows? "For neither does the Father judge any man, but all judgment he has given to the Son,
that all men may honor the Son, as they honor the Father."
And he added this in this way, as giving the reason for the
previous sentence. A very provocative question! Pay careful
attention. The Son gives life to whom he will, and the Father
gives life to whom he wishes; the Son raises the dead, as the
Father raises the dead. "For neither does the Father judge
any man." If the dead must be raised in the judgment, how
does the Father raise the dead if he does not judge any man?
For indeed "all judgment he has given to the Son." But in
that judgment the dead are raised; and some rise to life, some
to punishment. And if the Son does the whole of this but the
Father does not, for the reason that "The Father does not

judge any man, but all judgment he has given to the Son," it will seem contrary to what was said, "As the Father raises the dead and gives life, so also the Son gives life to whom he wishes." Therefore they raise together. If they raise together, they give life together. Therefore they judge together. How is it therefore true: "For neither does the Father judge any man, but all judgment he has given to the Son"? Let the questions proposed excite you for the time being; the Lord will provide that the solutions delight. For so it is, brothers; every question, unless it occupies one's mind intensely when propounded, will not delight when expounded.

(3) Therefore let the Lord himself continue, in case he may perhaps, in the words which he adds, make himself a little more clear. For he covered his light with a cloud;[4] and it is difficult to fly like an eagle over all the mist with which the whole earth is covered and to see the purest light in the words of the Lord. In case, therefore, by the heat of his rays he may perhaps disperse our darkness and deign to make himself a little more clear in his subsequent words, putting off these [questions], let us see what follows.

6. "He who does not honor the Son does not honor the Father who sent him." This is true and quite clear. For "all judgment he has given to the Son," as he said before, "that all men may honor the Son, as they honor the Father." What if they are found who honor the Father, but do not honor the Son? It is not possible, he says, for "He who does not honor the Son does not honor the Father who sent him." Therefore, no one can say, "I honored the Father because I did not know the Son." If you did not yet honor the Son, you did not honor the Father. For what is it to honor the Father except because he has the Son? For it is one thing when God is presented for your praise because he is God, and another when God is presented for your praise because he is the Father. When because he is God he is presented for your praise, the creator is presented for your praise, the omnipotent is presented for your praise, what might be called a supreme spirit, eternal, invisi-

---

4. Cf. Ecclus (Sir) 24.6 (LXX) (NAB 24.3).

ble, unchangeable, is presented for your praise. But when, because he is the Father he is presented for your praise, nothing other than the Son also is presented for your praise. For he cannot be called Father if he does not have a Son; just as neither can he be called Son if he does not have a Father. But in order that you may not perhaps honor the Father as greater but the Son as lesser so that you say to me, "I honor the Father, for I know that he has the Son, and I do not err in the name of Father, for I do not understand the Father without the Son; nevertheless, I honor the Son as lesser," the Son himself corrects you and calls you back, saying, "that all men may honor the Son," not in a lesser degree, but "as they honor the Father." Therefore "he who does not honor the Son does not honor the Father who sent him."

(2) I want, you say, to give greater honor to the Father, less to the Son. There you take honor away from the Father where you give less to the Son. For what else do you think when you reflect in that way except that the Father did not want or could not beget a Son equal to himself? If he did not want to, he was envious;[5] If he could not, he lacked the ability. Do you not see, therefore, that, by thinking this way, where you want to give greater honor to the Father, there you are insolent to the Father? Accordingly, honor the Son just as you honor the Father if you wish to honor both Father and Son.[6]

7. "Amen, amen, I say to you, that he who hears my word, and believes him who sent me, has life everlasting, and does not come into judgment, but has passed"—he does not say "now passes," but already—"has passed from death to life." And notice this, "he who hears my word," and he did not say, believes me, but "believes him who sent me." Therefore let him hear the Word of the Son that he may believe the Father.

5. Gibb translates, "He was unwilling." This is a possible connotation of the Latin verb *invidere,* but it normally and overwhelmingly has the meaning of "be jealous" or "begrudge." That divinity is not subject to emotions like envy is, of course, Platonic; but Berrouard, *Homélies XVII–XXXIII,* 172–173, suggests that Ambrose, *De Fide* 5.18.224 (PL 16.273; CSEL 78.302), may be Augustine's source for this idea.

6. Cf. *Tractate* 23.13 where this verse is interpreted in connection with the resurrection of the body; see Berrouard, *Homélies XVII–XXXIII,* 173.

(2) Why does he hear your word but believe another? When we hear someone's word, do we not believe him uttering the word, do we not give our credence to the one speaking to us? Why, then, did he want to say, "He who hears my word and believes him who sent me" except that his word is in me? And what does "hears my word" mean except "hears me"? But "he believes him who sent me" because when he believes him, he believes his Word; but when he believes his Word, he believes me because I am the Word of the Father.

(3) Therefore there is peace in the Scripture, and all things have been set in order, not at all in conflict. But you, cast aside the strife in your heart; understand the harmony of the Scriptures. Would truth ever utter contradiction?

8. "He who hears my word and believes him who sent me, has life everlasting, and does not come into judgment, but has passed from death to life." You remember what we had posited earlier, that "as the Father raises the dead and gives them life, so the Son also gives life to whom he wishes." Now he begins to make himself clear and to speak about the resurrection of the dead; and look, the dead are now rising. For "he who hears my word and believes him who sent me, has life everlasting, and will not come[7] into judgment." Demonstrate that he has risen. "But he has passed," he says, "from death to life." He who has passed from death to life has risen, of course; no one doubts it. For he would not pass from death to life unless he were first in death and were not in life; but when he passes, he will be in life and will not be in death. Therefore he had died and has come back to life; he had been lost and was found.[8]

(2) Accordingly, a kind of resurrection already happens, and men pass from a kind of death to a kind of life, from the death of unbelief to the life of faith, from the death of falsehood to the life of truth, from the death of iniquity to the life

7. In section 7 and at the beginning of section 8 this verb is given in the present tense, "does not come." The future tense is also cited in *Tractates* 22.3–4 and 23.14.
8. Cf. Lk 15.32.

of justice. There is also, therefore, this kind of resurrection of the dead.

9. Let him disclose that [resurrection] more fully and let it dawn upon us, as it has begun [to do]. "Amen, amen, I say to you, the hour is coming, and it is now." We were expecting the resurrection of the dead at the end; for so we have believed. Rather not, we were expecting, but we absolutely must expect it. For we do not believe it false that the dead will rise at the end. Therefore, when the Lord Jesus wanted to intimate to us a kind of resurrection of the dead before the resurrection of the dead, not as [that] of Lazarus,[9] or of the son of that widow,[10] or of the daughter of the ruler of the synagogue,[11] who all rose, to die again (for a kind of resurrection of these dead also happened before the resurrection of the dead), but as he says here, "he has life everlasting," he says, "and does not come into judgment, but has passed from death to life." To what life? To eternal [life]. Not, therefore, as the body of Lazarus; for he, too, passed from the death of the tomb to the life of men, but not eternal [life]; he was going to die again.

(2) But the dead who will rise at the end of the world will pass into eternal life. Therefore, when our Lord, Jesus Christ, the heavenly teacher, the Word of the Father, and the truth, wanted to show us a kind of resurrection of the dead into eternal life, before the resurrection of the dead into eternal life, he said, "The hour is coming." You, no doubt, imbued with a belief in the resurrection of the flesh, were expecting that hour of the end of the world, the day of judgment; and that you might not expect that in this passage, he added, "and it is now." Therefore, what he says, "the hour is coming," he does not say about that last hour when "The Lord himself with commandment and with the voice of an archangel and with the trumpet of God will come down from heaven; and the dead in Christ will rise first. Then we the living, who are left, will be caught up together with them in the clouds to

9. Cf. Jn 11.43–44.   10. Cf. Lk 7.14–15.
11. Cf. Mk 5.41–42; Mt 9.25; Lk 8.54–55.

meet Christ in the air, and so we shall always be with the Lord."[12]

(3) That hour will come, but it is not now. But notice what this hour is: "The hour is coming, and it is now." What happens in it? What except the resurrection of the dead? And what sort of resurrection? That they who rise may live forever. This will also be in the last hour.

10. Well now, how do we understand these two resurrections? Will those who now rise perhaps not rise then, so that there now occurs a resurrection of some, and then of others? It is not so. For, if we have believed rightly, we have risen by this resurrection; and we ourselves who have already risen await another resurrection at the end. But even now we have risen to eternal life, if we remain persevering in the faith itself; and we shall then rise to eternal life when we shall be made equal with the angels.[13] Therefore let him himself distinguish, let him himself make clear what I have made bold to say, how a resurrection occurs before the resurrection, not of some and of others, but of the same ones; not such as that of Lazarus, but into eternal life. He will make it absolutely clear. Hear the teacher, shining the dawn light [upon us], and hear our sun flowing into our hearts, not one whom the eyes of the flesh long for, but one to whom the eyes of the heart seethe to be opened.[14] Therefore let us hear him: "Amen, amen, I say to you, the hour is coming, and it is now, when the dead," see the resurrection being expressed, "when the dead shall hear the voice of the Son of God, and they who hear shall live."

(2) Why did he add, "they who hear shall live"? For could they hear if they were not alive? Therefore it should be enough, "The hour is coming, and it is now, when the dead shall hear the voice of the Son of God." We would then understand them as living since they could not hear if they were not alive. They do not hear, he says, because they live,

12. 1 Thes 4.15–16 (NAB 4.16–17).
13. Mt 22.30; Lk 20.36.
14. The Christian metaphorical use of the sun for Jesus is contrasted with the Manichaean teaching that the sun is Jesus. See *Tractate* 34.2.

but by hearing they live anew, [therefore, he says,] "they shall hear, and they who hear shall live."

(3) What does it mean, then, "they shall hear" except "they shall obey"? For as far as pertains to the hearing of the ear, not all who hear shall live; for many hear and do not believe. By hearing and not believing, they do not obey; by not obeying, they do not live. And therefore, here, "who shall hear" is nothing other than "who shall obey." Therefore, they who obey shall live; let them be assured, let them be free from anxiety, they shall live. Christ is being proclaimed, the Word of God, the Son of God, through whom all things were made, born of the virgin with flesh assumed, for the sake, surely, of the divine economy,[15] a baby in the flesh, a youth in the flesh, suffering in the flesh, dying in the flesh, rising in the flesh, ascending in the flesh, promising resurrection to the flesh, promising resurrection to the mind, to the mind before the flesh, to the flesh after the mind. He who hears and obeys will live; he who hears and does not obey, that is, who hears and scorns, who hears and does not believe, will not live. Why will he not live? Because he does not hear. What does "he does not hear" mean? He does not obey. Therefore, "they who hear shall live."

11. Consider now what we had said had to be deferred, that it may now possibly be made clear. Immediately he added, about this very resurrection, "For as the Father has life in himself, so he has given to the Son also to have life in himself." What does it mean, "the Father has life in himself"? He has life not somewhere else but in himself. For, in fact, his own living is in him; it is not from elsewhere, it is not someone else's. He does not, as it were, borrow life, nor does he become, as it were, a sharer in life, in that life which is not what he is, but he "has life in himself," so that life itself is for him, he himself. If I shall be able to say even a little more on this point, by citing examples to instruct your under-

15. The Latin reads *dispensationis gratia.* The Latin *dispensatio,* "the Dispensation," is used in the *Vulgate* for Paul's *oeconomía* in Eph 1.10 and 3.9. I have given the term its Greek sense as a less ambiguous technical term than "dispensation." See NCE 5.86.

standing, I shall be able [to do so] with the Lord's help and the kindness of your attention.

(2) God lives; the soul, too, lives. But the life of God is immutable; the life of the soul is mutable. God neither improves nor succumbs to weakness,[16] but he is himself always in himself, he is just so as he is, not one way now, another way afterwards, another way before. But the life of the soul acts very differently on different occasions. It lived foolishly; it lives wisely. It lived unjustly; it lives justly. Now it remembers, now it forgets. Now it learns, now it cannot learn. Now it loses what it had learned, now it perceives what it had lost. The life of the soul is mutable. And when the soul lives in iniquity, [that] is its death; but when it becomes just, it becomes a sharer in another's life which is not what it itself is. For by uplifting itself to God and by adhering to God, it is justified from him. For it has been said, "To him who believes in him who justifies the ungodly, his faith is reputed to justice."[17]

(3) By succumbing to weakness apart from him the soul becomes wicked; by progressing towards him it becomes just. Does it not appear to you as something cold becoming warm when moved to the fire [and] growing cold when removed from the fire? Does it not appear to you something dark, becoming bright when moved to the light [and] growing dark when removed from the light? The soul is some such thing; God is not any such thing.

(4) Man, too, can say that he has light now in his own eyes. Then let your eyes speak with a kind of voice of their own, so to speak, if they can, "we have light in ourselves." An objection is raised: "You do not say properly that you have light in yourselves; you have light, but in the sky; you have light, if, perchance, it is night, but in the moon, in lamps, not in yourselves. For you, when [your eyes have been] closed, lose

16. Browne's translation, "For God is neither proficiency nor deficiency," and Gibb's, "In God is neither increase nor decrease," have the advantage of reflecting the word play in the verbs *proficit* and *deficit*, but do not seem to convey the meaning adequately.

17. Cf. Rom 4.5.

what you, when [they have been] opened, perceive. You do not have light in yourselves. When the sun sets, keep the light, if you can. It is night, and you are enjoying the nocturnal light; when the lamp is removed, keep the light. But since, after the lamp is removed, you remain in darkness, you do not have light in yourselves." Therefore to have light in oneself is this, not to need light from another.

(5) Look where, if anyone understand, he shows the Son equal to the Father, where he says, "As the Father has life in himself, so he has given to the Son also to have life in himself," so that there should be this difference only between the Father and the Son, that the Father has life in himself which no one has given him, but the Son has life in himself which the Father has given.

12. But here also rises another cloud to be dispersed. Let us not succumb to weakness; let us be keenly attentive. These[18] are the pastures of the mind; let us not loathe them, so that we may live. "Look," you say, "you yourself admit that the Father has given life to the Son, that he may, indeed, have life in himself, as the Father has life in himself, the one not needing, that the other also may not need; that the one should be life, so also the other should be, and both enjoined, one life, not two, because there is one God, not two gods, and this same thing is 'to be life.'" How therefore did the Father give life to the Son? Not in such a way as if the Son had been without life before and received life from the Father in order that he might live; for if this were so, he would not have life in himself.

(2) Look, I was talking about the soul. The soul exists. Although it may not be wise, although it may not be just, it is a soul; although it may not be devout, it is a soul. Therefore, it is one thing for it to be a soul; but it is another for it to be wise, to be just, to be devout. Therefore, there is something because of which it is not yet wise, not yet just, not yet devout; and yet it is not nothing, it is not non-life. For from certain works of itself it shows itself to be life, although it does not

18. That is, the Scriptures.

show itself to be wise, devout, just. For unless it were living, it would not move the body; it would not order steps to the feet, work to the hands, looking to the eyes, hearing to the ears; it would not open the mouth for the voice, it would not move the tongue for a distinction of sounds. And so by these works it shows that it lives and is something which is better than the body.

(3) But does it show itself to be wise, devout, just, by these works? Do not the stupid and the ungodly and the unjust walk, work, see, hear, speak? But when it elevates itself to something which it itself is not, and which is above it, and from which it itself is, it receives wisdom, justice, devotion; and when it was without these, it was dead and did not have the life by which it lived itself, but that by which it made the body live. For there is one thing in the soul by which the body is made to live, another by which it itself is made to live. For in fact it is better than the body; but God is better than it. Therefore, even if it is foolish, unjust, ungodly, it is itself the life of the body. But because God is its life, just as when it itself is in the body, it provides [the body] strength, beauty, movement, the functions of the members, so when God, its life, is in it, he provides it wisdom, devotion, justice, love.

(4) Therefore it is one thing which is provided the body from the soul; it is another which is provided the soul from God. It gives life and it is given life; even if dead, it gives life, even if it itself is not given life. And so, when the Word comes and has been infused in those who hear, and they become, not only hearing but also obedient, the soul rises from its death to its life, that is, from iniquity, from folly, from ungodliness, to its God who is wisdom, justice, illumination for it. Let it rise to him, let it be enlightened by him. "Draw near to him," [Scripture] says. And what will there be for us? "And be enlightened."[19] Therefore, if you are enlightened by drawing near, and darkened by withdrawing, your light was not in yourselves but in your God. Draw near, that you may rise; if you withdraw, you will die. Therefore, if by drawing near you

19. Cf. Ps 33.6 (LXXX).

live, by withdrawing you die, your life was not in you. For
that is your life which is your light. "For with you is the fountain of life, and in your light we shall see light."[20]

13. Therefore, not as the soul is something else before it is
enlightened and becomes better when it is enlightened by a
participation in a better, [not] thus was the Word of God, the
Son of God, also something else before he received life that
he might have life by participation; but he has life in himself,
and through this he himself is life itself.

(2) Why then does he say, "He has given to the Son to have
life in himself "? Let me state it briefly. He begat the Son. For
it is not that he was without life and received life; but he is
life by a "being born." The Father is life, not by a "being
born"; the Son is life by a "being born." The Father [is] from
no father; the Son, from God the Father. The Father, in that
he is, is from no one; but in that he is the Father, he is in
regard to the Son. But the Son, both in that he is the Son, is
in regard to the Father, and in that he is, is from the Father.
Therefore, he said this, "He has given life to the Son, that he
might have it in himself," as if he were to say, The Father
who is life in himself begat the Son who should be life in
himself. For he wanted "He has given" to be understood as
equivalent in meaning to "He has begotten." As if he were to
say to someone, "God has given you being."

(3) To whom did he give it? If he has given being to someone already existing, he did not give him being, because he
who could receive it was, before it was given to him. Therefore, when you hear, "He has given you being," you who were
to receive [being] were not in being and, by coming into
being, you have received that you should be. The builder has
given to this house that it should be. But what did he give it?
That it should be a house. To what did he give it? To this
house. What did he give it? That it should be a house. How
could he give to the house that it should be a house? For if it
was a house, to what would he give that it should be a house
since it already was a house? Therefore, what does it mean,

20. Ps 35.10.

he has given to it that it should be a house? He made it to be a house. What, then, did he give to the Son? He has given to him to be the Son; he begot him to be life, that is, "He gave to him to have life in himself," that he might be life, not needing life, that he not be understood to have life by participation. For if he had life by participation, he could also be without life by losing it. Do not accept this in the Son, do not think it, do not believe it. Therefore, the Father remains life, the Son also remains life; the Father, life in himself, not from the Son, the Son, life in himself, but from the Father. [He was] begotten by the Father to be life in himself, but the Father [is] life in himself, unbegotten.

(4) And he did not beget a lesser Son who by growing would become equal. For he was not aided by time for perfecting himself, through whom, being perfect, times were created. Before all times he was coeternal with the Father. For the Father never was without the Son; but the Father is eternal, therefore the Son [is] likewise coeternal.

(5) What about you, soul? You were dead, you had lost life. Hear the Father through the Son. Rise, receive life that in him who has life in himself you may receive life which you do not have in yourself. Therefore the Father gives you life, and the Son; and the first resurrection is effected when you rise to sharing life, a thing which you are not, and by participation you are brought alive. Rise from your death to your life which is your God, and pass from death to life everlasting. For the Father has life everlasting in himself, and unless he begot such a Son as had life in himself, then the Son would not also give life to whom he would wish, as the Father raises the dead and gives them life.

14. What, then, about that resurrection of the body? For these who hear and live, whence do they live except by hearing? For "the friend of the bridegroom stands and hears him, and rejoices with joy because of the bridegroom's voice,"[21] not because of his own voice; that is, by participating, not by existing, they hear and live. And all who hear live because all

21. Cf. Jn 3.29.

who obey live. Say something, Lord, also about the resurrection of the flesh. For there have been those who deny it and say that this alone is resurrection which occurs through faith.[22] The Lord just now made mention of this resurrection and set us on fire because some "dead shall hear the voice of the Son of God, and shall live." Not some of those who hear shall die and others live, but all "who hear shall live" because all who obey shall live. Look, we see a resurrection of the human soul;[23] let us not, therefore, lose faith in the resurrection of the flesh.

(2) And unless you, Lord Jesus, say it, whom shall we oppose to the objectors? For all the sects, which have presumed that they implant some religion in men, have not denied this resurrection of human souls, so that it not be said to them, "If the soul does not rise, why do you speak to me? What do you want to do in me? If you do not make a better person out of an inferior one, why do you speak? If you do not make a just person out of an unjust one, why do you speak? But if you make one just from unjust, devout from ungodly, wise from foolish, you admit that my soul rises if I obey you, if I believe you." Therefore, all who have established a sect of some religion, even a false one, wishing that they be believed, have not been able to deny this resurrection of human souls; all have agreed on that, but many have denied the resurrection of the flesh, and have said that resurrection has already taken place in faith. The Apostle resisted such men, saying,

22. Those who deny a resurrection of the body and interpret resurrection spiritually. Probably he only refers to those mentioned by Paul in 2 Tm 17–18 which is quoted below. However, the various Gnostic sects, the Manichaeans, and the Neo-Platonists all denied the resurrection of the body and Augustine may possibly have had these, of whom his congregation would be aware, in mind. In the *De Haeresibus* (PL 42.21–50; CCL 46.283–345) he mentions many heresies which denied the resurrection of the body. All of these are either Gnostic or very minor; it seems unlikely that any of them, except the Manichaeans, would have had any immediate impact upon the Christians of Hippo Regius.

23. The Latin word is *mens*, "the mind," the intellectual faculty of the human soul which distinguishes human life from other kinds of earthly life, plants and animals. I take it here as a synecdoche, a partial aspect of the human soul posited for the whole. Throughout the rest of the sermon "human soul" is *mens* and "soul" is *anima*.

"Of whom are Humenaeus and Philetus, who have gone far astray concerning the truth in saying that the resurrection has taken place already; and they are subverting the faith of some."[24] They said that resurrection had already taken place, but in such a way that another was not to be hoped for; and they reproached men who hoped for the resurrection of the flesh, as though the resurrection which had been promised was already fulfilled in the human soul by believing.

(3) The Apostle reproaches them. Why does he reproach them? Were they not saying this which the Lord just now said, "The hour is coming and it is now, when the dead shall hear the voice of the Son of God, and they who hear shall live"? "But I am still speaking about the life of human souls," Jesus is saying to you. "I do not yet speak about the life of bodies, but I am speaking about the life of the life of bodies, that is, about [the life] of souls in which is the life of bodies. For I know that there are bodies lying in tombs; I know, too, that your bodies will be in tombs. I am not yet speaking about that resurrection. I speak about this one; rise in this one that you may not rise in that one to punishment."

(4) "But that you may know that I speak about that one, what do I add? 'For as the Father has life in himself, so he has given to the Son also to have life in himself.' This life, the thing which the Father is, which the Son is, to what does it pertain? To the soul or to the body? For the body does not perceive that life of wisdom, but the rational human soul does. For not every soul can perceive wisdom. For a brute animal, too, has a soul; but the brute animal's soul cannot perceive wisdom. Therefore, the human soul[25] can perceive this life which the Father has in himself and has given to the Son to have in himself, because that is 'the true light which enlightens,' not every soul, but 'every man who comes into the world.'[26] Therefore, since I speak to the mind itself, let it hear, that is, obey, and live."

15. And so, Lord, do not keep silent about the resurrection

24. Cf. 2 Tm 2.17–18.   25. Here, *anima humana.*
26. Cf. Jn 1.9.

of the flesh, lest men do not believe it and we remain debaters, not preachers. Therefore "as the Father has life in himself, so he has given to the Son also to have life in himself." Let them who hear understand, let them believe that they may understand, let them obey that they may live. Let them hear still another thing, that they may not think that resurrection was limited here. "And he has given him power also to do judgment." Who? The Father. To whom has he given? To the Son. For to him to whom he has given to have life in himself, he has also given power to do judgment. "Because he is the Son of man." For this Christ is both Son of God and Son of man. "In the beginning was the Word, and the Word was with God, and the Word was God. He was in the beginning with God."[27] See how he has given him to have life in himself.

(2) But because "the Word was made flesh and dwelt among us,"[28] having been made man from the Virgin Mary, he is the Son of man. Accordingly because he is the Son of man, what did he receive? The power also to do judgment. What judgment? At the end of the world; and there you will have a resurrection of the dead, but of bodies. Therefore, God raises souls, through Christ, the Son of God; God raises bodies, through the same Christ, the Son of man. "He has given him power." He would not have this power unless he received it, and he would be a man without power. But the very same one is the Son of man who is also the Son of God. For by adhering to the unity of person, the Son of man with the Son of God was made one person; and the Son of God is the same person as the Son of man. But one must distinguish what he has [and] why. The Son of man has a soul, has a body. The Son of God, who is the Word of God, has human nature, as the soul has body. As a soul, having body, does not make two persons, but one man, so the Word, having human nature does not make two persons, but one Christ.

(3) What is human nature? A rational soul having body. What is Christ? The Word of God having human nature. I

27. Jn 1.1–2.   28. Cf. Jn 1.14.

see about what matters I speak, who I am who speaks, and to whom I speak.

16. Now hear about the resurrection of bodies; it is not I, but the Lord, who will speak, on account of those who have risen again, by rising from death, by adhering to life. To what life? That which knows not death. Why does it not know death? Because it does not know mutability. Why does it not know mutability? Because it is life in itself. "And he has given him power also to do judgment, because he is the Son of man." What judgment? What kind of judgment? "Do not wonder at this" because I said, "He has given him the power also to do judgment."

(2) "For the hour is coming." He did not add, "and it is now"; therefore, he intends to intimate a certain hour at the end of the world. Now there is the hour that the dead may rise; there will be an hour at the end of the world that the dead may rise. But let them rise now in the human soul, then in the flesh; let them rise now in the human soul through the Word of God, the Son of God; let them rise then in the flesh through the Word of God made flesh, the Son of man. For neither will the Father himself come to the judgment of the living and the dead; yet neither does the Father withdraw from the Son.

(3) How, then, will he not come himself? Because he himself will not be seen in the judgment. "They shall look on him whom they have pierced."[29] That form will be judge which stood before the judge; that [form] will judge which has been judged. For it has been judged wickedly; it will judge justly. Therefore the form of the servant will come and will itself appear. For how could the form of God appear to the just and the wicked? For if judgment were only to occur among the just alone, there would appear as to the just the form of God. But because there will be a judgment of the just and the wicked and it is not permitted that the wicked see God, for "blessed are the clean of heart, for they shall see God,"[30] the judge will appear such as can be seen both by those whom

29. Cf. Jn 19.37, quoting Zec 12.10.
30. Mt 5.8.

he will crown and by those whom he will condemn. Therefore the form of the servant will be seen, the form of God will be hidden.

(4) The Son of God will be hidden in the servant, and the Son of man will appear, because "He has given to him power also to do judgment because he is the Son of man." And because he alone will appear in the form of the servant, but the Father will not appear because he has not been clothed with the form of a servant, therefore he said earlier, "The Father does not judge any man, but all judgment he has given to the Son." Therefore it has been well deferred that he himself might be the expounder who was the propounder. For earlier it had been hidden; now, as I think, it is clear that "He has given him the power also to do judgment," that "The Father does not judge any man, but all judgment he has given to the Son," because judgment will be through that form which the Father does not have.

(5) And what kind of judgment? "Do not wonder at this, for the hour is coming," not that which now is, that souls may rise, but that which will be, that bodies may rise.

17. Let him say this more explicitly, that the heretic who denies the resurrection of the body may find no quibbling evasion, although the meaning already shines forth. When it was said earlier, "The hour is coming," he added, "and it is now." But just now [when it was said], "The hour is coming," he did not add, "and it is now." Nevertheless, let him with the clear truth smash to pieces all graspable opportunities, all the obstructing doorbolts of quibblings, all the knotty restraints of ensnaring objections.

(2) "Do not wonder at this, for the hour is coming in which all who are in the tombs. . . ." What is more evident? What is more explicit? There are bodies in the tombs; there are no souls in the tombs, neither of the just nor of the wicked. The soul of the just man was in the bosom of Abraham, the soul of the wicked man was being tortured in Hell;[31] in the tomb was neither the one nor the other. When he said earlier, "The hour is coming, and it is now"—I beg you, pay attention.

31. Cf. Lk 16.22–25.

(3) You know, brothers, that with work one procures the bread of the stomach; with how much more work the bread of the mind? You stand with work, and you hear; but we stand with greater work, and we speak. If we work for you, ought you not to work together with us for yourselves? So, earlier, when he said, "The hour is coming" and added, "and it is now," what did he put next? "When the dead shall hear the voice of the Son of God, and they who hear shall live." He did not say "All the dead will hear and they who hear shall live"; for he intended the dead to be understood as the wicked. And do all the wicked obey the gospel? The Apostle clearly says, "But all do not obey the gospel."[32] Nevertheless, they who hear will live, because all who obey the gospel will pass to life everlasting through faith; yet not all obey, and this is now. But truly at the end, "all who are in the tombs," that is, the just and the unjust, "shall hear his voice and shall come forth."

(4) Why did he not want to say, "and shall live?" For all shall come forth, but not all shall live. Indeed in what he said before, "And they who hear shall live," in this obedience he intended to be understood an eternal and happy life which not all who come forth from the tombs will have. Therefore now, both by the mention of the tombs and the setting forth of a coming forth from the tombs, we already understand the resurrection of bodies.

18. "All shall hear his voice and shall come forth." And where is the judgment if all shall hear and all shall come forth? It is as if the whole were run together; I see no distinction. To be sure, you have received the power of judging because you are the Son of man. Look, you will be present in judgment, the bodies will rise. Say something about the judgment itself, that is, about the separation of the evil and the good. And hear this: "They who have done good, in the resurrection of life;[33] they who have done evil unto the resur-

32. Cf. Rom 10.16.
33. The CCL text, following Migne (PL 35.1554), has *in resurrectione vitae;* the *Vulgate,* Berrouard, *Homélies XVII–XXXIII,* 216, and A. Caillu, *Sancti Au-*

rection of judgment." Earlier when he was speaking about the resurrection of minds and souls, did he make a separation? But all who shall hear shall live because they shall live by obeying. But truly by rising and coming forth from the tombs, not all shall go to eternal life, but those who have done well, however, those who [have done] ill, [will go] to judgment. For here he put judgment for punishment.

(2) And there will be a division, but not such as there is now. For even now we are separated not by places, but by habits, feelings, desires, faith, hope, love. For we live together with wicked persons; but all do not have one life. We are divided in secret; we are separated in secret, as the grains on the threshing-floor, not as the grains in the granary. The grains on the threshing-floor are both separated and mixed; they are separated when they are stripped from the husk, they are mixed because they are not yet winnowed. Then there will be an open separation, as of habits, so, too, of life; as of wisdom, thus, too, of bodies. They who have done well will go to live with the angels of God; they who have done ill will go to be tormented with the devil and his angels.[34]

(3) And the form of the servant will pass.[35] For, it was for this that he had shown himself, that he might do judgment; after the judgment, he will go from here; he will lead with him the body whose head he is, and will offer the kingdom to God.[36] Then plainly that form of God will be seen which cannot be seen by the wicked to whose sight the form of the servant had to be displayed. He says so elsewhere too: "These will go into everlasting burning" (about certain ones on the left), "but the just into everlasting life."[37] And in another place he says about this life: "Now this is everlasting life, that

gustini *Opera Omnia* 15, Patres Ecclesiae 122 (Paris, 1842) 206, have *in resurrectionem vitae*, "unto the resurrection of life." None of the editors indicate any variant readings.

34. Cf. Mt 25.41.

35. What this means is not clear here, that is, whether Augustine shared the view of those who held that after the final judgment Christ's human nature would be absorbed into his divine nature. See Berrouard, *Homélies XVII–XXXIII*, 218–219 and 827–828.

36. Cf. 1 Cor 15.24.   37. Cf. Mt 25.46.

they may know you, the only true God, and him whom you have sent, Jesus Christ."[38] Then there will appear there "He who, though he was in the form of God, thought it not robbery to be equal with God."[39]

(4) Then he will show himself as he promised he would show himself to those who love him. He said, "For he who loves me keeps my commandments; and he who loves me will be loved by my Father, and I will love him and will manifest myself to him."[40] He was present to those to whom he was speaking; but they saw the form of the servant, but did not see the form of God. On [his own] beast[41] they were being led to the inn of healing, and when healed, they will see; for, he said, "I will manifest myself to him."[42] How is he shown an equal to the Father? When he says to Philip, "He who sees me sees also the Father."[43]

19. "I cannot of myself do anything. As I hear, I judge; and my judgment is just." Because they were going to say, "You will judge and the Father will not judge, because 'all judgment he has given to the Son,' therefore, you will not judge according to the Father," he added, "I cannot of myself do anything. As I hear, I judge; and my judgment is just because I seek, not my own will, but the will of him who sent me."

(2) The Son does assuredly give life to whom he wishes. He does not seek his own will, but the will of him who sent him. Not mine, not my own, not mine, not the Son of man's, not mine, which may resist God. For men do their own will, not God's, when they do what they wish and not what God orders; but when they do what they wish in such a way that nevertheless they follow God's will, they do not do their own will even though they do what they wish. Willingly do what you are

38. Jn 17.3.   39. Cf. Phil 2.6.
40. Cf. Jn 13.21.
41. Cf. Lk 10.34 which Augustine interprets in *Quaestiones Evangeliorum* 2.19 (CCL 44B.63) as follows: His "beast" is the flesh in which he deigned to come to us. "To be put upon the beast" is to believe in the Incarnation of Christ. "The inn" is the Church where travelers returning from this journey abroad to their eternal homeland are refreshed.
42. Cf. Jn 14.21.   43. Cf. Jn 14.9.

ordered, and so you, too, will do this which you want, and you will not do your own will but that of him ordering.

20. What then? "As I hear, so I judge." The Son hears, and the Father shows him, and the Son sees the Father doing. And we had deferred these points, to treat them a little more clearly in accordance with our strength, if, when the reading was finished, time and strength remained to us. If I should say that I can still speak, you perhaps can no longer listen. Likewise, you perhaps say from your eagerness to hear, "We can." Therefore, it is better that I admit my weakness, that I am wearied and can speak no longer, rather than that, although you are well filled already, I should still pour out what you will not digest well. Accordingly, of this promise which I had put off to today, if time should be left, hold me a debtor for tomorrow,[44] with the Lord's help.

44. This promise is carried out in *Tractate* 23. As indicated in the introduction, D. Wright, "Tractatus 20–22," 317–330, and Berrouard, *Homélies XVII–XXXIII*, 42–46, demonstrate that *Tractates* 20, 21, and 22 were not originally part of the sequence of sermons on the Gospel of John, but later insertions, although these three were delivered on three successive days (see 20.13, 21.1, 22.1).

TRACTATE 20

On John 5.19

HE WORDS OF OUR LORD, Jesus Christ, especially those which John the Evangelist relates, are so special and of such deep meaning as to upset those misguided in their heart and to tax the upright of heart. Not without reason did [John] recline on the Lord's bosom[1] except to absorb the secrets of more profound wisdom and, by propagating the gospel, to give utterance[2] to what he had imbibed by his love. Accordingly, my beloved people, give your attention to these few words which have been read.[3] With the favor and aid of him who intended his words to be read out to us, words which at that time were heard and were written down that they might now be read, let us see if we can, in any way, say what that which you have just now heard him say means. "Amen, amen, I say to you, the Son cannot do anything of himself, but only what he sees the Father doing. For whatsoever things the Father does, these the Son also does in like manner."

2. Now, you must be reminded of the occasion for this discourse because of the previous parts of the reading, where the Lord had cured a certain man among those who were lying in the five porticoes of the well-known pool of Solomon and had said to him, "Take up your bed, and go into your

---

1. Cf. Jn 13.23–25 and 21.20.

2. The Latin verb here, *ructaret*, literally means "to belch." It is a strong verb widely used in Christian Latin with an ameliorative connotation, to express from deep within, and is regularly applied to prophetic or mystical pronouncements. See Blaise, 726, and Berrouard, *Homélies XVII–XXXIII*, 224–225.

3. This sermon is not part of the original series of sermons on John's Gospel, but a later insertion; see *Tractate* 19.20, note 44.

house."[4] But he had done this on the Sabbath; and as a result, the Jews were upset and were slandering him as a subverter and transgressor of the Law. Then he had said to them, "My Father works even until now, and I work."[5] For they, understanding the observance of the Sabbath carnally, thought that God, after the labor of making the world, slept, as it were, right down to this day, and therefore, that he had sanctified that day from which he began as if to rest from his labors.

(2) But the rite[6] of the Sabbath was taught to our ancient fathers[7] which we Christians observe spiritually so that we abstain from all servile work, that is, from all sin (for the Lord says, "Everyone who commits a sin is a slave of sin"),[8] and we have rest in our hearts, that is, spiritual tranquility. And, however we try it in this world, we shall, nevertheless, not arrive at that perfect rest except when we have departed from this life. But it was said that God rested for this reason, that he no longer made any creature after all things were completed.[9] And, therefore, the Scripture called it rest that it might remind us that we shall rest after good works. For so we have it written in Genesis, "and God made all things exceedingly good, and God rested on the seventh day,"[10] so that you, man, when you observe that God himself rested after good works, may not hope for rest for yourself, except when you have performed good works. And just as God, after he made man to his image and likeness on the sixth day and on that day finished all his exceedingly good works, rested on the seventh day, so also you may not hope for rest for yourself except when you have returned to the likeness in which you were made, which you have lost by sinning.

(3) For God, who spoke and they were made, ought not to be said to have worked.[11] Who is there who, after such ease

---

4. These exact words appear in Mk 2.11, but the context of the sermon calls for Jn 5.8.

5. Cf. Jn 5.17.

6. *sacramentum.* See Blaise, 730, s.v. 6, and A. Souter, *A Glossary of Later Latin to 600 A.D.* (Oxford, 1949), 360, for this connotation.

7. Cf. Ex 20.8–11.   8. Cf. Jn 8.34 and *Tractate* 3.19.

9. Cf. *Tractate* 17.15.   10. Cf. Gn 1.31 and 2.2.

11. Cf. Ps 32.9; also Ps 148.5 (LXX).

of work would want to rest as if after labor? If he ordered and someone resisted him, if he ordered and it was not done, and he labored that it might be done, it may be rightly said that he rested after labor. But when in the very same book of Genesis we read, "God said, 'Let light be made,' and light was made; God said, 'Let there be a firmament made,' and a firmament was made,"[12] and the rest of things were made instantly at his word, to which the Psalm also attests, saying, "He spoke and they were made; he commanded and they were created,"[13] then how, after the creation of the world, did he need rest as if so that he might cease who in giving orders had never labored?[14] Therefore those words are mystical and so put for this reason, that we may hope for rest for ourselves after this life—but [only] if we have done good works.

(4) Thus the Lord, restraining the shamelessness and error of the Jews, and showing that they did not have a correct understanding of God, said to them who were scandalized because he worked a healing of men on the Sabbath, "My Father works even until now, and I work." Do not, therefore, think that my Father has so rested on the Sabbath that he does not work thereafter; but as he himself now works, I also work. But as the Father works without labor, so the Son also works without labor. God "said, and they were made"; Christ said to the sick man, "Take up your bed and go into your house," and it was done.

3. Now the Catholic faith holds that the works of the Father and the Son are not separable. This is what I want to say, if I can, to you, my beloved people, but according to those words of the Lord, "He who can take it, let him take it."[15] But he who cannot take it, let him ascribe this, not to me but to his own dullness, and let him turn himself to him who opens the heart that he may pour in what he gives. And, lastly, if anyone does not understand for the reason that it has not been said by me as it ought to have been said, let him pardon human frailty and implore divine goodness. For

12. Cf. Gn 1.3 and 6.
13. Cf. Ps 32.9; also Ps 148.5 (LXX).
14. Cf. *Tractate* 17.14.   15. Cf. Mt 19.12.

within we have Christ as our teacher.[16] Whatever you cannot take through your ear and my mouth, in your heart turn to him who both teaches me what I am saying and apportions to you as he sees fit.[17] He who knows what he gives and to whom he gives will provide support for one who asks and will open to one who knocks.[18] And if, perchance, he does not give, let no one say that he has been abandoned. For perhaps he delays in giving something, but he leaves no one hungering. For if he does not give at the hour, he exercises the seeker and does not scorn the asker. Therefore consider and observe what I want to say, even if, perhaps, I should not be able to.

(2) The Catholic faith, made firm by the Spirit of God in its saints, holds this against every heretical depravity: The works of the Father and the Son are inseparable. What is it that I have said? Just as the Father himself and the Son himself are inseparable, so also the works of the Father and the Son are inseparable. How is it possible that the Father and the Son are inseparable? Because he himself said, "I and the Father are one."[19] For the Father and the Son are not two gods, but one God, the Word and he of whom the Word is, the one and the only one, one God, Father and Son, having embraced in love, and the one of their love is their Spirit,[20] so that there is found the Trinity, Father and Son and Holy Spirit. Therefore, as there is an equality and inseparability of the persons, not only of the Father and the Son, but also of the Holy Spirit, so also the works are inseparable. I shall say still more clearly what this means, the works are inseparable.

(3) The Catholic faith does not say that God the Father did something and the Son did something else; but what the Father did, this the Son also did, this the Holy spirit also did. For all things were made through the Word; when he spoke and they were made,[21] they were made through the Word, they were made through Christ. For "in the beginning was

---

16. Cf. *Tractate* 1.7, note 23.   17. Cf. *Tractate* 11.7.
18. Cf. Mt 7.7.   19. Jn 10.30.
20. Cf. *Tractates* 9.8, 14.9, and 18.4.
21. Cf. Ps 32.9; also Ps 148.5 (LXX).

the Word, and the Word was with God, and the Word was God; all things were made through him."[22] If all things were made through him, "God said, 'Let light be made,' and light was made";[23] he did it in the Word, he did it through the Word.

4. So look, we have now heard the gospel when he answered the Jews who were boiling with rage "because he not only broke the Sabbath, but also said God was his Father, making himself equal to God."[24] For so it was written in the previous section. Therefore when the Son of God and the truth replied to such mistaken indignation of theirs, he said, "Amen, amen, I say to you, the Son cannot do anything of himself, but only what he sees the Father doing." As if he were to say, "Why were you scandalized because I said, God is my Father, and because I make myself equal to God? I am equal in such a way that he begot me; I am equal in such a way that he is not from me, but I am from him." For this is understood in those words, "The Son cannot do anything of himself, but only what he sees the Father doing." That is, whatever the Son has to do, of the Father he has it to do.

(2) Why does he have it of the Father? Because of the Father he has that he is the Son. Why does he have of the Father that he is the Son? Because he has of the Father that he is able to do, because he has of the Father that he is. For "to be" is for the Son the same as "to be able to do."[25] It is not so for man. From the depths of human frailty, which lies at a far lower level, as best you can, lift up your hearts; and in the event, perchance, some one of us should touch upon the secret and, trembling with excitement at the flash, as it were, of the great light, should gain some understanding, let him not remain unwise; nevertheless, let him not think that he understands all, so that he may not be too proud and lose what understanding he has gained. As regards man, what he is is one thing, what he is able to do is another. For sometimes man is and is not able to do what he wants; but at other times

22. Cf. Jn 1.1 and 3.
24. Cf. Jn 5.18.
23. Gn 1.3.
25. Cf. *Tractate* 18.10.

man is in such wise that he is able to do what he wants. And so his "to be" is one thing, his "to be able to do" is another. For if his "to be" were the same as his "to be able to do," when he wanted he would be able to do.

(3) But as regards God to whom there is not one substance for "to be" and another power for "to be able to do," but whatever is his, and whatever he is, is consubstantial with him, because he is God, it is not that he is in one way and he is able to do in another way, but he has "to be" and "to be able to do" at one and the same time because he has "to will" and "to do" in one and the same act. Therefore, because the Son's power is from the Father, for that reason the Son's substance also is from the Father; and because the Son's substance [is] from the Father, for that reason the Son's power is from the Father. For in the Son the power is not one and the substance another, but his power is the very same as his substance, substance for "to be," power for "to be able to do." Therefore because the Son is from the Father, for that reason he said, "The Son cannot do anything of himself." Because he is not the Son of himself, for that reason he cannot do of himself.

5. Now it seems as if he made himself lesser when he said, "The Son cannot do anything of himself, but only what he sees the Father doing." Here heretical vanity stiffens the neck, of those, of course, who, not understanding the mystery of Christ's words, and say that the Son is lesser than the Father, of lesser power, majesty, capability.[26] But pay attention, my beloved people, and see how in their carnal understanding they are now troubled in the very words of Christ. And I said this just a little while ago, that the Word of God distresses all perverse hearts as he exercises devout hearts, especially [the word] which is said through John the Evangelist. For deep things are said through him, not any kind whatever, not those which may be easily understood. Look, right now if a heretic, perchance, hears these words, he stiffens himself and says to us, "Look, the Son is lesser than the Father; look, hear the words of the Son who says, 'The Son cannot do any-

26. The Arians. See *Tractate* 1.11, note 27.

thing of himself, but only what he sees the Father doing.'" Wait now! As it was written, "Be meek to hear the word, that you may understand."[27]

(2) For suppose that I was disturbed by these words, because I say that the power and majesty of the Father and the Son are equal, when I heard, "The Son cannot do anything of himself, but only what he sees the Father doing." Troubled by these words, I ask of you who seem to yourself to have already understood, "We know in the gospel that the Son walked upon the sea.[28] Where did he see the Father walking upon the sea?" Here now that man is troubled. Therefore put aside what you had understood and let us seek together. What, then, do we do? We heard the words of the Lord. "The Son cannot do anything of himself, but only what he sees the Father doing." He himself walked upon the sea; the Father never walked upon the sea. Yet surely "the Son does not do anything, but only what he sees the Father doing."

6. Therefore, return with me to that which I was saying; in case, perchance, it may possibly be understood in such a way that we may both have a way out of the question. For according to the Catholic faith I see how I may have a way out without offense, without scandal; but you, trapped in, are seeking a way out. See where you had entered. Perhaps you also did not understand this which I said, see where you had entered. Hear him speaking himself, "I am the door."[29] Not without reason, therefore, do you seek a way out, and you only find that you did not enter by the door but you dropped in by the wall. Therefore, as far as you can, gather yourself together from your fall, and enter by the door, that you may enter without offense and have a way out without error. Come by Christ; and do not assert what you would say from your heart, but speak this which he shows.

(2) See how the Catholic faith has a way out of this problem. The Son walked upon the sea; he put his feet of flesh on the waves. The flesh walked and the divinity guided its

27. Ecclus (Sir) 5.13 (LXX).
28. Cf. Mt 14.25; Mk 6.48; Jn 6.19.
29. Cf. Jn 10.7.

course. Therefore, when the divinity guided its course and the flesh walked, was the Father absent? If he was absent, how does the Son himself say, "But the Father abiding in me, he does his works"?[30] Therefore, if the Father abiding in the Son does his works, that walking of the flesh upon the sea was done by the Father, [yet] was done through the Son. Therefore, that walking is the inseparable work of the Father and the Son. I see both working there; neither has the Father abandoned the Son, nor has the Son withdrawn from the Father. Thus whatever the Son does, he does not do without the Father because whatever the Father does, he does not do without the Son.

7. We have found our way out of this. See that we say correctly that the works of the Father and the Son and the Holy Spirit are inseparable. For as you understand, look, God made light, and the Son saw the Father making light, according to the carnal understanding you have who, therefore, wish to understand him as lesser because he said, "The Son cannot do anything of himself, but only what he sees the Father doing." God the Father made the light; what other light did the Son make? God the Father made a firmament, the sky between the waters and the waters;[31] the Son saw him according to your dull and crass understanding. Because the Son saw the Father making the firmament and [because] he said, "The Son cannot do anything of himself, but only what he sees the Father doing," give me another firmament. Or is it that you have lost the foundation? But they who were built upon the foundation of the apostles and prophets with Christ Jesus himself as the cornerstone are at peace in Christ and do not contend and go astray in heresy.[32] Therefore, we understand that the light was made by God the Father, but through the Son; the firmament was made by God the Father, but through the Son. For "all things were made through him, and without him was made nothing."[33]

(2) Cast out your understanding—and it ought not be

---

30. Cf. Jn 14.10.
32. Cf. Eph 2.14–22.

31. Cf. Gn 1.6–8.
33. Cf. Jn 1.3.

called understanding but clearly stupidity. God the Father made the world; what other world did the Son make? Give me a world of the Son. This world in which we are, whose is it? Tell us, by whom was it made? If you say, "By the Son, not by the Father," you have erred concerning the Father. If you say, "By the Father, not by the Son," the gospel answers you, "And the world was made through him, and the world knew him not."[34] Therefore acknowledge him through whom the world was made, and be not among those who do not know him who made the world.

8. Inseparable, therefore, are the works of the Father and the Son. But this, "The Son cannot do anything of himself " is what would be if he were to say, "The Son is not of himself." For if the Son is, he was born; if he was born, he is of him from whom he was born. But, nonetheless, he begot an equal to himself. For nothing was lacking to him who begot; neither did he who begot one coeternal search for a time to beget, nor did he who brought forth the Word from himself search for a mother to beget, nor had the Father in begetting preceded in age so that he might beget the Son lesser [in age]. And, perhaps, someone says that after many centuries, in his old age, God had a Son. As the Father [is] without old age, even so the Son [is] without growth; neither has the one grown old nor has the other grown. But an equal begot an equal; an eternal, an eternal.

(2) How does an eternal, someone says, beget an eternal? As temporal flame generates temporal light. For the generating flame is of the same duration as the light which it generates, nor does the generating flame precede in time the generated light; but the light begins from the instant when the flame begins. Give me flame without light, and I give you God the Father without the Son. This is, therefore, "The Son cannot do anything of himself, but only what he sees the Father doing," because the "seeing" of the Son is to have been born of the Father.

(3) His vision is not one thing and his substance another;

34. Cf. Jn 1.10.

nor is his power one thing, his substance another. The whole
that he is is from the Father; the whole that he is able to do
is from the Father, because what he is able to do and what he
is—this is one, and the whole is from the Father.

9. He himself also continues in his own words and disturbs
those who understand incorrectly, that he may recall the erring to the right understanding. When he said, "The Son cannot do anything of himself, but only what he sees the Father
doing," in order that no carnal understanding might creep in
and divert the mind, and that man might not make for himself two craftsmen, one a teacher, the other an apprentice
watching the master closely, so to speak, making a chest, for
example, so that, as the one made the chest, so the other may
also make another chest according to the visual image which
he looked at carefully with regard to his teacher as he was
working—but that the carnal understanding might not du-
plicate some such idea for itself in that simple divinity, he
continued and said, "For whatsoever things the Father does,
these same things the Son also does in like manner."

(2) The Father does not do some things, and the Son other
similar things, but the same things in like manner; but, he
said, "Whatsoever things the Father does, these same things
the Son also does in like manner." What the one does, these
the other, also. The Father [made] the world, the Son [made]
the world, the Holy Spirit [made] the world. If [there are]
three gods, [there are] three worlds; if [there is] one God,
Father and Son and Holy Spirit, one world was made by the
Father through the Son in the Holy Spirit. Therefore the Son
does these things which the Father also does, and he does
them not in a dissimilar manner; he both does them, and
does them in like manner.

10. He had already said, "These he does," why did he add
"He does in like manner"? That no other distorted understanding or error might arise in the mind. For you see man's
work. There is mind and body in man, the mind commands
the body, but there is much difference between body and
mind. The body is visible; the mind, invisible. Between the
power and the capability of the mind and of any body at all,

even a heavenly body, there is much difference. Yet the mind commands its body and the body does; and what the mind seems to do, this the body also does. Therefore the body seems to do this same thing as the mind, but not in like manner. How does it do this same thing, but not in like manner? The mind makes[35] a word in itself; it orders the tongue, and it utters the word which the mind made. The mind made, and the tongue made; the master of the mind made, and the servant made. But that the servant might make, it received from the master what it was to make, and under the master's order, it made. This same thing was made by both. But in a like manner?

(2) "How not in a like manner?" someone says. Look, the word which my mind made remains in me; the [word] which my tongue made struck the air and passed through it and is not. When you have said a word in your mind and have sounded it with your tongue, return to your mind and see that the word which you made is there. As it remained in your mind, did it remain on your tongue? What sounded through your tongue, the sounding tongue made and the thinking mind made. But what the tongue sounded has passed away; what the mind thought remains. Therefore the body made the same thing as the mind, but not in like manner. For the mind made what the mind would keep; but the tongue made what sounds and strikes the ear through the air. You don't follow after the syllables and cause them to remain, do you? Therefore, not so the Father and the Son; but [the Son] does these same things and he does in like manner.

(3) If God made the sky which remains, the Son made this sky which remains. If God the Father made man who dies, the Son made the same man who dies. Whatever the Father made lasting these the Son made lasting because he made them in like manner; and whatever the Father made temporary, these same things the Son made temporary, because he not only made the same things, but also made them in like

---

35. The semantic range of the Latin verb *facere* includes both "make" and "do," a variation necessary to the English translation but which somewhat blunts the force of Augustine's argument; see *Tractate* 18.5, note 18.

manner. For the Father made through the Son, because the Father made all things through the Son.

11. Look for separation in the Father and the Son, you do not find it; even if you have soared high, then you do not find it; if you have touched something beyond your intellect, then you do not find it. For if you busy yourself in these things which the erring mind makes for itself, you speak with your own images, not with the Word of God; your images deceive you. Transcend the body also and savor the mind. Transcend the mind also and savor God. You do not reach out and touch unless you also have passed beyond the mind. You do not reach out and touch God unless you have also passed beyond the mind. How much less do you touch him if you have remained in the flesh? Therefore, those who savor the flesh, how far are they from savoring what God is because they would not be there even if they savored the mind! Man withdraws far from God when he savors carnally, and there is much difference between flesh and mind; yet there is more difference between mind and God.

(2) If you are in the mind, you are in the middle. If you look below, there is body; if you look above, there is God. Raise yourself up from the body, pass beyond even yourself. For see what the Psalm said and be advised how God is to be savored. It says, "My tears have become my bread day and night, when they say to me daily, where is your God?"[36] As though the pagans should say, "Look! Our gods! Where is your God?" For they show what is seen; we worship what is not seen.

(3) And to whom are we to show? To a person who does not have the means to see? For, of course, if these see their own gods with the eyes, we also have other eyes with which we may see our God. The eyes themselves must be cleansed by our God for us to see our God; for "blessed are the clean of heart, for they shall see God."[37] Therefore, when he said that he was troubled when they say to him daily, "Where is your God?" he said, "These things I have remembered," because "they say to me daily, 'Where is your God?'"

36. Ps 41.4.   37. Mt 5.8.

(4) And as if wishing to take hold of his God, he said, "These things I have remembered and I have poured out my soul over me."[38] Therefore that I might touch my God about whom they said to me, "Where is your God?" I poured out my soul not over my flesh, but over me; I transcended myself that I might touch him. For he is over me who made me; no one touches him except he who passes beyond himself.

12. Think of the body: it is mortal, it is earthly, it is frail, it is corruptible. Cast it aside! But perchance the flesh is temporal? Think of other bodies, think of heavenly bodies. They are bigger, better, magnificent. Observe these too; they revolve from east to west and do not stand still; they are seen by the eyes, not only by mankind, but also the brute animal. Go beyond these too! And how, you will say, do I go beyond heavenly bodies when I walk on earth? You go beyond, not in the flesh, but in the intellect. Cast aside these too! Although they shine, they are bodies; although they glisten from the sky, they are bodies.

(2) Come, because, perhaps, you do not think that you have somewhere to go when you consider all these things. "And where will I go beyond the heavenly bodies," you say, "and what shall I go beyond with the intellect?" Have you considered all these things? "I have considered," you say. With what have you considered them? Let the one who considers appear himself. For the one who considers all these things, who distinguishes, who differentiates, who in some way weighs them in the scale of wisdom, is the mind. Without doubt the mind by which you thought of all these things is better than all these things which you thought of.

(3) Therefore this mind of yours is spirit, not body; pass beyond it too! Compare the mind itself first, that you may see to what place you are to pass beyond; compare it to the flesh. God forbid that you so compare it. Compare it to the brightness of the sun, the moon, the stars; the mind's brightness is greater. Look first at the swiftness of the mind itself. See if

38. Cf. Ps 41.5. The same text is found in *En in Ps* 41.8 (CCL 38.465–466).

the spark of the thinking mind is not more intense than the brightness of the shining sun. You see the rising sun in your mind; how slow is its movement in comparison with your mind! Swiftly you could think what the sun will do. It will come from east to west; tomorrow it rises from another position. When your thought did this, the sun is still slow and you have made the whole journey. A great thing, then, is the mind.

(4) But how do I say "is"? Pass beyond it too! For the mind itself also is mutable even though it is better than every single body. Now it knows, now it does not know. Now it forgets, now it remembers. Now it wishes, now it does not wish. Now it sins, now it is just.

(5) Therefore pass beyond all mutability, not only everything which is seen but also everything which is changed. For you have passed beyond the flesh which is seen, you have passed beyond the sky, the sun, the moon, and the stars, which are seen. Pass also beyond everything which is changed! For when these things had already been passed by, you had come to your mind, but there also you found the mutability of your mind. Is God mutable? Therefore pass beyond your mind too! Is God mutable? Pour out your soul over you, that you might reach God, about whom they say to you, "Where is your God?"[39]

13. Do not suppose that you are going to do anything which a human being cannot do. John the Evangelist himself did this. He passed out beyond the flesh, he passed out beyond the earth upon which he trod; he passed out beyond the seas which he saw, he passed out beyond the air where the birds fly about. He passed out beyond the sun, he passed out beyond the moon, he passed out beyond the stars. He passed out beyond all the spirits who are not seen; he passed out beyond his own intellect by the very reasoning power of his mind. Passing out beyond all these things, pouring out his soul over himself, where did he arrive? What did he see? "In the beginning was the Word, and the Word was with God."[40]

39. Cf. Ps 41.4.   40. Cf. Jn 1.1.

(2) Therefore, if you do not see separation in light, why do you look for separation in work? See God; see his Word inhering in the Word speaking;[41] for he himself, in speaking, does not speak by syllables. But to shine with the brightness of wisdom, this is "to speak."

(3) What was said about his wisdom? "She is the brightness of eternal light."[42] Observe the brightness of the sun. It is in the sky and spreads its brightness through all lands, through all seas, and for certain, it is a bodily light. If you separate the brightness of the sun from the sun, separate the Word from the Father. I speak about the sun. One slight little flame of a lamp, which can be extinguished with one breath, spreads its own light over everything which lies under it. You see the light, generated by the little flame, spread; you see the emission; you do not see separation. Understand, therefore, dearest brothers, that the Father and the Son and the Holy Spirit cohere to one another inseparably, this Trinity, one God; and that all the works of the one God, these are of the Father, these are of the Son, these are of the Holy Spirit.

(4) The rest which comes next, which pertains to the discourse of our Lord, Jesus Christ himself, in the gospel, because a discourse is also due you tomorrow, be present that you may hear.

41. There is an alternate reading to this puzzling sentence which some editors follow: "See his Word; adhere to the Word speaking." Berrouard, *Homélies XVII–XXXIII*, 263, gives a version of this sentence which does clarify its meaning: "See his Word, intimately united to him who speaks through the Word." His translation, however, involves some very strange syntax, making *Verbo* an ablative of means dependent upon the dative participle *dicenti*, but immediately following a verb which governs a dative. It seems better to adhere to the normal syntax in spite of the obscure sense.

42. Cf. Wis 7.26.

TRACTATE 21

On John 5.20–23

ESTERDAY,[1] as far as the Lord deigned to grant, we discussed with what ability we could, and we understood with what capacity we could, how the works of the Father and the Son are inseparable, and how the Father does not do some and the Son others, but the Father does all through the Son, as through his Word about whom it was written, "all things were made through him and without him was made nothing."[2] Today let us look at the following words, and let us both pray for his mercy from the same Lord, and hope that first, if he judges it appropriate, we may understand what is true, but that if we cannot do this, we may not resort to that which is false. For it is better not to know than to err; but to know is better than not to know. And so before all else we ought to strive to know. If we can, thanks be to God; but if we cannot, for the time being, attain to the truth, let us not resort to falsehood.

(2) For we ought to consider what we are and what we are discussing. We are human beings carrying flesh, walking in this life. And if we have already been reborn from the seed of the word of God,[3] still we have been renewed in Christ in such a way that we have not yet been utterly stripped of Adam.[4] For this mortal and corruptible part of us which burdens the soul[5] is clearly from Adam; and that is evident. But

---

1. See *Tractate* 20.1, note 3.
2. Cf. Jn 1.3. The difficulty in translating *facere* which means both "make" and "do" continues in this sermon. See *Tractates* 18.5, note 18, and 20.10, note 35.
3. Cf. 1 Pt 1.23.
4. Perhaps a reminiscence of Col 3.9–10.
5. Cf. Wis 9.15.

the spiritual part of us which uplifts the soul [is clearly] from the gift of God and his mercy who sent his only one to share our death with us and to lead us to his immortality. We have this one as a teacher, that we may not sin, and as a defender if we have sinned[6] and confessed and converted, and as an intercessor for us if we have desired any good from the Lord, and as a giver together with the Father because the Father and the Son are one God.

(3) But he, as a man, was speaking these words to men: God hidden, man manifest that he might make [those who are] manifest men gods, and the Son of God, become the Son of man that he might make the sons of men the sons of God. By what art of his wisdom he does this, we come to know in his words. For a little one speaks to little ones, but he is little in such a way that he is also great;[7] we, however, are little, but great in him. Therefore he speaks as one fostering and nourishing suckling infants[8] and those growing by loving.

2. He had said, "The Son cannot do anything of himself, but only what he sees the Father doing." Now we understood that the Father does not do something separately which when the Son has seen it, he, too, does some such thing after having examined the work of his Father; but that he said, "The Son cannot do anything of himself, but only what he sees the Father doing," because the whole Son is from the Father, and his whole substance and power is from him who begot him. But now when he had said that he does in like manner these things which the Father does, so that we do not understand that the Father does some things, the Son other things, but that with like power the Son does the very same things which the Father does, when the Father does them through the Son, he continued and said what we heard read today: "For the Father loves his Son, and shows him all that he himself does."

(2) Again mortal thought is troubled. The Father shows the Son what he himself does. "Therefore," someone says, "the Father does separately, that the Son may be able to see what

6. Cf. 1 Jn 2.1.   7. Cf. *Tractate* 14.12.
8. Cf. 1 Thes 2.7.

he does." Again there occur to human thought two crafts-men, as it were, as though an artisan would teach his son his artistic skill and show him whatever he does that he also may be able to do it himself. He says, "He shows him all that he himself does." Therefore when the Father does, does the Son not do in order to be able to see what the Father is doing? This, at any rate is certain, that "all things were made through him and without him was made nothing."[9] From this we see how the Father shows the Son what he makes although the Father makes nothing except what he makes through the Son.

(3) What did the Father make? The world. Did he show the Son the world when made so that he, too, might make some such thing? Then let the world which the Son also made be put before us. But "all things were made through him and without him was made nothing" and "the world was made through him."[10] If the world was made through him and all things were made through him, and the Father does nothing which he might not do through the Son,[11] where does the Father show the Son what he does except in the Son himself through whom he does? For what [is] the place where the Father's work may be shown to the Son, as if on the outside he should do it and on the outside he should sit and the Son should look at the Father's hand [to see] how it does [the work]?

(4) Where is that inseparable Trinity? Where is the Word about whom it was said that he is the power and wisdom of God?[12] Where is that which Scripture says about wisdom her-self: "For she is the brightness of eternal light"?[13] Where is that which again is said about wisdom: "She reaches from end to end mightily and orders all things sweetly"?[14] If the Father does anything, he does it through the Son; if he does it through his wisdom and his power, he does not show him on

9. Cf. Jn 1.3.   10. Cf. Jn 1.3 and 10.
11. I.e., which he might do by himself alone, not through the Son.
12. Cf. 1 Cor 1.24.   13. Cf. Wis 7.26.
14. Cf. Wis 8.1.

the outside what he may see, but he shows him in himself what he does.

3. What does the Father see, or rather what does the Son see in the Father that he himself may also do? Perhaps I may be able to say it, but give me someone who may be able to grasp it; or perhaps I may be able to think it and not to say it, or perhaps not even to think it. For that divinity surpasses us as God [surpasses] men, as the immortal mortals, as the eternal temporal beings. Let him inspire and grant; let him deign from that fountain of life now to besprinkle or trickle something for our thirst that we may not wither in this desert. Let us say to him, "O Lord," to whom we have learned to say "Father." For we dare this because he himself wanted us to dare, yet, if only we should so live that he does not say to us, "If I am a father, where is my honor? If I am a master, where is my fear?"[15]

(2) Let us, then, say to him, "our Father." To whom do we say, "our Father"? To the Father of Christ. Therefore, he who says to the Father of Christ, "our Father," what does he say to Christ except, "our Brother?" Yet, not as [he is] the Father of Christ [is he] thus our Father too; for Christ never brought us into so close an association that he made no distinction between us and himself. For he [is] the Son equal to the Father, he [is] eternal with the Father and coeternal with the Father; but we were made through the Son, adopted through the only one. Accordingly, never was it heard from the mouth of our Lord, Jesus Christ, when he spoke to his disciples, that he said about the highest God, his Father, "our Father," but he said either "my Father" or "your Father." He did not say "our Father," but he said either "my Father" or "your Father." He did not say "our Father" even so, at a certain passage, he used these two phrases; he said, "I go to my God and your God."[16] Why did he not say "our God"? He said, "my Father and your Father";[17] he did not say, "our Father."

(3) He so joins that he distinguishes; he so distinguishes

15. Cf. Mal 1.6.   16. Cf. Jn 20.17.
17. Ibid.

that he does not disjoin. He wants us to be one in himself, but the Father and himself [to be] one.

4. Therefore, however much we understand and however much we see, even when we have become equal to the angels,[18] we shall not see as the Son sees. For even when we do not see, we are something. And what else are we when we do not see but the non-seeing? Nevertheless, even non-seeing, we do exist; and that we may see, we turn to him whom we may see; and there comes to be in us a vision, which was not, at a time when we, nevertheless, were. For there is a man non-seeing, and the same man when he sees is called man seeing. Therefore, for him to see is not the same thing as to be a man. For if for him to see were the same thing as to be a man, he would never be man except when seeing. But since there is a non-seeing man and he seeks to see what he does not see, there is one who seeks and there is one who turns himself to see; and when he has turned himself well and seen, he becomes man seeing who before was man non-seeing. Therefore "to see" comes to him and departs from him; it comes to him when he turns himself, it departs from him when he turns himself away.

(2) Can it be said that the Son is like this? Far from it. The Son was never non-seeing and later became seeing; but "to see the Father" this is for him "to be the Son." For we, by turning aside to sin, lose our enlightenment; and by turning ourselves to God, we acquire enlightenment. For the light by which we are enlightened is one thing, but we who are enlightened are another. But the light itself by which we are enlightened is neither turned away from itself nor loses its source of light, because it is the source of light.[19]

(3) So, therefore, the Father shows to the Son the thing

18. Cf. Mt 22.30; Lk 20.36.

19. Augustine here distinguishes between the Latin *lumen* and *lux*. In Latin the noun-creating suffix *-men* designates either an act or the result of an act. Thus strictly *lumen* designates "the radiance of a light source" or "the brightness produced by the light source," although by metonymy it is not uncommon for *lumen* also to designate "the light source." In this passage Augustine makes *lumen* "the light resulting from a source of light" and *lux* "the source of light"; but he does not do this consistently in the *Tractates*.

which he does, so that the Son sees all things in the Father
and the Son is all things in the Father. For by seeing he was
born and by being born he sees. But not, at any time, was he
not born and later born, just as not, at any time, did he not
see and later did see; but in that which for him is "to see," in
the same way is for him "to be," in the same way is for him
"not to be changed," and in the same way is for him "to continue without beginning and without end."

(4) Therefore let us not interpret carnally that the Father
sits and does work and shows it to the Son, and that the Son
sees the work which the Father does and does that in another
place or from another material. For "all things were made
through him, and without him was made nothing."[20] The
Word of the Father is the Son; God has said nothing that he
has not said in the Son. For by saying in the Son what he was
going to do through the Son, he begot the Son himself
through whom he might do all things.

5. "And greater works than these he will show him, that
you may wonder." Here again he disturbs. And who is there
who can worthily investigate so great a secret as this? But
now, because he has deigned to speak to us, he himself makes
it clear. For he would not want to say what he did not want to
be understood; because he deigned to speak, without a doubt
he has provoked attentive listening. Can it be said that he
deserts one who has been aroused to listen, after he has been
aroused? We have said, as best we could, that the Son does
not know in time, that the knowledge of the Son is not one
thing and the Son himself another, that the vision of the Son
is not one thing and the Son himself another, but that the
vision itself is the Son, and the knowledge itself or the wisdom
of the Father is the Son, and that this wisdom and this vision
are eternal from an eternal, and are coeternal with him from
whom it is; nor does anything there vary in time nor is anything born which was not, nor does anything which was,
perish.

(2) We have said it, as best we could. Therefore what does

20. Cf Jn 1.3.

time do in the statement just now made, so that he should say, "Greater works than these he will show him"? That is, he is going to show, that is, he will show. "Has shown" is one thing; "will show" is another. We say "has shown" about the past; we say "will show" about the future.[21] What, then, are we dealing with here, brothers? Look, he whom we had said [is] coeternal with the Father, that nothing in him varies in time, that nothing is moved through the intervals of time or place, but that he always remains seeing with the Father, seeing the Father and by seeing, existing, again mentioning times to us, he said, "Greater [works] than these he will show him." Therefore is he still going to show something to the Son which the Son does not know? What do we do, then? How do we understand this? Look, our Lord, Jesus Christ, was above, he is below. When was he above? When he said, "Whatsoever things the Father does, these same things the Son also does in like manner." How is he now below? "Greater works than these he will show him."

(3) O Lord, Jesus Christ, our Savior, the Word of God through whom all things were made, what is the Father going to show you that you still do not know? What of the Father is still hidden from you? What in the Father is hidden from you from whom the Father is not hidden? What greater works is he going to show you? Or greater than what works are the ones which he is going to show? For when he said, "greater than these," we ought first to understand greater than which.

6. Let us recall the sources of this discourse—when that man who was thirty-eight years in his infirmity was healed and [Christ] ordered him, now in sound condition, to take up his bed and go into his house. For the Jews with whom he was speaking were upset by this. (He was speaking with words but kept silence with respect to the understanding; in a certain way he gave a sign to those who understood, he concealed from those who were angry.) Therefore when the Jews

21. This problem in colloquial or dialectical phonology, a confusion between v and b which made it difficult to distinguish between the perfect and future in some verb forms, was discussed earlier in regard to the same verse in *Tractate* 19.4, note 3.

had been upset by this, because the Lord did it on the Sabbath, they provided the occasion for this discourse. Therefore let us not hear these words as though having forgotten what was said earlier, but let us look back at that man, sick for thirty-eight years, who was suddenly made well, to the wonder and anger of the Jews. They sought darkness from the Sabbath rather than light from the miracle. Speaking to them in their indignation, therefore, he said this, "Greater works than these he will show him."

(2) "Greater than these!" Than which? Because you saw a man made well whose illness has lasted even thirty-eight years, greater works than these the Father will show the Son. What works are greater? He continues and says, "For as the Father raises the dead and gives them life, so the Son also gives life to whom he will." Clearly these are greater things. For it is exceedingly more that a dead man rise than that a sick man regain his health; these are greater things.

(3) But when is the Father going to show them to the Son? For does the Son not know them? And did not he who was speaking know how to bring the dead to life again? Did he still have to learn how to raise the dead, through whom all things were made? Did he who gave life to us, who were not, still have to learn how, in order that we might be brought to life again? Therefore, what is it that he means to say?

7. For he descended to us; and he, who a little before was speaking as God, has begun to speak as man. Nevertheless, he who [is] God is man because God was made man, but he was made what he was not without losing what he was. Therefore, man was added to God that he who was God might be man, not that he might now be man and not be God. Therefore, let us who heard him as maker hear him also as a brother. [He was] maker because [he was] the Word in the beginning, brother because born of the Virgin Mary; maker before Abraham, before Adam, before earth, before heaven, before all things corporal and spiritual, but brother from the seed of Abraham, from the tribe of Juda, from an Israelite virgin. Therefore, if we know this one who is speaking to us as both God and man, let us understand the words of God

and man; for he speaks such things to us sometimes as pertain to his majesty and sometimes as pertain to his lowliness. For he [is] lofty who [was] lowly that he might make us lowly men lofty. Why, then, did he say, "Greater works than these the Father will show" to me "that you may wonder"? Therefore he is going to show us, not him. Therefore, since the Father is going to show us, for that reason he said, "that you may wonder." For he explained what he meant to say, "The Father will show" to me. Why did he not say, "The Father will show to you," but "[the Father] will show" to the Son? Because we also are members of the Son. And, as if what we, the members, learn, he himself in a way learns in his members.

(2) How does he learn in us? As he suffers in us. How do we prove that he suffers in us? From that voice from heaven, "Saul, Saul, why do you persecute me?"[22] Is it not he who will preside as judge at the end of the world; and, putting the just on the right but the wicked on the left, he will say, "Come, blessed of my Father, take possession of the kingdom; for I was hungry and you gave me to eat."?[23] And when they reply to him, "Lord, when did we see you hungry?" He is going to say to them, "When you gave it to one of the least of my own, you gave it to me." Therefore, let him who said, "When you gave it to one of the least of my own, you gave it to me," now be asked by us, and let us say to him, "Lord, when will you be a learner, since you teach all things?" For immediately he answers us in our faith, "When one of the least of my own learns, I learn."

8. Therefore, let us rejoice and give thanks, not only that we have been made Christians, but that we have been made Christ. Do you understand, brothers, do you comprehend the grace of God upon us? Be in awe. Rejoice. We have been made Christ. For if he is the head, we are the members—a whole man, he and we. This is what the Apostle Paul says, "that we may be now no longer children, tossed to and fro and beset by every wind of doctrine."[24] But just previously he

22. Cf. Acts 9.4.   23. Cf. Mt 25.31–40.
24. Cf. Eph 4.14.

had said, "until we all attain to the unity of the faith, and to the knowledge of the Son of God, to a perfect man, to the mature measure of the age of the fullness of Christ."[25]

(2) The fullness of Christ, therefore, head and members. What does it mean, head and members? Christ and the Church. For we would proudly claim this[26] for ourselves if he had not deigned to promise this who says through the same Apostle, "Now you are the body and members of Chist."[27]

9. Therefore, when the Father shows to the members of Christ, he shows to Christ. There occurs a kind of miracle, great, but still true; there is shown to Christ what Christ knew and it is shown to Christ through Christ. It is a wondrous thing and great, but so Scripture says. Are we going to contradict divine utterances and not rather understand them and in consequence of his gift give thanks to him who gave them? Why is it that I said, it is shown to Christ through Christ? It is shown to the members through the head. Look, see that in yourself.

(2) Suppose that, with your eyes closed, you wish to pick up something; the hand does not know where to go, and, of course, your hand is a member of yours, for it has not been separated from your body. Open your eyes; now the hand sees where to go. With the head showing the way, the member followed. Therefore if some such thing could be found in you, that your body showed to your body, and through your body something was shown to your body, do not be amazed that it was said, it is shown to Christ through Christ. For the head shows that the members may see, and the head teaches that the members may learn. Still head and members are one man.

(3) He did not wish to separate himself but deigned to be attached [to us]. He was far apart from us, and very far apart. What is so far apart as justice and iniquity? What is so far apart as eternity and mortality? See how far apart was the Word in the beginning, God with God, through whom all

25. Cf. Eph 4.13.
26. The CCL text erroneously reads *hos* for *hoc*.
27. Cf. 1 Cor 12.27.

things were made.[28] How, then, did he come to be near, that he might be what we [are] and we in him? "The Word was made flesh and dwelt among us."[29]

10. Therefore he is going to show us this; he showed this to his disciples who saw him in the flesh. What is this? "As the Father raises the dead and gives them life, so the Son also gives life to whom he wishes." Does the Father [give life] to some, the Son to others? Yet certainly all things were made through him.

(2) What are we saying, my brothers? Christ raised Lazarus; what dead man did the Father raise so that Christ might see how to raise Lazarus? Can it be that when Christ raised Lazarus, the Father did not raise him, but the Son did it alone without the Father? Read the reading itself, and see that there he calls upon the Father that Lazarus may rise.[30] As a man, he calls upon the Father; as God, he does together with the Father. Therefore Lazarus, who rose, was raised both by the Father, and by the Son, and by the gift and grace of the Holy Spirit; and the Trinity did that miraculous work.

(3) Let us not, therefore, understand "As the Father raises the dead and gives them life, so the Son also gives life to whom he wishes," so that we think that some are raised and given life by the Father, others by the Son; but the same ones whom the Father raises and gives life, these the Son also raises and gives life, because "all things were made through him and without him was made nothing."[31] And that he might show that he had power, although given by the Father, yet equal, he said, "so the Son also gives life to whom he wishes," that he might show there his will, and that no one might say, "The Father raises the dead through the Son; but the one as powerful, as having power, the other as from another's power, as a minister does something, as an angel," he signified power when he said, "so the Son also gives life to whom he wishes." For the Father does not wish anything other than the Son, but as they have one substance, so, too, they have one will.[32]

28. Cf. Jn 1.1 and 3.
30. Cf. Jn 11.41–44.
32. Cf. *Tractate* 19.5.

29. Cf. Jn 1.14.
31. Cf. Jn 1.3.

11. And who are these dead to whom the Father and the Son give life? Are they those about whom we have spoken, Lazarus, or the son of that widow,[33] or the daughter of the ruler of the synagogue?[34] For we know that these were raised by Christ, the Lord. He wanted to intimate something else to us, namely, the resurrection of the dead which we are all waiting for; not that which some had that the rest might believe. For Lazarus rose to die [again]; we shall rise to live forever. Does the Father effect such a resurrection, or the Son? No, rather the Father in the Son. Therefore the Son, and the Father in the Son.

(2) Whence do we prove that he speaks about this resurrection? That we might not understand that resurrection of the dead which he does as a miracle, not for eternal life when he said, "For as the Father raises the dead and gives them life, so the Son also gives life to whom he wishes," he continued and said, "For neither does the Father judge any man, but all judgment he has given to the Son." What does this mean? He was speaking about the resurrection of the dead, because "as the Father raises the dead and gives them life, so the Son also gives life to whom he wishes." Why immediately did he add as a reason [this] concerning judgment, saying, "For neither does the Father judge any man, but all judgment he has given to the Son," except that he had spoken about that resurrection of the dead which will be at the judgment?

12. He said, "For neither does the Father judge any man, but all judgment he has given to the Son." A little while ago we were thinking that the Father did something which the Son does not do when he said, "For the Father loves the Son, and shows him all that he himself does," as if the Father was doing and the Son seeing. So there was a carnal understanding, creeping into our mind, as if the Father would do what the Son would not do, but the Son would see the Father showing what was done by the Father. Therefore, just as the Father was doing what the Son was not doing, now we see the Son

33. Cf. Lk 7.11–15.
34. Cf. Lk 8.41–56; Mt 9.18–26; Mk 5.21–43.

doing something which the Father does not do. How he whirls us about and keeps our mind busy, leads us here and there, does not allow us to remain in one place of the flesh, that by the whirling about he may exercise us, by the exercising cleanse, by the cleansing render us capable of understanding, [and] fill us who have become capable of understanding. What do these words do with regard to us? What was he saying? What is he saying?

(2) A little before he said that the Father shows the Son whatever he does. I saw, as it were, the Father doing, the Son watching; now again I see the Son doing, the Father being unoccupied: "For the Father does not judge any man, but all judgment he has given to the Son." Therefore, when the Son is going to judge, will the Father be unoccupied and not judge? What does this mean? What am I to understand? O Lord, what are you saying? You are God, the Word; I am a man. Do you say that "the Father does not judge any man, but all judgment he has given to the Son"? In another place I read that you say, "I judge no one; there is one who seeks and judges."[35] About whom do you say "There is one who seeks and judges" except about the Father? He seeks to know about wrongs against you; he passes judgment on wrongs against you. How here "does the Father not judge any man, but all judgment he has given to the Son"? Let us also ask Peter; let us hear him speaking in his epistle. He said, "Christ has suffered for us, leaving us an example that we may follow his steps: 'He who did not sin, neither was guile found in his mouth.' When he was reviled, he did not revile in return; when he suffered wrong, he did not threaten, but entrusted to him who judges justly."[36] How is it true that "the Father does not judge any man, but all judgment he has given to the Son"?

---

35. Cf. Jn 8.15 and 50. This interesting conflation is presented as though it were a single verse. Jn 8.15 reads: "You judge according to the flesh; I judge no one." Jn 8.50 reads: "But I seek not my own glory; there is one who seeks and judges." In *Tractates* 36.4 and 43.9 where he comments on these two verses in their proper place, he does not connect them with the passage under discussion here.

36. Cf. 1 Pt 2.21–23, quoting Is 53.9.

(3) Here we are troubled; being troubled, let us sweat greatly over it; by our sweating let us be freed of our troubles. Let us try, as far as we can, by his gift, to penetrate the deep secrets of these words. Perhaps we are acting rashly because we desire to pry into and examine the words of God. And why were they said except that they be known? Why were they uttered except that they be heard? Why were they heard except that they be understood? Let him strengthen us, therefore, and grant to us something as far as he deigns; and if we do not yet penetrate to the headwater, let us drink from the brook.

(4) Look, John himself has flowed, as a brook, for us; he has led the Word from on high to us; he has lowered him and, in a way, has brought him down to our level that we may not tremble before the high but approach a lowly one.

13. At all events there is a meaning, a true one, a strong one, if we can in some way grasp hold of it, that "the Father does not judge any man, but all judgment he has given to the Son." For this was said because in the judgment the Son only will appear to men. The Father will be hidden, the Son manifest.[37] In what will the Son be manifest? In the form in which he ascended. For in the form of God he is hidden with the Father; in the form of the servant he is manifest to men. Therefore, "the Father does not judge any man, but all judgment he has given to the Son"; but it is manifest in what manifest judgment the Son will judge because he himself will appear to those to be judged.

(2) Scripture shows us more clearly that he himself will appear. On the fortieth day after his resurrection he ascended into heaven, with his disciples watching; and an angel's voice said to them, "Men of Galilee, why do you stand looking up to heaven? This one who has been taken up from you into heaven, shall come just as you have seen him going to heaven."[38] How did they see him go? In the flesh which they touched, which they felt, the scars of which they even probed by touching; in that body in which he went in and went out

37. Cf. *Tractate* 19.16.   38. Cf. Acts 1.11.

with them for forty days, manifesting himself to them in truth, not in any falsehood, not as an apparition, not as a shadow, not as a spirit, but as he himself said, not deceiving, "Handle and see; for a spirit does not have flesh and bones, as you see me to have."[39]

(3) Now, indeed, that body is worthy of a heavenly dwelling-place, not subject to death, not changeable through ages. For as he had grown to that age from infancy, so he does not decline to old age from the age which was young adulthood. He remains as he ascended; he is going to come to those to whom, before he comes, he wanted his word to be preached. So, therefore, he will come in a human form. The ungodly, too, will see this; those placed to the right will see it too; those separated to the left will see it too, as it was written, "They shall see him whom they have pierced."[40] If they will see him whom they have pierced, they will see the same body which they thrust through with a spear; [for] the Word is not struck by a spear.

(4) Therefore, the ungodly will be able to see this which they were also able to wound. They will not see the God lying hidden in the body; after the judgment he will be seen by these who will be on the right. This, therefore, is why he said, "The Father does not judge any man, but all judgment he has given to the Son," because the Son will come, clearly visible, to the judgment, appearing in human body to human beings, saying to those on the right, "Come, blessed of my Father, take possession of the kingdom," saying to those on the left, "Go into the everlasting fire which was prepared for the devil and his angels."[41]

14. Look, the form of the man will be seen by the godly and the ungodly, by the just and the unjust, by the believers and the unbelieving, by those rejoicing and by those lamenting, by the confident and by the confounded: look, it will be seen. When that form has been seen in the judgment and the judgment has been completed, wherein it was said that the

39. Cf. Lk 24.39.
40. Cf. Jn 19.37, quoting Zec 12.10.
41. Cf. Mt 25.34 and 41.

Father does not judge any man, but all judgment he has given to the Son, for this reason, that the Son will appear at the judgment in the form which he received from us, what will be afterwards?

(2) When will the form of God be seen, for which all believers thirst? When will there be seen that which was in the beginning the Word, God with God, through whom all things were made?[42] When will there be seen that form of God about which the Apostle says, "Though he was in the form of God, he thought it not robbery to be equal to God."?[43] For great is that form wherein the equality of the Father and the Son is still recognized, ineffable, incomprehensible, especially for little ones. When will it be seen? Look, the just are on the right, the unjust are on the left; they all equally see the man. They see the Son of Man; they see him who was pierced, they see him who was crucified. They see him made lowly; they see him born of a virgin. They see the Lamb of the tribe of Juda.[44] When will they see the Word, God with God? Even then he will be the very same one, but the form of the servant will appear.

(3) The form of the servant will be shown to the servants; the form of God will be saved for the sons. Therefore, let the servants become sons. Let them who are on the right go to the eternal inheritance, promised of old, which the martyrs, although not seeing, believed, for the promise of which they poured out their blood without hesitation; let them go there and see there. When will they go there? Let the Lord himself say, "So those will go into everlasting burning, but the just into life everlasting."[45]

15. Look, he has named life everlasting. Did he say this to us so that we shall see and know the Father and Son there? What if we shall live forever but not see that Father and Son? Hear in another place where he named life everlasting and described what life everlasting is: "Do not fear; I am not deceiving you. Not without reason have I promised to those who

---

42. Cf. Jn 1.1 and 3.
44. Cf. Apoc (Rv) 5 and 6.

43. Cf. Phil 2.6.
45. Cf. Mt 25.46.

love me, saying, 'He who has my commandments and keeps them, he it is who loves me; and he who loves me will be loved by my Father, and I will love him and reveal myself to him.' "[46] Let us respond to the Lord and say, "What great thing, O Lord, our God, [is it]? What great thing [is it]? Are you going to show yourself to us? Well, now, and did you not show yourself to the Jews? Did not even they who crucified you see you? But you will show yourself at the judgment when we shall stand at your right; and will not also they who stand at the left see you? What is it, that you will show yourself to us? For do we not see you now when you speak?"

(2) He answers, "I shall show myself in the form of God; now you see the form of the servant. I shall not cheat you, O man of faith; believe that you will see. You love and you do not see; will not love itself lead you to see? Love, persist in loving; I who have cleansed your heart shall not," he says "cheat your love. For why have I cleansed your heart except that God may be able to be seen by you? For 'blessed are the clean of heart, for they shall see God.' "[47]

(3) "But," says the servant as though arguing with the Lord, "You did not describe this when you said, 'The just will go into life everlasting.'[48] You did not say, 'They will go to see me in the form of God, to see that Father to whom I am equal.' " Observe what he said elsewhere: "Now this is life everlasting, that they may know you, the only true God, and him whom you have sent, Jesus Christ."[49]

16. Even now, therefore, after the mention of the judgment, all of which the Father, judging no man, has given to the Son, what will be? What follows? "That men may honor the Son as they honor the Father." The Father is honored by the Jews, the Son is scorned. For the Son was seen as a servant; the Father is honored as God. The Son also will appear, equal to the Father, "that all may honor the Son as they honor the Father." Now, therefore, we hold this in faith. Let the Jew not say, "I honor the Father; what do I have to do with the Son?"

46. Jn 14.21.
48. Cf. Mt 25.46.

47. Mt 5.8.
49. Jn 17.3.

Let him answer that man, "He who does not honor the Son does not honor the Father."

(2) You lie completely; you blaspheme the Son; you do wrong to the Father. For the Father sent the Son; you scorn him whom he sent. How do you honor the sender, you who blaspheme the one sent?[50]

17. "Look," someone says, "the Son was sent; and the Father is greater because he sent." Move away from the flesh. The old man suggests oldness; but you, in the new man acknowledge the newness![51] Let the man, new to you, ancient so far as concerns the world, everlasting, eternal, call your understanding back to this. Is the Son lesser because he was said to have been sent? I heard sending, not separation. "But we see this," he says, "in human affairs, that he who sends is greater than the one who is sent." But human affairs deceive man; divine affairs purge him. Pay no attention to human affairs where he seems greater who sends and he lesser who is sent, although even human affairs themselves give evidence against you.

(2) As, for example, if someone should wish to seek a wife and cannot by himself, he sends a greater friend to seek for him. And there are many things in which the greater is chosen to be sent by a lesser. Why, therefore, do you want to make a quibbling objection, that the one sent, the other was sent? The sun sends a ray and does not separate it; the moon sends its glow and does not separate it. A lantern pours forth its light and does not separate it. I see sending there and I see no separation. For if you seek examples from human affairs, O heretical vanity, although even human affairs, as I just now said, in certain instances argue against you and confute you, yet observe what a difference there is in human affairs from which you want to draw examples for divine affairs. The man who sends himself remains and he who is sent goes. Does the man go with him whom he sends?

(3) But the Father who sent the Son did not withdraw from

50. Cf. *Tractate* 19.6 where there is a variant interpretation of Jn 5.23.
51. Cf. Col 3.9–10.

the Son. Hear the Lord himself, saying, "Behold, the hour will come that every man shall depart to his own and you shall leave me alone. But I am not alone, because the Father is with me."[52] How did he send him with whom he came? How did he send him from whom he did not withdraw? In another place he said, "But the Father abiding in me, he does his works."[53] See, he is in him. See, he works. The one sending did not withdraw from the one sent because the one sent and the one sending are one.[54]

---

52. Cf. Jn 16.32.   53. Cf. Jn 14.10.
54. Cf. Jn 10.30. Augustine clearly has the Arians in mind in this sermon; see Berrouard, *Homélies XVII–XXXIII*, 757–759.

TRACTATE 22

On John 5.24–30

ODAY'S GOSPEL READING continues the discourses delivered to you on the day before yesterday and yesterday[1] and, keeping with the sequence, let us examine it, not as befits its importance, but in view of our strength because you too grasp, not in proportion to the abundance of the overflowing fountain, but to your limited capacity. And we direct our words to your ears, not so much as the fountain itself pours forth, but as much as we can take which we may transmit to your minds, with the fountain himself working more abundantly in your hearts than us upon your ears. For a great matter is being discussed, and not by great men, but rather by very small ones.

(2) Nevertheless, he gives to us hope and confidence who, though great, became small for us. For, if we were not encouraged by him, nor invited to understand him, but rather, he were to forsake us as contemptible, because we cannot take his divinity if he himself did not take our mortality and come to us to speak his gospel to us, if what is ignoble and least in us he had not wished to share with us, we would think that he did not wish to give us his greatness, who took on our smallness.

(3) I have said these things that no one may either censure us for discussing these things, as if we were too brash, or may despair of himself that he can grasp, by the gift of God, what the Son of God has deigned to say to him. Therefore what he has deigned to say to us we ought to believe because he meant for us to understand. But if we cannot, he who, unasked, offered his word, when asked, offers understanding.

1. See *Tractate* 20.1, note 3.

2. Look at what these secrets of [his] words are. Pay attention. "Amen, amen, I say to you, that he who hears my word, and believes him who sent me, has life everlasting." We all, of course, are aiming for life everlasting; and he said, "He who hears my word, and believes him who sent me, has life everlasting." Can it be, then, that he wanted us to hear his word and not to understand it? Seeing that if life everlasting is found in hearing and believing, much more [is it] in understanding. But faith is a step toward devout love, understanding the fruit of faith[2] that we may attain to life everlasting where the gospel is not left to us as a legacy but [where he is] who recently dispensed[3] it to us. When the pages of the text and the voice of the reader and the exegete have been set aside, may he appear to all his own, as they stand before him with purified heart, and with an immortal body never more to die, and may he enlighten them, now living and seeing that which "in the beginning was the Word, and the Word was with God."[4]

(2) Now then, let us observe who we are and let us reflect on whom we are hearing. Christ is God and he speaks with men; he wishes to be understood. Let him make us capable of understanding. He wishes to be seen; let him open our eyes. Nevertheless, not without good reason does he speak to us, but because what he promises us is true.

3. He says, "He who hears my word and believes him who sent me, has life everlasting and will not come to judgment, but has passed from death to life." Where, and when do we come from death to life, so that we may not come to judgment? In this life one passes from death to life; in this life which is not yet life, from here one passes from death to life. What is that passing? "He who hears my words," he said, "and believes him who sent me." Keeping these words, you believe and you pass.

2. Cf. *Tractate* 8.6–7.

3. *dispensavit.* I take this to be an application of the concept of the Dispensation or Divine Economy whereby the gospel is part of God's plan for man's salvation; hence my translation. Cf. *Tractate* 19.10, note 15.

4. Cf. Jn 1.1.

(2) And is there one who passes by standing? There certainly is! For he stands in body, he passes in mind. Where was he from which he might pass, and to what does he pass? He passes from death to life. See a man standing in whom all this which is said may be worked. He stands; he hears. Perhaps he was not believing; by hearing he believes. A little before he did not believe, now he believes. He has made a passing, as if from the region of unbelief to the region of faith, with his heart moved, while his body was unmoved, moved to something better, because those who again abandon the faith are moved to something worse. Look, in this life which, as I said, is not yet life, there is a passing from death to life that there may be no coming into judgment.

(3) But why have I said that there is not yet life? If there were life, the Lord would not say to a certain man, "if you wish to come into life, keep the commandments."[5] For he did not say to him, "if you wish to come into life everlasting"; he did not add everlasting, but only said "life." And therefore this [life] is not even to be called life because it is not true life. What is true life except that which is everlasting? Hear the Apostle speaking to Timothy: "Charge the rich of this world not to be haughtily high-minded, nor to trust in the uncertainty of riches, but in the living God who provides us all things in abundance to enjoy. Let them do good, let them be rich in good works; let them give easily, let them share." Why this? Hear what follows: "Let them treasure up for themselves a good foundation against the time to come, that they may lay hold on the true life."[6]

(4) If they ought to treasure up for themselves a good foundation against the time to come that they may lay hold on the true life, surely this life in which they were is false life. For why would you wish to lay hold on true life if you now hold true life? Must true life be laid hold on? You must travel away from false life. And by what road must one travel? Where? Hear, believe; and you pass from death to life, and you do not come into judgment.

5. Cf. Mt 19.17.   6. Cf. 1 Tm 6.17–19.

4. What does this mean, "and you do not come into judgment"? And who will be better than the Apostle Paul who said, "All of us must be revealed before the judgment seat of Christ, that there every one may receive what he has done through the body, whether good or evil."[7] Paul says, "All of us must be revealed before the judgment seat of Christ." And do you dare to promise yourself that you will not come into judgment? "Far be it," you say, "that I dare to promise myself this; but I believe his promise. The Savior speaks, truth promises, he himself said to me, 'He who hears my word and believes him who sent me, has life everlasting, and passes from death to life, and will not come into judgment.' I, then, have heard the words of my Lord; I have believed. Although I was an unbeliever, I have now become a believer. As he instructed me, I have passed from death to life, I do not come into judgment, not by my presumption, but by his promise."

(2) But does Paul speak against Christ, the servant against the Lord, the disciple against the teacher, the man against God, so that, whereas the Lord says, "He who hears and believes passes from death to life and will not come into judgment," the Apostle says, "All of us must be revealed before the judgment seat of Christ"? But if he who is revealed at the judgment seat does not come into judgment, I do not know how to understand it.

5. Therefore the Lord, our God, reveals and through his Scriptures teaches us how one is to understand judgment when it is said. Therefore I urge you to pay attention. Sometimes judgment is called punishment, sometimes judgment is called distinction. According to that mode whereby judgment is called distinction, "All of us must be revealed before the judgment seat of Christ so that there" a man "may receive what he has done through the body, whether good or evil"; for it is distinction that good things be distributed to the good, evil things to the evil. For if judgment were received always in regard to evilness, the Psalm would not say, "Judge me, O God."[8]

---

7. Cf. 2 Cor 5.10.   8. Cf. Ps 42.1.

(2) Some one, perchance, hears a person saying, "Judge me, O God," and he is amazed. For a man usually says, "May God pardon me; spare me, O God." Who is there who says, "Judge me, O God"? And sometimes in the Psalm this very verse is placed at a pause point,[9] that it may be proffered by the reader and answered by the people. Is there perhaps anyone whose heart is not deeply affected and who is not afraid to sing to God and say, "Judge me, O God"? And yet the people sing it, believing, and do not think that they wrongly desire what they have learned from the divinely inspired text; and if they little understand, they believe that what they sing is something good. And yet even this Psalm itself did not send man away without understanding. For it continued and showed in the words coming next what kind of judgment it meant, that it is not [the judgment] of damnation but of discerning. For the Psalm says, "Judge me, O God." What does it mean, "Judge me, O God"? "And discern my cause from an unholy nation."[10] Therefore, according to this judgment of discerning "all of us must be revealed before the judgment seat of Christ."

(3) But according to the judgment of damnation he says, "He who hears my words and believes him who sent me, has life everlasting, and will not come into judgment, but passes from death to life." What does it mean, "he will not come to judgment"? He will not come to damnation. Let us prove from Scriptures that judgment was said where punishment is understood, although even in this reading itself you will hear a little later the very word "judgment" put only for damnation and punishment.[11] Nevertheless, the Apostle says in a certain place, writing to those who were treating evilly the body which you, the faithful, know, and because they were treating it wrongfully, they were being chastised by the scourge of the

9. *diapsalma*. This is a Greek word which occurs at certain places in the Psalms in the *Septuagint*. Its meaning was uncertain and much disputed in Augustine's time (and still is). In *En in Ps* 4.4 (CCL 38.15–16), while Augustine acknowledges the possibility of Jerome's interpretation of the word as an "amen" (see *Epistula* 28, PL 22.433–435; CSEL 54(1).227–232), he clearly prefers the meaning which has been given the term here.

10. Cf. Ps 42.1.   11. At Jn 5.29.

Lord; for he says to them, "This is why many weak and sick among you sleep in goodly number."[12] For many were even dying for that reason. And he continued, "For if we were to judge ourselves, we would not be judged by the Lord." That is, if we chastised ourselves, we would not be chastised by the Lord. "But when we are judged, we are being chastised by the Lord that we may not be condemned with this world." Therefore, there are those who are being judged according to punishment here that they may be spared there; there are those who are being spared here that they may be more fully tormented there. But there are those to whom the very punishments are distributed without the scourge of punishment, if they have not been reproved by the scourge of God, so that since they have scorned the Father lashing them here, they may perceive the judge punishing them there.

(4) Therefore, there is a judgment to which God, that is, the Son of God, will send at the end the devil and his angels, and all the unbelievers and the ungodly with him;[13] to this judgment he will not come who, believing now, passes from death to life.

6. For that you might not think that by believing you will not die according to the flesh, and that by understanding carnally you might not say to yourself, "My lord has said to me, 'He who hears my words and believes him who sent me has passed from death to life.' Therefore I have believed; I shall not die," know you that you will pay the death which you owe from the punishment of Adam; for he in whom then we all were received [this judgment]: "You shall die the death."[14] And the divine sentence cannot be voided. But when you have paid the death of the old man, you will be taken into the life everlasting of the new man[15] and you will pass from death to life. Only for the time being make the passage of life. What is your life? Faith. "The just man lives by faith."[16]

(2) What about the faithless? They are dead. Among such

12. Cf. 1 Cor 11.23–34, especially 30–32.
13. Cf. Mt 25.41.   14. Cf. Gn 2.17.
15. Cf. Col 3.9–10 and *Tractate* 21.17.
16. Cf. Rom 1.17 and Gal 3.11, quoting Hb 2.4.

dead was that one, still in his body, about whom the Lord said, "Leave the dead; let them bury their dead."[17] Therefore, even in this life there are the dead, there are the living; yet all live in a way. Who are the dead? They who have not believed. Who are the living? They who have believed. What is said to the dead by the Apostle? "Rise, you who sleep." But, someone says, he said sleep, not death. Hear what follows. "Rise, you who sleep, and arise from the dead." And as if he were to say, where shall I go? "And Christ will enlighten you."[18] Now when Christ has enlightened you believing, you pass from death to life; remain in that to which you have passed and you will not come to judgment.

7. He himself now explains that, and continues, "Amen, amen, I say to you." In case, because he said, "He has passed from death to life," we may, perhaps, understand this in regard to the future resurrection, wishing to show how he who believes passes and that to pass from death to life is this, to pass from unbelief to belief, from injustice to justice, from pride to humility, from hate to love, he now says, "Amen, I say to you, the hour is coming,[19] and it is now." What is more evident? Now, indeed, he has made clear what he was saying because right now that to which Christ encourages us is taking place. "The hour is coming." What hour? "And now is when the dead shall hear the voice of the Son of God, and those who have heard shall live." We have already spoken about these dead.[20]

(2) What do we think, my brothers? In this crowd which hears me, are there no dead? They, indeed, who believe and act according to true faith do live and are not dead; but they who either do not believe or believe like the demons, trembling[21] and living evilly, proclaiming the Son of God and not having love, must rather be accounted dead. And yet this hour is still occurring. For the hour about which the Lord spoke will not be one hour of the twelve hours of one day.

17. Cf. Mt 8.22; Lk 9.60.
18. Cf. Eph 5.14; also Is 26.19 and 60.1.
19. Some codices read *veniet*, "the hour will come."
20. In *Tractate* 19.9–10.   21. Cf. Jas 2.19.

From the time that he spoke even to this time, and even to
the end of the world, this one hour is occurring about which
John in his epistle says, "Little children, it is the last hour."[22]
Therefore, it is now. He who lives, let him live; he who was
dead, let him live. Let him who was lying dead hear the voice
of the Son of God; let him rise and live.

(3) The Lord cried out at the tomb of Lazarus and a man
dead for four days arose. He who was stinking came forth
into the open air; he had been buried, a rock had been put
over him, the voice of the Savior broke through the hardness
of the rock. And your heart is so hard that that divine voice
does not yet break through to you! Rise in your heart; come
forth from your tomb. For you were lying dead in your heart
as in a tomb, and you were weighted down as by the rock of
evil habit. Rise, and come forth. What does this mean, rise
and come forth? Believe and confess. For he who believed
arose; he who confesses has come forth.

(4) Why did we say that he came forth confessing? Because
before he confessed, he had been hidden; but when he confesses, he comes forth from darkness to light. And when he
has confessed, what is said to the servants? What was said
beside the corpse of Lazarus, "Loose him, and let him go."[23]
How? It was said to the Apostles as servants, "What you shall
loose on earth shall be loosed also in heaven."[24]

8. "The hour is coming, and it is now when the dead shall
hear the voice of the Son of God, and those who have heard
shall live." From what will they live? From life. From what
life? From Christ. From what do we prove that it is from
Christ as the life? He says, "I am the way, the truth, and the
life."[25] Do you wish to walk? "I am the way." Do you wish not
to be deceived? "I am the truth." Do you wish not to die? "I
am the life." Your Savior says this to you, "There is no place
where you may go except to me; there is no way by which you
can go except through me."

(2) Therefore, this hour is now occurring, and this is as-

suredly occurring and is not at all ceasing. Men who were
dead are rising, they are passing to life, they live at the voice
of the Son of God, from him persevering in his faith. For the
Son has life; he has that by which the believers may live.

9. And how does he have it? As the Father has it. Hear
him speaking himself: "For as the Father has life in himself,
so he has given to the Son also to have life in himself." Brothers, to the best of my ability, I shall speak. For these are those
words which trouble our meager understanding. Why did he
add "in himself "? It would suffice for him to say, "For as the
Father has life, so he has given to the Son also to have life."
He has added "in himself."

(2) For the Father has life in himself, the Son also has life
in himself. He intended for us to understand something in
what he said, "in himself." And a secret is locked up here in
this word; let there be knocking that it may be opened.[26] O
Lord, what is it that you said? Why did you add, "in himself "? For did not the Apostle Paul whom you made to live
have life? "He had," he says. As for dead men that they may
live again and may pass by believing in your word, when they
have passed, will they not have life in you? "They will have;
for I said a little before, 'He who hears my words and believes
him who sent me has life everlasting.'" Therefore, those who
believe in you have life; and you did not say, in themselves.
But when you were speaking about the Father, "As the Father
has life in himself." Again when you were speaking about
yourself you said, "So he has given to the Son also to have
life in himself." As he has, so he has given to have. Where
does he have it? "In himself." Where has he given to have it?
"In himself." Where does Paul have it? Not in himself, but in
Christ. Where do you, a man of faith, have it? Not in yourself,
but in Christ. Let us see if the Apostle says this: "And I live,
now not I, but Christ lives in me."[27]

(3) Our life as our own, that is, from our own proper will,
will only be evil, sinful, wicked; but the good life from God
is in us, not from ourselves; from God it is given to us, not

26. Cf. Lk 11.9.   27. Cf. Gal 2.20.

from ourselves. But Christ has life in himself as the Father [does] because [he is] the Word of God. He does not now live wickedly, and now live well; but man [lives] now wickedly, now well. He who was living wickedly was in his own life; he who lives well has passed to the life of Christ. Having become a sharer in life, you were not what you received, you were as one who received; but the Son of God was not as if at first without life and [then] he received life. For, if he so received it, he would not have it in himself. For what does "in himself " mean? That he himself is life itself.[28]

10. I shall say another thing still more clearly perhaps. Some one lights a lamp. For example, that lamp, as far as regards the little flame which shines there, that fire has light in itself. But your eyes which, when the lamp was not there, were inactive and saw nothing, now they, too, have light, but not in themselves. Accordingly, if they turn themselves away from the lamp, they are darkened; if they turn toward it, they are enlightened. But that fire, as long as it exists, emits light; if you wish to take the light away from it, you extinguish it also at the same time; for without light it cannot remain in existence. But the Light, Christ, is inextinguishable and co-eternal to the Father, always glowing, always shining, always burning; for if he did not burn, would it be said in the Psalm, "There is no one who can hide from his heat"?[29]

(2) But in your sin you were cold; you turn that you may grow hot; if you move away, you will become cold. In your sin you were in darkness; you turn that you may be enlightened; if you turn yourself away, you will be darkened. Accordingly, because you were darkness in yourself, when you will be enlightened, you will not be light, though you are in light. For the Apostle said, "You were once darkness, but now you are light in the Lord."[30] When he said, "but now you are light" he added "in the Lord." Therefore there is darkness in you, "light in the Lord." Why light? Because by participation in that light you are light.[31] But if you withdraw from the

28. Cf. *Tractate* 19.11–13.
30. Cf. Eph 5.8.
29. Cf. Ps 18.7.
31. Cf. *Tractate* 2.6.

light by which you are enlightened, you return to your darkness. Not so Christ, not so the Word of God. But how?

(3) "As the Father has life in himself, so he has given to the Son also to have life in himself," so that he does not live by participation, but he lives without change and in every respect he, himself, is life. "So he has given to the Son also to have life." As he has, so he has given. What difference is there? That the one has given, the other has received. Did he already exist when he received? Do we understand that Christ was once without light when he is himself the wisdom of the Father about which it was said, "It is the brightness of eternal light"?[32]

(4) Therefore what is said, "He has given to the Son" is such as if it were said, "He begot a Son"; for he gave by begetting. As [the Father] gave that he might be, so he gave that he might be life and so he gave that he might be life in himself. What does it mean, he might be life in himself? He would not need life from another source, but he would be the fullness of life by which others, believing, might live while they live. Therefore "He has given to him to have life in himself." He has given as to whom? As to his Word, as to him who "in the beginning was the Word, and the Word was with God."[33]

11. And then, because he was made man, what did he give him? "And he has given him power to do judgment, because he is the Son of man." Insofar as he is the Son of God, "as the Father has life in himself, so he has given to the Son also to have life in himself"; but insofar as he is the Son of man, "He has given him the power of doing judgment." This is what I explained to you yesterday,[34] my beloved people, that in the judgment man will be seen, but God will not be seen; but after the judgment God will be seen by these who have prevailed in the judgment, but God will not be seen by the ungodly. Therefore because man will be seen in the judgment in that form by which he will come just as he ascended,[35] for

32. Cf. Wis 7.26.   33. Cf. Jn 1.1.
34. Cf. *Tractate* 21, especially sections 13 and 14.
35. Cf. Acts 1.11.

that reason, he had said above, "The Father does not judge any man, but all judgment he has given to the Son."[36]

(2) He repeats this also in this place when he says, "And he has given him the power of doing judgment because he is the Son of man." As if you were to say, "He has given him the power of doing judgment," but why? When did he not have the power of doing judgment? Since "in the beginning was the Word, and the Word was with God, and the Word was God," since "all things were made through him,"[37] did he not have the power of doing judgment? But according to this I say, "He has given him the power of doing judgment because he is the Son of man"; according to this he has received the power of judging, "because he is the Son of man." For in regard to the fact that he is the Son of God, he always had this power. He who was crucified received it. He who was in death is in life; the Word of God was never in death, was always in life.

12. Now then, perhaps someone of us said about this resurrection, "Look, we have arisen. He who hears Christ, who believes, both passes from death to life and will not come to judgment. The hour is coming, and it is now, that he who hears the voice of the Son of God may live. He was dead, he heard, he arises. Why is it that the future resurrection is mentioned later?" Spare yourself; do not abruptly throw off an opinion, lest you go rushing after it. There is, indeed, this resurrection which happens now. The unbelieving were dead, the wicked were dead; the just live, they pass from the death of unbelief to the life of faith. But from that do not believe that there is, afterwards, no future resurrection of the body; believe the future resurrection of the body also.

(2) For, hear what follows after this resurrection which happens through faith so that no one might think that this is the only one and might fall into that hopelessness and error of men who subvert the understanding of others, "saying that the resurrection has taken place already," about whom the Apostle says, "and they are subverting the faith of some."[38]

36. Jn 5.22.   37. Cf. Jn 1.1 and 3.
38. Cf. 2 Tm 2.18.

For, I believe that they said to them some such words as, "Look, where the Lord says, 'And he who believes in me has passed from death to life,' a resurrection has already taken place in men of faith who were unbelievers; how is another resurrection mentioned?"

(3) Thanks be to the Lord, our God. He props up the wavering; he guides the uncertain; he strengthens the doubters. Hear what follows, since you do not have the means to make the darkness of death for yourself. If you have believed, believe the whole. "What whole," you say, "do I believe?" Hear what he says, "Do not wonder at this," at the fact that he has given to his Son the power of doing judgment. "I mean at the end," he says. How at the end? "Do not wonder at this, for the hour is coming."

(4) Here he did not say, "and it is now." In that resurrection of faith what did he say? "The hour is coming, and it is now." In this resurrection which he points to as the future resurrection of dead bodies, he said, "The hour is coming." He did not say, "and it is now," because it will come at the end of the world.[39]

13. And how, you say, do you prove to me that he spoke about resurrection itself? If you listen patiently, you yourself will now prove it to yourself. Let us continue therefore. "Do not wonder at this, for the hour is coming in which all who are in the tombs." What is more evident than this resurrection? Before he had not said, "who are in the tombs" but "the dead shall hear the voice of the Son of God, and they who have heard shall live." He did not say, "Some will live, some will be damned," because all who believe will live. But about the tombs what does he say? "All who are in tombs shall hear his voice, and they shall come forth." He did not say, "they shall hear and live." For if they have lived badly and were lying in the tombs, they will rise to death, not to life.

(2) Therefore, let us see who shall come forth. Although a little before the dead were living by hearing and believing, there no distinction was made. It was not said, the dead will

---

39. Cf. *Tractate* 19.15–18.

hear the voice of the Son of God; and when they hear, some
will live, some will be damned; but "all who have heard shall
live," because they who believe will live, they who have love
will live, and no one will die. But from the tombs, "they shall
hear the voice. And they who have done well shall come forth
to the resurrection of life; they who have done ill, unto the
resurrection of judgment." This is the judgment, that punishment about which he had said a little before, "He who believes
in me has passed from death to life, and will not come to
judgment." ·

14. "I cannot of myself do anything. As I hear, I judge;
and my judgment is just." If you judge as you hear, from
whom do you hear? If from the Father, yet, indeed, "The
Father does not judge any man, but all judgment he has given
to the Son."[40] To what extent do you, the herald of the Father,
in a sense, say this which you hear? What I hear, this I say
because what the Father is, this I am; for speaking is my
proper function because I am the Word of the Father. For
Christ says this to you in your heart. What does it mean, "As
I hear, so I judge," except, as I am? For how does Christ
hear? Brothers, let us search it out, I ask of you. Does Christ
hear from the Father? How does the Father speak to him? Of
course, if he speaks to him, he utters words to him; for everyone who says anything to anyone says it with a word. How
does the Father speak to the Son when the Son is the Word
of the Father? Whatever the Father says to us, he says by his
Word. The Word of the Father is the Son; with what other
word does he speak to the Word himself? God is one, he has
one Word, he contains all things in one Word. Therefore,
what does it mean, "As I hear, so I judge"?

(2) As I am from the Father, so I judge. Therefore "My
judgment is just." For if you do nothing of yourself, O Lord
Jesus, as carnal men suppose, if you do nothing of yourself,
how did you say a little before, "so the Son also gives life to
whom he wishes"?[41] Now you say, "I do nothing of myself."
But what does the Son point out except that he is from the

---

40. Jn 5.22.   41. Cf. Jn 5.21.

Father? He who is from the Father is not from himself. If the Son were from himself, he would not be the Son; he is from the Father. That he may be Father, he is not from the Son; that he may be Son, he is from the Father. Equal to the Father, but still [the Son] is from him, but he is not from [the Son].

15. "Because I seek not my own will, but the will of him who sent me." The only Son says, "I seek, not my own will," and men want to do their own will! So greatly does that one who is equal to the Father humble himself; and so greatly does he extol himself who lies in the depths, and he does not rise unless a hand should be stretched to him! Therefore let us do the will of the Father, the will of the Son,[42] the will of the Holy Spirit, because of this Trinity there is one will, one power, one majesty.

(2) And yet the Son says, "I have not come to do my own will, but the will of him who sent me"[43] for the reason that Christ is not from himself but is from his Father. But what he had that he might appear as a man he assumed from the creature which he himself formed.

42. The codices read, "the will of Christ." The CCL reading is that of various early editions and of the Maurists.
43. Cf. Jn 6.38.

TRACTATE 23

On John 5.19–40

I N A CERTAIN PLACE in the gospel the Lord says that the wise hearer of his word ought to be like a man who, wishing to build, digs rather deeply until he comes to bedrock, and there without anxiety he establishes what he builds against the onrush of a flood, so that when it comes, rather it may be pushed back by the solidity of the building than that by its impact it causes the collapse of that house.[1] Let us consider the Scripture of God as being a field where we want to build something. Let us not be lazy nor content with the surface. Let us dig more deeply until we come to rock: "Now the rock was Christ."[2]

2. Today's reading spoke to us about the witness of the Lord, that he does not find witness from men necessary, but that he has a greater [witness] than men are; and he said what that witness is. He said, "The works that I do give witness of me." Then he added, "And the Father who has sent me gives witness of me." He says that also the works themselves which he does he has received from the Father. Therefore the works give witness, the Father gives witness. Did John give no witness? Clearly he gave witness, but as a lamp, not for satisfying friends, but for confounding enemies;[3] for it had already been foretold by the person of the Father: "I have made ready a lamp for my Christ; his enemies I will clothe with confusion, but upon him shall my sanctification flourish."[4]

(2) Let it be as if you were put in [the darkness of] the night; you have looked toward the lamp, and you have mar-

---

1. Cf. Mt 7.24–27; Lk 6.48–49.   2. Cf. 1 Cor 10.4.
3. Cf. *Tractates* 2.8–9 and 5.14.   4. Cf. Ps 131.17–18 (LXX).

veled at the lamp, and you have rejoiced at the light of the lamp. But that lamp declares that it is the sun in which you ought to rejoice; and although it burns in the night, it bids you to look forward to the day. Not, therefore, that there was not need for the testimony of that man. For why would he be sent if there were no need? But so that man not stay by the lamp and not think that the light of the lamp is sufficient for him, therefore, the Lord says that that lamp was not super-fluous and he says, nevertheless, that you ought not to stay by the lamp.

(3) The Scripture of God mentions another witness; there, of course, God gave witness to his Son, and in that Scripture the Jews placed hope, namely in the Law of God, ministered to them by Moses, the servant of God.[5] "Search the Scrip-ture," he says, "in which you think to have life everlasting; the same gives witness of me, and you are unwilling to come to me that you may have life." Why do you think that you have life everlasting in Scripture? Ask it to whom it gives wit-ness and understand what life everlasting is. And because they wanted to repudiate Christ on account of Moses, as if he were an adversary to the traditions and teachings of Moses, again he himself convicts these same ones as from another lamp.

3. For all men are lamps because they can both be lighted and extinguished. And, indeed, when the lamps smell well, they give light and are fired up with spirit;[6] then, too, if they were burning and have been extinguished, they also smell badly. For the servants of God have remained good lamps from the oil of his mercy, not from their own strength. For, in fact, the grace of God is gratuitous; that is the oil of the lamps. "In fact, I have labored more than all those" says a certain lamp; and that he might not seem to burn by his own strength, he added, "yet not I, but the grace of God with me."[7] And so every prophecy before the Lord's coming is a lamp; and about this the Apostle Peter says, "And we have a

---

5. Cf. Jn 5.45–47.
7. Cf. 1 Cor 15.10.

6. Cf. Acts 18.25; Rom 12.11.

more sure prophetical word, to which you do well to attend, as to a lamp shining in a dark place, until the day dawns and the morning star rises in your hearts."[8] And so the prophets are lamps, and all prophecy is one great lamp.[9]

(2) What about the apostles? Are they not also lamps themselves? Certainly they are lamps. For only he is not a lamp. For he is not lighted and extinguished, because "as the Father has life in himself, so he has given to the Son to have life in himself." Therefore, the apostles, too, are lamps; and they give thanks because they both have been kindled by the light of truth and burn with the Spirit of love, and the oil of God's grace is available to them. If they were not lamps, the Lord would not say to them, "You are the light of the world."[10] For after he said, "You are the light of the world," he shows that they should not think they were such a light as that of which it is said, "It was the true light that enlightens every man who comes into this world."[11]

(3) But this was said then about the Lord, when he was being distinguished from John. For indeed, about John the Baptist it had been said, "He was not the light, but was to give testimony of the light."[12] And that you might not say, "How was he not light about whom Christ says, 'He was a lamp'?" [you should know that] in comparison with the other light, he was not a light. For "it was the true light that enlightens every man who comes into the world." Therefore, when he said to the apostles also, "You are the light of the world," that they might not think that something had been attributed to them which must be understood about Christ alone, and that thus the lamps might not be extinguished by the wind of pride, when he had said, "You are the light of the world," he immediately added, "A city set upon a mountain cannot be hidden. Neither do men light a lamp and put it under a bushel basket, but upon a lampstand, so that it may shine to all who are in the house."[13]

(4) But what if he did not call the apostles a lamp but the

8. Cf. 2 Pt 1.19.   9. Cf. *Tractate* 35.6–8.
10. Cf. Mt 5.14.   11. Jn 1.9.
12. Jn 1.8.   13. Cf. Mt 5.14–15.

lighters of the lamp which they were to place on the lamp-stand? Hear that he called them a lamp. He said, "Let your light so shine before men, that, seeing your good works, they may give glory" not to you, but "to your Father who is in heaven."[14]

4. Therefore Moses gave witness to Christ, and John gave witness to Christ, and the rest of the prophets and the apostles gave witness to Christ. Before all these witnesses he placed the witness of his own works. For, even through them it was only God who gave witness to his Son. But God gives witness to his Son in another way; God reveals the Son through his Son himself; he reveals himself through the Son. If man can come to him, he will not need lamps; and by truly digging more deeply, he will bring his building to the rock.

5. Today's reading, therefore, brothers, is easy; but because of yesterday's debt[15] (for I know what I put off, not put aside, and the Lord has deigned also today to grant that [I] speak to you) recall what you ought to claim, if perhaps, with devotion and solitary humility preserved, we may somehow extend ourselves not against God, but to God,[16] and may lift up our soul to him, pouring it out over ourselves as that man in the Psalm to whom it was said, "Where is your God?" He said, "On these things I meditated and I poured out my soul over me."[17]

(2) Therefore let us lift up the soul to God, not against God, because this, too, was said, "To you, O Lord, I have lifted up my soul."[18] And let us lift it up, with his help; for it is heavy. But why is it heavy? Because the body which is corruptible weighs upon the soul and the earthly habitation

---

14. Cf. Mt 5.16.

15. Berrouard and Wright maintain that this *Tractate* was the one delivered on the day after *Tractate* 19 and that *Tractates* 20, 21, and 22 are insertions into this series of *Tractates* delivered at another time. See Introduction and *Tractate* 19.20, note 44.

16. Cf. Phil 3.13–14.

17. Cf. Ps 41.4–5. Augustine also has *super me* rather than the *in me* of the *Vulgate* for the Greek *ep' emè* of the LXX in *En in Ps* 41.8 (CCL 38.465–466).

18. Cf. Ps 24.1.

presses down the mind thinking about many things.[19] Can it perhaps be, therefore, that we can bring our intellect from many thoughts to one, and, when it has been torn away from the many, lift it up to the one (a thing which, indeed, we cannot do, as I said, unless he should help who wishes our souls to be lifted to him) and that we may to some extent arrive at how the Word of God, the only one of the Father, coeternal and equal to the Father, only does what he has seen the Father doing although the Father himself, nevertheless, does not do anything except through the Son who sees?

(3) It seems to me that the Lord Jesus, in this passage, wished to intimate something great to the attentive, to impart it to those capable of understanding, but to arouse those not capable to ardent exertion so that, though not yet understanding, by living well, they may become capable of understanding. He intimated to us that the human soul and rational mind which is in the human being and is not in the brute animal, are not enlivened, are not made happy, are not enlightened except by the very substance of God. [He intimated], too, that this soul does something through the body and from the body and yet holds the body subject, and through bodily things the body's senses can be soothed or offended, and for this reason, that is, because of a sort of partnership of soul and body in this life, and mutual embracement, the soul is delighted when the body's senses are calmed or it is saddened when they are offended. Yet its happiness, by which the soul itself is made happy, only comes about by participation in that life of an always living, unchangeable, and eternal substance which is God, so that, just as the soul which is inferior to God causes that which is inferior to it, that is, the body, to live, so only that which is superior to the soul itself causes the same soul to live happily. For the soul is superior rather than the body, and God is superior rather than the soul. It offers something to its inferior; something is offered to it by its superior. Let it serve its Lord that it be not despised by its servant.

19. Cf Wis 9.15.

(4) This, my brothers, is the Christian religion which is preached through the whole world, with its enemies trembling in fear and, when they are defeated, murmuring, and when they prevail, raging. This is the Christian religion: that one God be worshipped, not many gods, because only one God makes the soul happy. It becomes happy by participation in God. Not by participation in a holy soul does a weak soul become happy, nor by participation in an angel does a holy soul become happy; but if a weak soul seeks to be happy, let it seek the means whereby the holy soul is happy. For you will not be made happy from an angel; but you too [will become so] from the source from which the angel [is so].

6. With these concepts set out first and very firmly established, that the rational soul is made happy only by God, that the body is given life only through the soul, and that there is something intermediate between God and the body, the soul, pay attention and recall with me, not today's reading, about which we have spoken enough, but yesterday's which, lo and behold, we are now reflecting upon and discussing for the third day,[20] and in proportion to our strength we are digging until we reach the rock.

(2) The Word, Christ, the Word of God, Christ, with God; the Word Christ and God the Word; Christ and God and the Word, one God. Go there, soul, despising, or also transcending, all else. Go there. Nothing is more powerful than this creature which is called the rational mind; nothing is more sublime than this creature. Whatever is above it is the creator. But I was saying that the Word is Christ, and the Word of God is Christ, and God the Word is Christ. But not only is the Word Christ, but because "the Word was made flesh and dwelt among us"[21] therefore both the Word and the flesh are Christ. For, although "He was in the form of God, he thought it not robbery to be equal with God."[22]

(3) And what about us down at the bottom who, being weak

---

20. If one follows Berrouard's excision of *Tractates* 20, 21, and 22 from the series of sermons (see note 15), Augustine is referring to *Tractates* 18 and 19. *Tractate* 20 also discusses Jn 5.19.

21. Cf. Jn 1.14.   22. Cf. Phil 2.6.

and crawling on the ground, were unable to reach God, were we to be left behind? Far from it. "He emptied himself, taking the form of a servant."[23] Not consequently losing the form of God. So he who was God became man, by receiving what he was not, not by losing what he was; so God became man. There you have something in view of your weakness; there you have something else in view of your perfection. Let Christ raise you up through the fact that he is man, let him lead you through the fact that he is God-man; let him bring you to that which is God. And this is the whole preaching and dispensation through Christ, brothers, and there is no other, that souls may rise and bodies may rise. Both, of course, were dead, the body from infirmity, the soul from wickedness. Because both were dead, let both rise. Both what? Soul and body.

(4) Through what, then, does the soul [rise] except through God, Christ? Through what does the body [rise] except through the man, Christ? For there was also in Christ a human soul, a whole soul, not only the irrational element of soul but also the rational element which is called mind. For there have been some heretics, and they have been expelled from the Church, who thought that Christ's body did not have a rational mind, but only, as it were, an animal soul.[24] Of course, when the rational mind is removed, there is animal life. But because they were expelled, and were expelled by the truth, accept the whole Christ, Word, rational mind, and flesh. This whole is Christ. Let your soul rise from its depravity through that which is God; let your body rise from its decay through that which is man.

23. Cf. Phil 2.7.
24. Apollinarianism was a fourth-century Christological heresy. In attempting to defend the divinity of the Logos against the Arians, Apollinaris or Apollinarius, bishop of Laodicea, c. 310–c. 390 A.D., denied that Christ had a human soul, asserting that the Divine Logos did not assume the complete human nature but only the body and Plato's sensitive soul, itself replacing the rational soul. See F. Chiovaro, "Apollinarianism," NCE 1.665–667; "Apollinarius and Apollinarianism," ODCC², 72–73. See also Augustine, De Haeresibus 55 (CCL 46.325), and Berrouard, Homélies XVII–XXXIII, 765–767.

(5) Accordingly, dearest people, hear the great profundity of this reading, as it seems to me; and see how Christ says here nothing else than why Christ came, that souls may rise from depravity, bodies may rise from decay. I have already said through what souls rise, through the very substance of God; and through what bodies rise, through economy of the human incarnation[25] of our Lord, Jesus Christ.

7. "Amen, amen, I say to you, the Son cannot do anything of himself, but only what he sees the Father doing. For whatsoever things he does, these the Son also does in like manner." Sky, land, sea, the things in the sky, the things on the land, the things in the sea, visible things, invisible things, animals on the lands, bushes in the fields, swimming things in the water, flying things in the air, shining things in the sky, and, besides all these things, the Angels, the Virtues, the Thrones, the Dominions, the Principalities, the Powers, "all things were made through him."[26] Did God make all these things and show them, when made, to the Son that he, too, might make another world filled with all these things? Certainly not! But what? "For whatsoever things he does, these," not other things but "these the Son also does," not in a dissimilar manner but "in like manner."

(2) "For the Father loves the Son, and shows him all things that he himself does." The Father shows the Son that souls may be restored to life because souls are restored to life through the Father and the Son and souls cannot live if God is not their life. Therefore, if souls cannot live if God is not their life, as they themselves are the life of bodies, what the Father shows to the Son, that is, what he does, he does through the Son. For not by doing does he show the Son, but by showing he does through the Son. For the Son sees the Father showing before anything is done, and from the showing of the Father and the seeing of the Son there is done what is done by the Father through the Son. So souls are restored

---

25. *per humanam dispensationem.* See *Tractate* 19.1, note 15.

26. Cf. Jn 1.3. Once again the verb *facere* must be translated both "do" and "make," losing some of the forcefulness of the argument. See *Tractate* 18.5, note 18.

to life if they can see that bond of unity, the Father showing, the Son seeing, and that through the Father's showing and the Son's seeing the creature is made, and that that thing made through the Father's showing and the Son's seeing, which is neither the Father nor the Son, but whatever is made by the Father through the Son, is inferior to the Father and the Son. Who sees this?

8. Look once more in terms of sensual concepts; look, again we humble ourselves and descend to your level if yet, in any respect, at any time, we had ascended from you. You want to show something to your son that he may do what you are doing; you will do and thus show. Therefore what you will do in order to show your son, you, of course, do not do through your son, but you alone do what he himself may see done and may do another such thing in like manner. This is not there. Why do you go to your own likeness and expunge the likeness of God in yourself? This is absolutely not there. Find some way that you can show to your son what you are doing before you do it, so that when you have shown, you do through your son what you are doing.

(2) Perhaps an explanation has already occurred to you something like this. "Look," you say, "I plan to make a house and I intend that it be built through my son; before I myself build it, I show my son what I want to make, and he makes it and I through him, to whom I have shown my wish." You have indeed retreated from the first comparison, but you are still situated in a great dissimilarity. For, look, before you make a house, you indicate to your son and show him what you wish to make so that, by your showing it before you make it, he himself may make what you have shown, and then you [may make it] through him. But you will say words to your son; words will move between you and him. And between the one showing and the one seeing, or between the one speaking and the one hearing, there flies articulate sound which is not what you are, and is not what he is. For that sound which goes out of your mouth and, after striking the air, touches your son's ear, and, when the sense of hearing has completed

its work, brings your thought to his heart—well, that sound is neither you yourself nor your son himself.

(3) A sign has been given by your mind to your son's mind, but a sign which is neither your mind nor your son's mind, but something else. Do we think that the Father spoke in this way with the Son? Were there words between God and the Word? How is this? Or, whatever the Father would wish to say to the Son, if he should wish to say it with a word (the Son himself is the Word of the Father), would he speak to the Word through a word? Or, because the Son is the great Word, would lesser words move between Father and Son? Would some sound and, so to speak, some temporal and flitting creature, go out of the mouth of the Father and strike the ear of the Son? Does God have a body so that this may go forth as if from his lips? And does the Word have a body's ears into which sound may come?

(4) Take away all bodily things; see simplicity, if you are simple. But how will you be simple? If you do not entangle yourself in the world, but if you untangle yourself from the world; for by untangling yourself, you will be simple. But how will you be simple? If you do not entangle yourself, you will be simple. And if you can, see what I am saying; or, if you cannot, believe what you do not see. You speak to your son, you speak with a word; the word which sounds is neither you nor your son.

9. "I have," you say, "another way to show. For my son is so well instructed that, even when I do not speak, he hears; but only with a nod I show him what to do." Look, show what you want with a nod; surely your mind wants to show what it has in it. From what do you make the nod? From your body, of course, with your lips, face, eyebrows, eyes, hands. All these things are not what your mind is. These also are intermediaries. Something has been understood through these signs which are not what your mind is, nor what your son's mind is. But this whole thing which you do with your body is inferior to your mind and inferior to your son's mind; and your son cannot know your mind unless you give him signs

from your body. What, then, do I do? This is not there; simplicity is there.

(2) The Father shows the Son what he is doing and by showing begets the Son. I see what I have said; but because I see also to whom I have said it, may this understanding be effected in you at some time or other. But, if you cannot now comprehend what God is, at least comprehend what God is not; you will have progressed far if you perceive of God as not something else than he is. You cannot yet attain to what he is; attain to what he is not. God is not body, not earth, not sky, not moon, not sun, not stars, not these bodily things. For if he is not heavenly things, how much less earthly? Remove all body. Hear still another thing; God is not mutable spirit. For I admit, and it must be admitted, because the gospel says it, "God is a spirit."[27] But pass beyond all changeable spirit, pass beyond the spirit who now knows, now does not know, now remembers and forgets, wishes what he did not wish, does not wish what he wished. If [a spirit] should now suffer these changes or if it should be able to suffer them, pass beyond all these things! You do not find in God anything changeable, not anything which is now one way and a little before was another way. For where you find one way and another way, there has occurred there a kind of death; for it is death when what was is not.[28]

(3) The soul is said to be immortal; indeed it is, because the soul lives always, and there is in it a kind of permanent life, but changeable life. According to the changeability of this life, it, too, can be said to be mortal, because if it was living wisely and loses its wisdom, it is dead for the worse; but if it was living foolishly and became wise, it is dead for the better. For Scripture teaches us that there is a death for the worse, and there is a death for the better. Certainly they were dead for the worse about whom it is said, "Leave the dead alone, let them bury their own dead;"[29] and "Rise, you who sleep, and

27. Cf. Jn 4.24.
28. A commonplace of ancient philosophy. Cf., e.g., Lucretius, *De Rerum Natura* 1.670–671; "For whatsoever has been changed and departs from its own limits, immediately this is the death of that which was before."
29. Cf. Mt 8.22; Lk 9.60.

arise from among the dead, and Christ will enlighten you;"[30] and from this reading, "When the dead shall hear, and they who have heard shall live." They were dead for the worse; therefore they live again. By living again, they die for the better, because by living again they will not be what they were; but not to be what was is death. But perhaps, if it is for the better, it is not called death? The Apostle called that death: "But if you are dead with Christ from the elements of this world, why do you, as though still living, judge concerning this world?"[31] And again, "For you are dead and your life is hidden with Christ in God."[32] He wishes us to die that we may live, because we have lived that we might die.

(4) Therefore, whatever dies both from the better for the worse and from the worse for the better, this is not God, because neither can the highest good pass to the better nor can true eternity pass to the worse. For, it is true eternity where there is not time. But was there now this and now that? Now time has been admitted and it is not eternal. For that you may know that God is not as the soul is (yet, indeed, the soul is immortal), therefore why is it that the Apostle said about God, "Who alone has immortality"[33] except that he clearly said this, he alone has immutability because he alone has true eternity? Therefore there is no mutability there.

10. Acknowledge in yourself something which I wish to say, within, within in you, not in you as if in your body, for there, too, "in you" can be said. For health is in you, any age at all is in you, but according to the body; your hand, your foot is in you. But there is one thing in you, within, another thing in you, as in your clothing. But leave outside both your clothing and your flesh; descend into yourself, enter your secret place, your mind, and there see what I want to say, if you can. For, if you are yourself far from yourself, how can you draw near to God? I was speaking about God, and you thought you would understand. I am speaking about the soul, I am speaking about you. Understand; there I shall test you.

30. Cf. Eph 5.14; also Is 26.19 and 60.1.
31. Cf. Col 2.20.   32. Col 3.3.
33. Cf. 1 Tm 6.16.

For, I do not go very far for examples when I want to give some likeness to your God from your mind, because, of course, not in body but in mind itself man was made according to the image of God. Let us seek God in his likeness, let us recognize the creator in his image.

(2) There within, if we can, let us find this which we are saying, how the Father shows the Son and the Son sees what the Father shows, before anything is done by the Father through the Son. But when I have spoken and you have understood, you should not even then think that that [sc. the showing-seeing of Father and Son] is something of just such a kind, in order that you may keep there the devoutness which I want to be kept by you and [which I] especially advise: that is, that, if you cannot comprehend what God is, you do not think that it is too little for you to know what he is not.

11. Look, in your mind I see two things, your memory and your thought, that is, so to speak, a kind of perception and vision of your soul. You see something; you perceive it through your eyes and you commit it to memory. There, what you committed to memory is within, shut up in secret as though in a storehouse, as though in a treasure vault, as though in some secret place and inner chamber. You think about something else, your attention is elsewhere; that which you saw is in your memory and is not seen by you because your thought is concentrated on another thing.

(2) Right now I prove my case; I speak to you who know. I mention Carthage by name. All of you, whoever of you know it, right now, with yourselves, have seen Carthage. Are there as many Carthages as your souls? You all saw it by means of these two[34] syllables well known to you, bursting forth from my mouth, your ears were touched, and the sense of your soul was touched through the body, and from attention to something else your mind was turned back to that which was there and it saw Carthage. Was Carthage at that moment made there? It was already there, but it was hidden. Why was

34. The Latin text reads "four" because the Latin form, *Carthaginem*, has four syllables.

it hidden there? Because your mind was attending to something else; but when your thought was turned back to that which was in the memory, from there it was formed and a kind of mental seeing was done. Before there was no seeing, but there was memory. When the thought was turned back to memory, a seeing was done. Therefore your memory showed Carthage to your thought; and what was in it before you paid attention to it, it showed to the attention of your thought once it had been turned to it. Look, a showing was done by the memory, a seeing was done in the thought; and no words sped in between, no sign from the body was given. You did not nod, nor write, nor make a sound; and yet the thought saw what the memory showed.

(3) But both that which showed and that to which it showed are of the same substance. But that your memory might have Carthage, this image was drawn through the eyes; for you saw what you stored in the memory. So you saw a tree which you remember, so a mountain, so a river, so a friend's face, so an enemy's, so your father's, your mother's, your brother's, your sister's, your son's, your neighbor's, so [the shape] of letters written in a book, so of the book itself, so of this basilica; all these things you saw, and because they had already been seen, you committed them to memory. And, as it were, you have placed there things which you might see by thinking whenever you wish, even when they were absent from the body's eyes. For you saw Carthage when you were at Carthage; your soul received a mental picture [of it] through the eyes. This mental picture was stored in your memory; and, a man who had been at Carthage, you kept something within which you could see within yourself even when you were not there. You received all these things from the outside.

(4) What the Father shows the Son, he does not receive from without. The entirety is done within; for there would be no creatures without unless the Father had made them through the Son. Every creature was made by God; before it was made it did not exist. Therefore it was not [first] made and [then] seen and retained in the memory so that the Father might show it to the Son as the memory to the thought;

but the Father showed it to be made and the Son saw it to be made, and the Father made it by showing it because he made it through the Son seeing it.[35] And, thus, it ought not to be disturbing because it was said, "but only what he sees the Father doing"; it was not said "showing." For through this it was signified that for the Father "to do" is the same as "to show," so that from this it may be understood that he does all things through the Son seeing. Neither that showing nor that seeing is temporal. For because all times are made through the Son, things to be made could obviously not be shown to him, at some time. But the Father's showing begets the Son's seeing in the same way as the Father begets the Son. Showing, of course, generates seeing; not seeing showing. But if we could look more purely and more perfectly, we would perhaps find that the Father is not one thing and his showing another, nor is the Son one thing and his seeing another.[36] But if we have barely grasped this [and] could barely explain how memory shows to the thought what it has taken from the outside, how much less will we be able to grasp or explain how God the Father shows to the Son what he does not have from elsewhere, or what is not other than himself?

(5) We are little ones. I speak to you what God is not; I do not show what he is. Therefore what shall we do that we may grasp what he is? Will you be able to from me, through me? I shall say this to little ones, to you and to me: there is one through whom we may be able. We have just sung, we have just heard, "Cast your care upon the Lord, and he will nourish you."[37] For you are not able, O man, for the very reason that you are a little one. If you are a little one, you must be nourished; after you have been nourished, you will be full-grown. And what you could not see as a little one, as one fullgrown you will see. But to be nourished, "Cast your care upon the Lord, and he will nourish you."

12. Now then, let us briefly run through what remains, and see how the Lord intimates here what I have mentioned.

---

35. Cf. *Tractate* 19.3.   36. Cf. *Tractate* 18.10.
37. Cf. Ps 54.23 and *Tractate* 14.7.

"The Father loves the Son, and shows him all things which he himself does." He himself restores souls to life, but through the Son, so that souls that have been restored to life may enjoy the substance of God, that is, of the Father and the Son. "And greater works than these he will show him."

(2) Greater than what? [Greater] than the healings of bodies. This we have also already discussed previously,[38] and we ought not to tarry. For the resurrection of the body to eternity is greater than this healing of the body which was done for a time in that sick man.[39] "And greater works than these he will show him, that you may wonder." "He will show" as if temporally, therefore as if to a man made in time, because God the Word was not made, through whom all times were made; but Christ was made man in time. It is clear under what consul and on what day the Virgin Mary gave birth to Christ who had been conceived of the Holy Spirit; therefore he was made man in time through whom as God times were made. And so, as if in time, he will show him greater works, that is, the resurrection of bodies, that you may wonder at the resurrection of bodies accomplished through the Son.

13. Next, he returns to that resurrection of souls. "For as the Father raises the dead and gives them life, so the Son also gives life to whom he wishes," but according to the Spirit. The Father gives life, the Son gives life, the Father to whom he wishes, the Son to whom he wishes, but the Father to the same as the Son because all things were made through him. "For, as the Father raises the dead and gives them life, so the Son also gives life to whom he wishes."

(2) This was said about the resurrection of souls; what about the resurrection of bodies? He returns and says, "For neither does the Father judge any man, but all judgment he has given to the Son." The resurrection of souls is done through the eternal and immutable substance of the Father and the Son; but the resurrection of bodies is done through the temporal economy[40] of the Son's humanity, [an economy]

---

38. In *Tractate* 19.4–5; see also *Tractate* 21.5–10.
39. The sick man beside the pool in Jn 5.1–9; cf. *Tractate* 17.1–9.
40. See section 6 and note 25.

not coeternal with the Father. And so when he mentioned judgment wherein a resurrection of bodies should occur, he said, "For the Father does not judge any man, but all judgment he has given to the Son"; but about the resurrection of souls, "As the Father raises the dead and gives them life, so the Son also gives life to whom he wishes." Therefore the Father and the Son do the one together; but the other about the resurrection of bodies, "The Father does not judge any man, but all judgment he has given to the Son, that all men may honor the Son as they honor the Father."

(3) Now this has been brought back to the resurrection of souls. "That all men may honor the Son." How? "As they honor the Father." For the Son works the resurrection of souls just as the Father does; the Son gives life just as the Father does. Therefore, in the resurrection of souls "let all men honor the Son, as they honor the Father." But what about the giving of honor on account of the resurrection of bodies? "He who does not honor the Son, does not honor the Father who sent him." He did not say, "as," but "does not honor" and "does not honor." For Christ the man is honored, but not *as* God the Father is. Why? Because in regard to this he said, "The Father is greater than I."[41] But when is the Son honored *as* the Father is honored? When "in the beginning was the Word, and the Word was with God" and "all things were made through him."[42] Therefore in this second giving of honor what did he say? "He who does not honor the Son, does not honor the Father who sent him." The Son was not sent except because he was made man.

14. "Amen, amen, I say to you." Again he returns to the resurrection of souls, that we may understand him from his constantly repeated utterances, because we could not follow, so to speak, a fleeting word. Look, God's word lingers with us, look, it dwells, as it were, with our infirmities. He again returns to a mention of the resurrection of souls. "Amen, amen, I say to you, that he who hears my word, and believes him who sent me, has life everlasting," but as from the Father.

41. Cf. Jn 14.28.   42. Cf. Jn 1.1 and 3.

"He who hears my word, and believes him who sent me," from the Father "has life everlasting," by believing in him who sent him. "And he will not come into judgment, but has passed from death to life," but he is given life from the Father whom he believes. What? Do you not give life? See that "the Son also gives life to whom he wishes."

(2) "Amen, amen, I say to you, that the hour is coming, when the dead shall hear the voice of the Son of God, and those who have heard shall live." He did not say here, "They will believe him who sent me, and therefore shall live"; but, by hearing the voice of the Son of God, "those who have heard," that is, who have obeyed the Son of God, "shall live." Therefore they shall both live from the Father when they believe the Father and they shall live from the Son when they hear the voice of the Son of God. Why shall they live both from the Father and from the Son? "For as the Father has life in himself, so he has given to the Son to have life in himself."

15. He finished [speaking] about the resurrection of souls; it remains to speak more plainly about the resurrection of bodies. "And he has given him power to do judgment" not only to restore souls to life through faith and wisdom, but also to do judgment. But why this [power]? "Because he is the Son of man." Therefore the Father does something through the Son of man which he does not do from his substance to which the Son is equal, as for him to be born, as for him to be crucified, as for him to die, as for him to rise—for not any of these things happened to the Father. So, too, the resurrection of bodies. For the Father effects the resurrection of souls from his own substance through the substance of the Son by which [the Son] is equal to him;[43] in fact, souls become participators in that immutable light, bodies do not. But the Father effects the resurrection of bodies through the Son of man. For "And he has given him the power to do judgment, because he is the Son of man," according to that which he

---

43. Some codices have an alternate reading: "The Father effects the resurrection of souls from his own substance; the Son, from his own substance by which he is equal to him.

said earlier, "for neither does the Father judge any man." And that he may show that he has said this about the resurrection of bodies, "Do not wonder at this, for the hour is coming." Not "and it is now" but "the hour is coming in which all who are in the tombs" (you have already heard this quite well enough yesterday)[44] "shall hear his voice and come forth."

(2) And where? Into judgment? "They who have done well, unto the resurrection of life; they who have done ill, unto the resurrection of judgment." And do you alone do this because the Father has given all judgment to the Son and does not judge any man? "I do it," he says. But how do you do it? "I cannot of myself do anything. As I hear, I judge; and my judgment is just." When the resurrection of souls was being dealt with, he did not say, "I hear" but "I see." For "I hear" as if the command of the Father giving instructions. Now, therefore, as a man, as one than whom the Father is greater, now from the form of the servant, not from the form of God, "As I hear, I judge; and my judgment is just." Why is the judgment of the man just? My brothers, listen carefully: "Because I seek not my own will, but the will of him who sent me."

44. In *Tractate* 19.17–18; cf. also *Tractate* 22.13.

TRACTATE 24

On John 6.1–14

THE MIRACLES which our Lord, Jesus Christ, performed are indeed divine works; and from things that can be seen they prompt the human mind to an understanding of God. For because he is not such a substance as can be seen with the eyes, and [because] his miracles, by which he governs the whole world and administers all creation, have lost their impressiveness by constant repetition, so that almost no one deigns to notice the wondrous and stupendous works of God in any grain of seed, in accordance with his very own mercy he has reserved for himself certain works which he might do at an opportune time outside the usual course and order of nature, so that, by seeing [works], not greater but irregular, they might be amazed for whom the daily ones had become unimpressive.[1]

(2) For the governance of the whole world is a greater miracle than the satisfying of five thousand men from five loaves.[2] Yet, at the former [miracles] no one is amazed; at the latter one, men are amazed, not because it is greater but because it is rare. For who even now feeds the whole world except he who creates crops from a few grain seeds? Therefore, he did as God does. For, by the same means by which he multiplies crops from a few grains, he multiplied in his hands the five loaves. The power was in fact in Christ's hands;[3] but those five loaves were like seeds, not entrusted to the earth, to be sure, but multiplied by him who made the earth.

1. Cf. *Tractates* 8.1, 9.1, 17.1, and 49.1.
2. This miracle of the five loaves and two fishes, the subject of this *Tractate,* is related in all four Gospels: here in Jn 6.1–14 and also in Mt 14.15–21; Mk 6.35–44; Lk 9.12–17.
3. Cf. *Tractate* 9.5.

(3) Therefore this [miracle] was put before the senses, that
the mind might be lifted up to him by it, and it was displayed
to the eyes, that the understanding might be put to work
upon it so that we might revere the invisible God through
visible works, and so that we, lifted up to faith and purged
by faith, might desire to see him even invisibly whom, though
invisible, we have come to know from visible things.

2. And yet, it is not enough to look at these things in
Christ's miracles. Let us ask the miracles themselves what
they say to us about Christ; indeed, if they are to be understood, they have a tongue of their own. For, because Christ
himself is the Word of God, even a deed of the Word is a
word for us.[4] Therefore, as to this miracle, as we have heard
how great it is, let us seek also how profound it is; let us
delight not only in its surface, but let us also search out its
depth. For it has something interior, this at which we wonder
on the outside. We have seen, we have watched something
great, something magnificent, and completely divine, which
cannot be done except by God. We have praised the doer
from the deed.

(2) But just as if we were to look at beautiful letters somewhere, it would not be enough for us to praise the writer's
hand[5] because he made the letters uniform, even, and ele-
gant, if we were not also to read what he made known to us
through them, so he who only looks at this deed is delighted
by the deed's beauty so that he admires the artist; but he who
understands also reads, so to speak. For a picture is seen in
one way, letters are seen in another way. When you have seen
a picture, to have seen it, to have praised it, is all that is.
When you have seen letters, this is not all that is because you
are put in mind also to read them. For you say, when you
have seen letters, if, perchance, you do not know how to read

4. Augustine in this *Tractate* sees miracles as serving two purposes: to
demonstrate Christ's divine power by extraordinary visible deeds which are
well-adapted to the nature and psychology of the human witnesses, and to
serve as symbolic signs conveying divine revelations to us. See Berrouard,
Homélies XVII–XXXIII, 771–773.
5. The Latin word *articulum* literally means "the finger."

them, "What do we think it is which was written here?" You ask what it is although you already see something.

(3) He, from whom you seek to discern the meaning of what you have seen, is going to show you something else. He has different eyes from you. Do you not see the letter forms similarly? But you do not understand the signs similarly. Therefore, you see and praise; he sees, praises, reads, and understands. Therefore, because we have seen, because we have praised, let us read and understand.

3. The Lord on the mountain; let us much rather understand that the Lord on the mountain is the Word on high. Accordingly, what was done on the mountain does not, as it were, lie on low ground, nor is it, in passing by, to be passed up unnoticed, but it must be looked up to from below. He saw the masses; he realized they were hungry; mercifully he fed them, by virtue not only of his goodness, but also of his power. For of what benefit would goodness alone be where there was no bread with which the hungry crowd might be fed? If power were not to assist goodness, that crowd would remain fasting and hungry.

(2) Then the disciples also, who together with the Lord were hungry, they, too, wanted to feed the masses that they might not remain empty, but did not have [anything] with which to feed them.[6] The Lord asked [what resources they had] from which loaves of bread might be bought to feed the crowd. And Scripture says, "But he said this, testing him," the Apostle Philip, namely, whom he had asked. "For he himself knew what he would do." Therefore, what was the benefit for which he was testing him except that he was pointing out the disciple's ignorance? And, perhaps, in this demonstration of the disciple's ignorance he signified something. It will be clear then when this very mystery of the five loaves begins to speak to us and to disclose what it signifies; for there we shall see why the Lord in this deed wanted to show the ignorance of the disciple by asking what he knew.

6. Berrouard, *Homélies XVII–XXXIII*, 411 points out that this is a reference to the account of the miracle given in the synoptic Gospels; see Mt 14.15, Mk 6.35–36, and Lk 9.12.

(3) For we sometimes ask what we do not know, wishing to hear in order that we may learn; sometimes we ask what we know, wishing to know whether he whom we are asking also knows. The Lord knew both; he knew both what he was asking (for he himself knew what he was going to do) and he, likewise, knew that Philip didn't know this. Why, therefore, did he ask except that he was pointing out that man's ignorance? Later, as I have said, we shall understand why he did this.

4. "Andrew says, 'There is a boy here who has five loaves and two fishes; but what are these for so many?'" When Philip had been asked and had said that two hundred *denarii*[7] worth of bread would not be enough with which so great a crowd as that might be refreshed, there was a boy there, carrying five barley loaves and two fishes. "And Jesus said, 'Make the people recline.' Now there was much grass there, and they reclined, almost five thousand men. And the Lord Jesus took the loaves, and he gave thanks"; he ordered, the loaves were broken, they were placed before those reclining. No longer [were there] five loaves, but what he had added who had created what had been increased.

(2) "And of the fishes, as much as was enough." It is not enough that that crowd was filled; there also remained fragments, and these were ordered to be gathered that they might not go to waste. "And they filled twelve baskets of fragments."

5. To run through it briefly, the five loaves are understood as the five books of Moses; rightly they are not wheat but barley because they belong to the Old Testament.[8] For you

7. The *denarius* was a Roman silver coin worth 16 *asses*, the *as* being a copper coin of the lowest value and serving as base value for other coins. NAB's "a day's wages" for *denarius* provides a closer estimation for the value of the coin than Douay's "pennyworth" and is supported by Mt 20.2, "the wages of the laborers in the vineyard." I have kept *denarius* because it is an exceedingly difficult and complex task to find modern equivalents for ancient monetary value designations. Two hundred *denarii* constituted a huge sum of money.

8. Cf. *DDQ* 61.1 and 4. The two testaments have the same content but differ in manner of expression; the Old Testament is barley, its grain hidden by the husk and hard to get at, whereas the wheat kernel of the New Testa-

know that barley was created in such a way that one can scarcely get to its kernel; for this kernel is clothed with a covering of husk, and this husk is tenacious and adhering, so that it is stripped off with effort. Such is the letter of the Old Testament, clothed with the coverings of carnal mysteries; but if one gets to its kernel, it feeds and satisfies.

(2) And so a boy was carrying five loaves and two fishes. If we should seek to know who this boy was, perhaps he was the people of Israel; [this people] was carrying them with a boyish understanding and was not eating. For those things which it was carrying, when kept shut, were a burden, but when opened, were food. Moreover, the two fish seem to us to signify those two sublime personages in the Old Testament who were anointed to make holy and rule the people, the priest and the king.

(3) And he himself came in mystery now at last, who was signified through them; he came now at last who was shown by the kernel of the barley but was hidden by the husk of the barley. He came, himself one person carrying both personages in himself, priest and king, priest through the victim which he offered for us to God—himself; king because we are ruled by him. And those things which were being carried shut up are opened. Thanks be to him; through himself he fulfilled what was promised in the Old Testament. And he ordered the loaves to be broken; by breaking, they were multiplied.

(4) Nothing is truer. For those five books of Moses, how many books have they made when they are explained, as if by breaking [them], that is, by discussing [them]? But because the ignorance of the first people was covered in that barley, and about this first people it was said, "When Moses is read, a veil has been placed over their hearts,"[9] (for the veil had

---

ment is easy to harvest. The Old Testament requires the reader to put aside carnal desires and understandings to gain the spiritual insight that enables him to see prophecy about Christ hidden in it. See also *Tractate* 9.3 and 5, and Berrouard, *Homélies XVII–XXXIII*, 414–415 and 773–774. The same ideas are also briefly expressed in *Sermo* 130.1 (PL 38.725).

9. Cf. 2 Cor 3.15.

not yet been taken away because Christ had not yet come; the
veil of the temple had not yet been torn in pieces when he
was hanging on the cross),[10] because, therefore, the ignorance
of the people was in the Law, for that reason that testing of
the Lord showed the ignorance of the disciple.

6. Therefore, nothing is without meaning, all things give
signs, but they require one who understands.[11] For also this
number of the people who were fed signifies the people
placed under the Law. For why were there five thousand except that they were under the Law and this Law is set out in
the five books of Moses? On this account also the sick were
brought forth from those five porticoes,[12] but were not
healed. But there he cured a sick man, who also here fed the
masses from five loaves. Then, too, they were reclining in the
grass; therefore they understood[13] carnally and rested in carnal things. For all flesh is grass.[14] But what are the fragments
except what the people could not eat? Therefore they are
understood as certain matters more hidden in meaning which
the multitude cannot grasp. Therefore, what remains except
that the matter more hidden in meaning which the multitude
cannot grasp be entrusted to those who are suited also to
teach others, as were the apostles?[15]

10. Cf. Mt 27.51; Mk 15.38; Lk 23.45. The life and especially the death
of Christ remove the veil of non-comprehension from the Old Testament,
that is, provide the necessary means to achieve a true understanding of its
meaning. See Berrouard, *Homélies XVII–XXXIII*, 775–776.

11. The Latin has here simply a noun *intellector,* a Christian Latin word
little used before Augustine; see TLL 7.1.2089, Berrouard, *Homélies XVII–
XXXIII,* 418, and C. Mohrmann, *Die Altchristliche Sondersprache in den Sermones
des hl Augustin,* 2d ed. (Amsterdam, 1965) 1.219–220.

12. Sc. into the pool; cf. Jn 5.2–9; *Tractate* 17.2–3.

13. *Sapiebant.* This word involves a word play frequently used in these
Tractates. Its denotation is "taste" with "understand" as a connotation. They
"tasted" the corporeal bread but did not "taste," i.e. "understand," the spiritual meaning of the miracle. Cf. *Tractate* 9.3–4, notes 10 and 16.

14. Cf. Is 40.6.

15. Berrouard, *Homélies XVII–XXXIII,* 419 points out that this should not
be understood as some type of esoteric gnosticism but represents a practical
teaching methodology: those few capable of the profoundest understanding teach the others according to their varied capabilities. See also
M.-F. Berrouard, "Saint Augustin et le ministère de la prédication," RAug 2
(1962) 447–501.

(2) Accordingly twelve baskets were filled. This was done both miraculously, because a great thing was done, and usefully, because a spiritual thing was done. Those who then saw were amazed, but we are not amazed when we hear it. For it was written that we might hear. What the eyes had the capability [to do] in their case, this faith [has the capability to do] in our case. To be sure, we see with our mind what we could not see with your eyes; and we have been preferred to them because it has been said about us, "Blessed are they who do not see and believe."[16]

(3) I add, moreover, that, perhaps too, we have understood what that crowd did not understand. And we who could get at the kernel of the barley truly have been fed.

7. Finally, those men who saw this, what did they think? [The text] says, "Those men, when they had seen the sign which Jesus had done, said, 'This is truly the prophet.'" Perhaps they still regarded Christ as a prophet for this reason, that they had reclined upon the grass.[17] Now, he was the Lord of the prophets, the fulfiller[18] of the prophets; for it was said to Moses, "I shall raise up for them a prophet like you."[19] "Like" means according to the flesh, not according to the majesty. And that that promise of the Lord had meaning about Christ himself is clearly explained and read in the Acts of the Apostles.[20]

16. Cf. Jn 20.29.

17. I.e., their understanding was still carnal; they saw only Christ in the flesh. See section 6.

18. The Latin noun *impletor* does not occur before Augustine; see TLL 7.1.639. I have translated it "fulfiller" together with Gibb, 160, Browne, 377, and Mohrmann, *Die Altchristliche Sondersprache*, 1.161, because the verb *implere* in Christian Latin, as early as Tertullian, means "to fulfill," "to accomplish," "to achieve" (Blaise, 413); this meaning is also clearly found in *Tractate* 26.1. In this section a few lines down prophets are said to be "filled" with the word of God, using this verb. Berrouard, *Homélies XVII–XXXIII*, 420–421, however, translates the word as "inspirer." He maintains (779–780) that Augustine is uneasy about the title of prophet given to Christ lest, like the disciples at Emmaus (Lk 24.19), one should think of Christ as no more than a prophet. Augustine defends the title but indicates its inadequacy; those who see Christ only as a prophet have not achieved fullness of understanding about him. See also *Tractates* 15.23–24 and 44.9.

19. Cf. Dt 18.18.   20. Cf. Acts 7.37.

(2) And the Lord himself said about himself, "A prophet is not without honor except in his own country."[21] The Lord is a prophet, and the Lord is the Word of God, and no prophet prophesies without the Word of God; the Word of God is with the prophets and the Word of God is a prophet. Earlier times were granted the prophets inspired and filled with the Word of God; we have been granted the Word of God himself as the prophet. But Christ, the Lord of the prophets, [is] a prophet in the same way as Christ, the Lord of angels, [is] an angel. For he himself also was called an angel of great counsel.[22] But even so, what does the prophet say elsewhere? That not as a legate nor as an angel, but he himself, coming, will save them,[23] that is, for saving them he will not send a legate, he will not send an angel, but he himself will come. Who will come? The angel himself. Assuredly not through an angel, except that he is an angel just as he is also Lord of the angels. For in Latin angels are messengers (*nuntii*).

(3) If Christ were to announce nothing, he would not be called an angel; if he were to prophesy nothing, he would not be called a prophet. He has urged us to faith and to the attainment of eternal life. He announced something present and predicted something future. From the fact that he announced a present thing, he was an angel; from the fact that he announced a future thing, he was a prophet. And from the fact that the Word of God was made flesh,[24] he was the Lord of both angels and the prophets.

21. Cf. Mt 13.57; Mk 6.4; cf. also Lk 4.24; Jn 4.44.
22. Is 9.6 (LXX).
23. Cf. Is 35.4 and 63.9 (LXX).   24. Cf. Jn 1.14.

TRACTATE 25

On John 6.15–40

HIS IS TODAY'S [reading] which follows yesterday's reading from the gospel [and] from which today's homily is due. After that miracle was performed, where Jesus fed five thousand men from five loaves, when the crowd had been astonished and said that he was a great prophet who came into the world, this follows: "Jesus therefore, when he knew that they would come to take him by force and make him king, fled again into the mountain, himself alone."

(2) Therefore, it is given to be understood that when the Lord was sitting on the mountain with his disciples and saw the crowds coming to him, he had descended from the mountain and fed the masses near to its lower areas. For, how could he possibly flee there again if he had not descended from the mountain before? Therefore, that the Lord descended from the mountain to feed the crowds signifies nothing. He fed them and ascended.

2. But why did he ascend when he knew that they wanted to take hold of him by force and make him king? Why indeed? Was he not the king, who feared to be made a king? He was in every respect; but he was not such a king as one who would be made by men but as one who would give a kingdom to men. Can it perhaps be that Jesus, whose deeds are words,[1] here too, signifies something to us?

(2) Therefore, in the fact that they wanted to take hold of him by force and make him king and for this reason he fled

---

1. Words are signs which communicate meaning. Deeds can be signs which communicate meaning; such deeds are, then, words. Augustine sees Jesus's deeds as words in this sense. See *DDC* 2.3.

to the mountain, himself alone, is this deed in his case silent, does it say nothing, or does it signify nothing? Or, is it perhaps that to take hold of him by force was to want to anticipate the time of his kingdom? For he had come now, not to rule now as he will rule in regard to that which we say, "Your kingdom come."[2] He indeed always rules with his Father in accordance with the fact that he is the Son of God, the Word of God, the Word through whom all things were made.[3] But the prophets predicted his kingdom, even according to the fact that Christ became man and made his faithful ones Christians. Therefore, there will be a kingdom of Christians which is now being gathered, which is now being mustered, which is now being bought by the blood of Christ. One day his kingdom will be manifest when the splendor of his saints will be clear after the judgment rendered by him; and this is the judgment which he himself said earlier that he will make as the Son of man.[4] And about this kingdom also the Apostle said, "When he shall have delivered the kingdom to God the Father."[5] And about it he himself also said, "Come, blessed of my Father, take possession of the kingdom which has been prepared for you from the beginning of the world."[6]

(3) But the disciples and the crowds, believing in him, thought that he had come so as to rule them; to want to take hold of him by force and make him king is to want to anticipate his time which he himself was concealing in himself that he might produce it at the appropriate time and declare it at the appropriate time at the end of the world.

3. For, that you may know that they wanted to make him king, (that is, to anticipate, and, right then, to have manifest the kingdom of Christ for whom it was necessary first to be judged and then to judge), when he was crucified and those who hoped in him had lost hope for his resurrection, rising from the dead, he found two of them conversing with each other in hopelessness and talking over what had happened,

2. Cf. Mt 6.10; Lk 11.2.   3. Cf. Jn 1.3.

4. Cf. Jn 5.22 and 27; *Tractate* 19.5, 16 and 18–19; 21.11–15; and 23.13 and 15.

5. Cf. 1 Cor 15.24.   6. Cf. Mt 25.34.

with moaning;[7] and appearing to them as a stranger, since their eyes were restrained that he might not be recognized by them, he joined in their discussion.

(2) But they, telling him what they were conversing about, said that that prophet, great in deeds and words, had been killed by the chief priests. "And we," they say, "were hoping that it was he who would redeem Israel."[8] You were hoping rightly, you were hoping for the truth; in him is the redemption of Israel. But why do you make haste? You want to take hold by force. For the following also declares this meaning to us, namely, when the apostles asked him about the end, they said to him, "Is it that you will be presented at this time, and when will be the kingdom of Israel?"[9] For they desired it to be right then, they wanted it right then: this is to want to take hold of him and make him king.

(3) But he says to the disciples, because still he alone was going to ascend, "It is not," he says, "for you to know the times or moments which the Father has put in his own power; but you shall receive power from on high, the Holy Spirit coming upon you, and you will be witnesses for me in Jerusalem and in all Judea and Samaria, and even to the ends of the earth."[10] You want me to show my kingdom now, first I shall gather what I am to show. You love height, and you will acquire height; but follow me through lowliness.

(4) So also it was foretold about him, "And a congregation of peoples will surround you, and for its sake return on high,"[11] that is, that a congregation of peoples may surround you, that you may gather many, return on high. He did so; he fed and ascended.

4. But why was it said, "He fled"? For truly, if he were unwilling, he would not be held; if he were unwilling, he would not be taken hold of by force; and if he were unwilling, neither would he be recognized. For, that you may know that

7. Cf. Lk 24.13–35.   8. Cf. Lk 24.21.
9. Cf. Acts 1.6.
10. Cf. Acts 1.7–8. The words "or moments" in Augustine's text are added by several editors but are not found in the codices.
11. Cf. Ps 7.8.

this was done mystically, not out of necessity but out of a meaningful plan, now in what follows you will see that he appeared to the same crowds which sought him, and speaking with them, said many things to them, discussed many things about the heavenly bread. Was he not discussing about the bread with the very men from whom he had fled away that he might not be held? Could he not, therefore, have acted even then in such a way that he would not be seized by them, just as afterwards when he was speaking with them? Therefore he signified something by fleeing.

(2) What does it mean, "He fled"? His height could not be understood. For whatever you do not understand, you say, "It escaped[12] me." Therefore, "He fled again into the mountain, himself alone," the firstborn of the dead,[13] ascending above all the heavens,[14] and interceding for us.[15]

5. Meanwhile, when he was situated above, alone, the high priest who entered the interior of the veil while the people were outside (for that priest in the Old Law who did this once a year signified him),[16] therefore when he was situated above, what were the disciples experiencing on the boat? For, when he was on high, that boat prefigured the Church. If we do not, first of all, understand in the Church this thing which that boat experienced, those events were not significant but simply transient; but if we see the truth of those significations expressed in the Church, it is clear that the deeds of Christ are types of expressions.

(2) [The gospel] says, "But when evening was come, his disciples went down to the sea. And when they had gone up into a boat, they went across the sea to Capharnaum." [The text] quickly said that that was completed which happened afterwards. "They went across the sea to Capharnaum." And [the text] goes back and explains how they went, that they crossed,

12. In Latin the form *fugit* can mean "flees," "fled," "escapes," or "escaped" (especially in the sense "it escapes" or "escaped" me). This extension of meaning does not exist in the English word "flee" and this obscures Augustine's thought.

13. Cf. Col 1.18.   14. Cf. Eph 4.10.
15. Cf. Rom 8.34.
16. Cf. Heb 9.1–12, esp. 7 and 12.

sailing over the lake. And while they were sailing to that place where it already said that they had come, recapitulating, it explains what happened: "It was now dark, and Jesus had not come to them." Rightly was it dark because light had not come. "It was now dark and Jesus had not come to them."

(3) The closer the end of the world approaches, errors grow, terrors become frequent, iniquity grows, unbelief grows.[17] And consequently the light, which is sufficiently and clearly shown in John the Evangelist himself to be love, so that he says, "He who hates his brother is in darkness,"[18] is very often extinguished. This darkness of brotherly hatreds grows, it grows daily, and Jesus has not yet come. What makes it clear that it grows? "Because iniquity will abound, the love of many will grow cold."[19] The darkness grows and Jesus has not yet come.

(4) When darkness grows, when love grows cold, when iniquity abounds, these are the waves harrying the boat. Storms and waves are the shouts of slanderers. From these love grows cold, from these the waves are enlarged and the ship is harried.

6. "With a strong wind blowing, the sea arose." Darkness was increasing, comprehension was lessening, iniquity was growing. "But when they had, therefore, rowed about twenty-five or thirty stadia."[20] Meanwhile they were proceeding, they

17. This sentence contains two rhymes in Latin: *errores* and *terrores* and *iniquitas* and *infidelitas*; but to translate the latter pair as "iniquity" and "infidelity," as Gibb and Browne do, misleads since "infidelity" is ordinarily thought of as moral or marital disloyalty rather than unbelief.

18. Cf. 1 Jn 2.11.

19. Cf. Mt 24.12. Two observations need to be made here. First there is another rhyme in this verse, *iniquitas* and *caritas*, "iniquity" and "charity"; but "love" better suits the context in contemporary English than "charity" (see *Tractate* 3.5, note 20). Secondly the *Vulgate* has *abundavit*, "has abounded." This does not involve the *v* past tense, *b* future tense confusion as noted in *Tractate* 19.4, note 3, because the Greek original has the future and Greek allows no possibility of such a tense confusion. Notice that in the next section Augustine uses the perfect tense, but in an application, not a quotation of the text.

20. A *stadium* is 625 Roman feet, a bit less than an eighth of a mile; hence both Douay's "twenty-five to thirty furlongs" and NAB's "three or four miles" are good approximations of the distance rowed.

were moving forward; and those winds and storms and waves and darkness did not cause the boat either not to move forward or to break up and sink, but it was going amid all those troubles. For because iniquity has abounded and the love of many grows cold, the waves grow, the darkness is increased, the wind rages; but nevertheless, the ship proceeds. For "who shall persevere to the end, he shall be saved."[21]

(2) Nor is that number of stadia to be disregarded. For what was said could not, in fact, signify nothing: "When they had rowed twenty-five or thirty stadia, then Jesus came to them." "Twenty-five" would be enough, "thirty" would be enough, especially since it was a matter of estimation, not affirmation. For in an estimation would the truth be jeopardized if one were to say almost thirty stadia or almost twenty-five stadia? But from twenty-five he made thirty. Let us examine the number twenty-five. Whence is it established, whence does it come? From the fives. That number five pertains to the Law. There are five books of Moses, there are five porticoes containing the sick, and the five loaves feeding five thousand men.[22] Therefore the number twenty-five signifies the Law; for five by five, that is, five times five, makes twenty-five, the square number of five. But before the gospel came to this Law, perfection was lacking. But perfection is contained in the number six.[23] For that reason God "perfected" the world in six days.[24] And the fives are multiplied by six, that the Law may be fulfilled by the gospel, that six times five may be thirty.

(3) Therefore, to them who fulfill the Law, Jesus came. And he came, how? Treading on the waves, having all the swellings of the world under his feet, pressing upon all the heights of [this] age.[25] This is done as long as [time] is added to time and as long as the life of [this] age continues. Tribulations are

---

21. Cf. Mt 10.22 and 24.13.   22. Cf. Jn 5.2–3, 6.9–10.
23. See *DDQ* 57.3.   24. Cf. Gn 1.31–2.2.
25. Augustine in these sermons distinguishes between *mundus,* the physical world and various groupings of people who live therein, and *saeculum,* one of the six subdivisions of human history as given in *Tractates* 9.6 and 15.9. Hence this age is the sixth, from John the Baptist through the present until the end of the world.

increased in this world, evils are increased, afflictions are increased, all these things are piled up; Jesus crosses over, treading upon the waves.

7. And yet, so great are the tribulations that even they themselves who have believed in Jesus and who try to persevere even to the end fear that they may fail; while Christ treads upon the waves and presses down the ambitions and highnesses of [this] age, the Christian fears. Were not these things foretold to him? Rightly too, when Jesus was walking on the waves, "they were frightened," just as Christians, although they have hope in a future age, when they see the highnesses of this age being pressed down, are very often troubled about the affliction of human affairs.[26] They open the gospel, they open the Scriptures; and there they find all these things predicted, because the Lord does this.

(2) He presses down the heights of [this] age that he may be glorified by the lowly. And about their highness it was predicted, "You shall destroy very strong cities"[27] and "The swords of the enemy have failed unto the end, and their cities you have destroyed."[28] Why, then, do you fear, Christians? Christ says, "It is I, do not be afraid." Why do you tremble at these things? Why are you afraid? I have predicted these things, I do them, they must needs happen. "'It is I, do not be afraid.' They wanted, therefore, to take him into the ship," recognizing him and rejoicing, having become secure. "And immediately the ship was at the land to which they were going." An end is made at the land, from the watery to the solid, from the troubled to the firm, from trip to destination.

26. Berrouard, *Homélies XVII–XXXIII*, 440 sees here the dismay felt by Christians at the fall of Rome to Alaric and the Goths.

27. An unclear scriptural reference. Berrouard, *Homélies XVII–XXXIII*, 441 suggests perhaps Ecclus (Sir) 28.14 (LXX) or Mi 5.11 (NAB 5.10).

28. Cf. Ps 9.7. *Framea* in classical Latin was "a spear" of a Germanic type, but in Christian Latin the word was used for the Greek *rhomphaía*, originally a large Thracian sword, then commonly, "a sword." In *En in Ps* 9.8 on this verse Augustine equates *framea* with the Latin *gladius;* so, too, when he writes on Ps 21.21 in *En in Ps* 21.2.21, *Sermo* 312.4 (PL 38.1421) and *Epistula* 140.16.41 (PL 33.555; CSEL 44.189–190; and FOTC 20.92). However, in *En in Ps* 149.12 when he writes on Ps 149.6 he defines *framea* as *spatha* or *machaera* because here it has two edges and the *gladius* has only one; still it is "a sword" and not "a spear." See Blaise, 363, and TLL 6.1.1239–1240.

8. "The next day, the crowd which stood on the other side of the sea" (from which they had come) "saw that there was no boat there but one and that he had not entered into the ship with his disciples, but that his disciples had gone away alone. But other ships came in from Tiberias near the place where they ate the bread when the Lord gave thanks.[29] When, therefore, the crowd saw that Jesus was not there, nor his disciples, they embarked in the boats and went to Capharnaum, seeking Jesus." Yet an inkling of so great a miracle had worked its way into their [thoughts]. For they saw that the disciples had embarked in a boat alone and that there was no other boat there. But boats also came from there near that place where they ate the bread, in which crowds followed him. Therefore, he had not embarked with his disciples; there was no other boat there.

(2) How did Jesus suddenly come to be across the sea unless he walked upon the sea, to show a miracle?

9. "And when the crowds found him." Look, he presents himself to the crowds by which he had feared that he was to be seized by force and [from which] he had fled to the mountain. Most assuredly he affirms to us and conveys that all these things have been said in mystery and have been done in grand symbolism[30] that they might signify something.

(2) Look, that is he who had fled the crowds to the mountain; does he not speak with these very crowds? Now let them hold him, now let them make him king. "And when they had found him on the other side of the sea, they said to him, 'Rabbi, when did you come here?'"

10. After the symbolic mystery of the miracle he also delivers a discourse, that, if it is possible, they who have been fed may be fed, and that he may, with his discourses, fill the minds of those whose bellies he had filled with bread; but

29. Some manuscripts read, "where they, giving thanks to the Lord, ate the bread." Willems, CCL 36.252, accepts this reading; the translated text is better attested.

30. *in magno sacramento*. The word *sacramentum* is rich in connotations as Blaise, 729–731, shows. Those connotations indicating mystery, symbolism, hidden signification, are very common in Augustine.

only if they grasp it. And if they do not grasp it, let what they do not grasp be taken up that the fragments may not be wasted. Let him speak, therefore, and let us listen.

(2) "Jesus answered and said, 'Amen, amen, I say to you, you seek me, not because you have seen signs, but because you have eaten of my loaves.'" You seek me on account of the flesh, not on account of the spirit. How many seek Jesus only that he may do them good temporally! One man has a business transaction; he seeks the intervention of the clergy.[31] Another is hardpressed by one more powerful; he flees to the Church.[32] Another wishes an intervention on his behalf with him with whom he has little influence. So one, so another. Today the Church is filled with such men. Jesus is scarcely sought for Jesus' sake. "You seek me, not because you have seen signs, but because you have eaten of my loaves. Do not labor for the food that perishes, but for that which endures unto life everlasting." You seek me for the sake of something else; seek me for my sake. For he suggests that he is himself that food; and this is clear in the following words: "which the Son of man will give you."

(3) You were waiting, I believe, to eat loaves again, to recline again, to be crammed full again. But he had said, "not for the food that perishes, but for that which endures unto life everlasting," just as had been said to that Samaritan woman,[33] "If you did know who asks of you to drink, you, perhaps, would have asked of him, and he would give you living water." When she said, "how can you, since you do not have a bucket and the well is deep?" Jesus answered the Sa-

31. Bishops had the right to provide arbitration and legal aid to citizens in civil cases; Augustine regularly did so and found them a terrible burden, distracting from spiritual duties but required nonetheless. See F. Van der Meer, *Augustine the Bishop*, tr. B. Battershaw and G. Lamb (New York, 1961), 255–270. See also Possidius, *Vita*, 19, *Verba Seniorum* 4 (Alba, 1955) 110–115; Berrouard, *Homélies XVII–XXXIII*, 789; P. Brown, *Augustine of Hippo* (Berkeley, 1969), 195–196; and, for an extensive account, J. Gaudemet, *L'Église dans l'Empire romain (iv–v siècles)* (Paris, 1958), 229–282.

32. Augustine was a stout defender of the Church as a place of asylum. See *DCD* 1.1–7; Van der Meer, 263–264; Berrouard, *Homélies XVII–XXXIII*, 446; and Gaudemet, 282–287.

33. Cf. Jn 4.5–15 and *Tractate* 15.12–16.

maritan woman, "If you did know who asks of you to drink, you would have asked of him, and he would give you water, and he who drinks of it will thirst no more, but he who drinks of this water will thirst again." And she rejoiced and wanted to receive it as if she, who was worn out with the labor of drawing water, would not suffer thirst of the body; and so, among conversations of this sort, he comes to a spiritual drink. It is completely in this way here also.

11. Therefore "not for" this "food which perishes, but for that which endures unto life everlasting which the Son of man will give you. For upon him God the Father has set his seal." Do not receive this Son of man just like other sons of men about whom it has been said, "But the sons of men will hope in the protection of your wings."[34] This Son of man [has been] set apart by a certain grace of the Spirit; and, Son of man according to the flesh taken from the number of men, he is the Son of man. This Son of man is also the Son of God; this man is even God. In another place, questioning his disciples, he says, "'Who do people say that the Son of man is?' And they said, 'Some John; others, Elias; others, Jeremiah, or one of the prophets.' And he said, 'But who do you say that I am?' Peter answered, 'You are Christ, the Son of the living God.'"[35] He said that he was the Son of man, and Peter said that he was the Son of the living God.

(2) Very aptly did he mention what he had shown [himself to be] in mercy; Peter mentioned that he continued to be in his glory. The Word of God shows his lowliness; the man acknowledges the glory of his Lord. And in very truth, brothers, I think it is just; he has humbled himself for us, let us glorify him. For he is the Son of man not for himself, but for us. Therefore he was the Son of man in that way when "the Word was made flesh, and dwelt among us."[36] For thus "upon him God the Father has set his seal."

(3) What is to set the seal except to put some [mark] exclusively one's own? For to set the seal is this, to apply some

34. Cf. Ps 35.8.
35. Cf. Mt 16.13–16; Mk 8.27–30; Lk 9.18–20.
36. Cf. Jn 1.14.

[mark] which would not be confounded with others. To set
the seal is to put a sign on a thing. You put a sign on something
or other; you put the sign precisely so that it may not be
confused with other things and can be recognized by you.
Therefore, "upon him the Father has set his seal." What does
"has set his seal" mean? He has given him something exclusively his own that he might not be compared to other men.
And so it was said about him, "God, your God, has anointed
you with the oil of gladness above your fellows."[37] Therefore
what is to set the seal? To have him set aside, that is, "above
your fellows." And so, he says, do not despise me because I
am the Son of man; and ask of me "not the food that perishes,
but that which endures unto life everlasting." For I am the
Son of man in such a way that I am not one of you; I am the
Son of man in such a way that God the Father has set his seal
upon me.

(4) What is "has set his seal"? He has given me something
exclusively my own whereby I might not be confused with the
human race, but the human race might be freed by me.

12. "They said, therefore, to him, 'What shall we do that
we may work the works of God?'" He had said to them, "Do
not labor for the food that perishes, but for that which endures unto life everlasting." "What shall we do?" they say. By
attending to what will we be able to fulfill this instruction?
"Jesus answered and said to them, 'This is the work of God,
that you believe in him whom he has sent.'" This, then, is to
eat "not the food that perishes, but that which endures unto
life everlasting." Why do you make ready your teeth and stomach? Believe, and you have eaten. Faith is, indeed, distinguished from works, as the Apostle says, "that a man is
justified by faith without works."[38] And there are works which
seem to be good, because they are not referred to that end
from which they are good; "for the end of the Law is Christ,
unto justice to everyone who believes."[39]

(2) Therefore, he did not wish to separate faith from work,

37. Cf. Ps 44.8.   38. Cf. Rom 3.28.
39. Rom 10.4.

but he said that faith itself is a work. For this is the faith which works by love.[40] He did not say, "This is your work," but "This is the work of God, that you believe in him whom he has sent," so that he who takes glory may take glory in the Lord.[41] Therefore, because he invited them to faith, they were still seeking signs in which they might believe. See if the Jews do not seek signs.[42] Therefore they said to him, "What sign, then, do you do, that we may see and believe you? What work do you do?" Was it not enough that they were fed from five loaves? They knew this, to be sure, but they preferred manna from heaven to this food. But the Lord Jesus said that he was such as was preferred to Moses. For Moses did not dare to say of himself that he would give "not food which perishes, but that which endures unto life everlasting."

(3) He promised something more than Moses. Through Moses, in fact, a kingdom was promised, a land flowing with milk and honey, temporal peace, an abundance of children, health of body, and all the rest, temporal things indeed, yet spiritual figuratively, because they were promised to the old man in the Old Testament.[43] Therefore, they noted the promises through Moses and they noted the promises through Christ. The one promised a full stomach on earth, but from the food that perishes; this one promised "not the food that perishes, but that which endures unto life everlasting." They noted that he promised more, but they did not yet, as it were, see him doing greater things. And so they noted what sort of things Moses had done and they wanted still greater things to be done by him who promised such great things. "What," they say, "do you do that we may believe you?"

(4) And, that you may know that they were comparing those miracles to this miracle and thus were judging these miracles which Jesus was doing as lesser, they say, "Our fathers ate manna in the desert." What is manna? Perhaps you despise it. "As it was written, 'Manna he gave them to eat.'" Through

40. Cf. Gal 5.6.
41. Cf. 1 Cor 1.31, quoting loosely Jer 9.23; also 2 Cor 10.17.
42. Cf. 1 Cor 1.22.
43. Cf. Eph 4.22, Col 3.9–11, and, perhaps, 2 Cor 5.17.

Moses our fathers received bread from heaven, and it was not said to them by Moses, "Do not labor for the food that perishes." You promise "not the food that perishes, but that which endures unto life everlasting," and you do not perform such works as Moses. He did not give barley loaves, but he gave manna from heaven.

13. "Then Jesus said to them, 'Amen, amen, I say to you, Moses did not give you the bread from heaven, but my Father gave you the bread from heaven. For the true bread is that which comes down from heaven and gives life to the world.'" Therefore, that is the true bread which gives life to the world, and this is the food about which I spoke a little before: "Do not labor for the food which perishes, but for that which endures unto life everlasting." Therefore that manna signified this and all those signs were signs of me. You loved the signs of me; do you despise him who was signified? Therefore, Moses did not give bread from heaven; God gives bread.

(2) But what bread? Manna, perhaps? No, but the bread which manna signified, namely, the Lord Jesus himself. "'My Father gives you the true bread. For the bread of God is that which comes down from heaven and gives life to the world.' They said, therefore, to him, 'Lord, give us always this bread.'" Just as that Samaritan woman to whom it was said, "He who drinks of this water will never thirst," and she, immediately understanding it according to the body and yet wishing to be free from her need, said, "Give me, sir, of this water,"[44] so, too, these said, "Lord, give us this bread," which may restore us and not run short.[45]

14. "But Jesus said to them, 'I am the bread of life. He who comes to me shall not hunger, and he who believes in me shall never thirst.'" "He who comes to me" means the same as "and he who believes in me." And his words "shall not hunger" must be understood as "shall never thirst." For there is signified by both that eternal satiety where there is no want. You are longing for bread from heaven; you have it before you and you

44. Cf. Jn 4.13–15.
45. My attempt to translate a rhyming word play, *reficiat nec deficiat.*

do not eat. "But I said to you that you also have seen me and you have not believed." But I have not therefore lost the people. For has your unbelief put an end to the faithfulness of God?[46] For see what follows: "All that the Father gives to me shall come to me, and him who comes to me I will not cast out."

(2) What sort of thing is that "within" from which there is no going out? A great inner chamber, a sweet secret place. O secret place without weariness, without the bitterness of evil thoughts, without the hindrance of temptations and sorrows! Is it not that secret place where he will enter to whom the Lord will say, to a servant having deserved well, "Enter into the joy of your Lord."?[47]

15. "And him who comes to me I will not cast out, because I have come down from heaven, not to do my own will, but the will of him who sent me." And will you, therefore, not cast out him who shall come to you for the very reason that you have come down from heaven, not to do your own will but the will of him who sent you? A great mystery! I beg of you, let us knock together.[48] There may come out to us something which may feed us, according to that which has delighted us.

(2) That is a great and sweet secret, "Him who shall come to me." Consider; consider, and ponder, "Him who shall come to me I will not cast out." Therefore he says, "Him who shall come I will not cast out." Why? "For I have come down from heaven, not to do my own will, but the will of him who sent me." Is this, then, the cause why you would not cast out him who comes to you because you have come down from heaven to do, not your own will, but the will of him who sent you? It is. Why do we ask whether it is? It is; he himself says it. For, it is not right for us to suspect something other than he says: "Him who comes to me, I will not cast out." And as if you were to ask why, "Because I have not come to do my own will but the will of him who sent me."

(3) I am afraid that the soul has gone away from God be-

---

46. Cf. Rom 3.3.   47. Cf. Mt 25.21 and 23.
48. Cf. Mt 7.7; Lk 11.9.

cause it was proud; rather I have no doubt about it. For it was written, "The beginning of all sin is pride" and "The beginning of the pride of man is to fall off from God."[49] It has been written, it is sure, it is true. Then, what is said about a proud mortal, girded in the clothes of the flesh, weighted down with the weight of a corruptible body,[50] and yet extolling himself, and forgetting with what garment he has been clothed,[51] what does Scripture say to him? "Why is earth and ashes proud?" Why is it proud? Let [Scripture] say why it is proud. "Because while he lives he has cast away his inmost parts."[52]

(4) What does "has cast away" mean except has cast far off? This is to go out. For to enter within is to seek the inmost parts; to cast out the inmost parts is to go out. The proud man casts out the inmost parts; the humble man seeks the inmost parts. If we are cast out by pride, we return by humility.

16. The source of all diseases is pride because the source of all sins is pride. When a physician clears up an illness, if he should heal what occurred through some cause and not heal the cause itself through which it occurred, the disease seems to be cured for a time, but since the cause remains, it strikes again. For example—let me express this more clearly— a fluid in the body produces a mange or sores; a high fever and no small pain develop in the body. Some medicines are employed which curb the mange and ease that burning of the sore; they are applied and bring results. You see a man who was covered with sores and mange healed; but because that fluid was not eliminated, the sore comes back again. The physician, knowing this, gets rid of the fluid, removes the cause, and there will be no sores.

(2) From what source does wickedness abound? From pride. Heal pride and there will be no wickedness. Therefore, in

---

49. Cf. Ecclus (Sir) 10.15 and 14 (LXX) (NAB 10.13 and 12).
50. Cf. Wis 9.15.
51. Berrouard, *Homélies XVII–XXXIII*, 463 cites Jb 10.11 as a scriptural reference here.
52. Cf. Ecclus (Sir) 10.9 (LXX).

order that the cause of all diseases, that is, pride, might be healed, he came down and the Son of God became humble. Why are you proud, man? God became humble for your sake. Perhaps, it would shame you to imitate a humble man; at least imitate a humble God. The Son of God came in [the form of] a man, and became humble; you are instructed to be humble, you are not instructed to become a brute animal instead of a man. That God became a man; you, man, know that you are a man. All your humility is this, that you know yourself.

(3) Therefore, because God teaches humility, he said, "I have not come to do my will, but the will of him who sent me." For this is a recommendation of humility. Pride, of course, does its own will; humility does the will of God. And so, "Him who comes to me I will not cast out." Why? "For I have not come to do my will, but the will of him who sent me." I have come, a humble man; I have come to teach humility; I have come, a master of humility. He who comes to me is embodied in me; he who comes to me becomes humble. He who adheres to me will be humble because he does not his own will, but God's. And, therefore, he will not be cast out because, when he was proud, he was cast out.

17. See that those interior things are commended in the Psalm: "But the children of men will hope in the protection of your wings."[53] See what it is to go within; see what it is to flee for safety to his protection. See what it is also to pass under the whippings of the Father; for he scourges every son whom he receives.[54] "But the children of men will hope under the covering of your wings."[55] And what is within? "They will be inebriated by the richness of your house." When you will have sent them within, entering into the joy of their Lord, "they will be inebriated by the richness of your house, and you will give them to drink from the torrent of your pleasure. For with you is the fountain of life."[56] Not without, outside you,

53. Cf. Ps 35.8.   54. Cf. Heb 12.6 and Prv 3.12.
55. Ps 35.8. Here Augustine uses *in tegmine,* the wording of the *Vulgate,* whereas at the beginning of the section and in section 11, he had *in protectione.* In *En in Ps* 35.12 he has *in tegmine,* although there is a less acceptable reading there, *in protectione(m).*
56. Cf. Ps 35.9–10.

but within, with you, there is the fountain of life. "And in your light we shall see light. Extend your mercy to them that know you, and your justice to these who are of upright heart."[57] They who follow the will of their Lord, not seeking the things that are their own, but those of the Lord, Jesus Christ,[58] these are upright of heart; their feet are not moved. For "the God of Israel is good to the upright of heart.

(2) But my feet," he said, "were almost moved." Why? "For I was envious of sinners, seeing the peace of sinners."[59] Therefore, to whom is God good except to the upright of heart? For God displeased me with my contorted heart. Why did he displease? Because he gave good fortune to the evil; and so my feet wavered for me, as if I had served God without reason. And so my feet were almost moved because I was not upright of heart. How, then, is one upright of heart? By following the will of God. One man is fortunate; another labors; one man lives evilly and is fortunate, another lives justly and labors. Let him who lives justly and labors not be indignant; he has within what the fortunate man has not. Therefore, let him not be sad, let him not be vexed, let him not fail. That fortunate man has gold in his trunk; this one has God in his conscience. Now compare gold and God, trunk and conscience. The one has that which perishes and has it there from where it perishes; the other has God who cannot perish and has him there from where he cannot be taken away, but only if he should be upright of heart; for then he enters and does not go out.

(3) And so what was [the Psalmist] saying? "For with you is the fountain of life," not with us. Therefore, we ought to enter that we may live, and we ought not, as it were, provide for ourselves that we may perish nor want to be sated from our own resources that we may wither, but [we ought] to put our mouth to the fountain itself where water fails not. For Adam wanted to live by his own counsel and he fell through him who had fallen before through pride, who offered the cup of

57. Cf. Ps 35.10–11.   58. Cf. Phil 2.21.
59. Cf. Ps 72.1–3.

his own pride for him to drink. Therefore, because "with you is the fountain of life and in your light, we shall see light," let us drink within, let us see within.

(4) For why was there a going out of there? Hear why: "Let not the foot of the proud man come to me." Therefore, he went out to whom the foot of the proud man came. Show that, therefore, he went out. "And let the hands of sinners not move me,"[60] on account of the foot of pride. Why do you say this? "There all who work evil have fallen." Where have they fallen? In pride itself. "They have been driven out and could not stand."[61] Therefore if pride drove out those who could not stand, humility sends within those who can stand forever. For he who said, "The bones which have been humbled shall rejoice," first said, "To my hearing you will give joy and gladness."[62]

(5) What does "to my hearing" mean? By hearing you, I am fortunate; from your voice I am fortunate. By drinking within, I am fortunate. And so I do not fall. And so "the bones which have been humbled shall rejoice." And so "the friend of the bridegroom stands and hears him."[63] He stands, therefore, because he hears. He drinks from the interior fountain, and so he stands. Those who did not wish to drink from the interior, "There they have fallen, they have been driven out, and they could not stand."

18. And so the teacher of humility came, not to do his own will, but the will of him who sent him. Let us come to him, let us enter to him, let us be embodied in him that neither may we do our own will, but the will of God. And he will not cast us out, because we are his members, because he wanted to be our head, by teaching us humility. Finally, hear him addressing the assembly: "Come to me, you who labor and are burdened. Take up my yoke upon you, and learn from me, because I am meek and humble of heart."[64] And when you have learned this, "you will find rest for your souls,"[65] wherefore you are not to be cast out, "for I have come down from

---

60. Cf. Ps 35.12.
62. Cf. Ps 50.10.
64. Cf. Mt 11.28–29.

61. Cf. Ps 35.13.
63. Cf. Jn 3.29.
65. Cf. Mt 11.29.

heaven, not to do my own will, but the will of him who sent me." I teach humility; only the humble man comes to me. Only pride sends out; how does he go out who keeps humility and does not slip away from truth?

(2) As much as could be said about the hidden meaning has been said, brothers; for here the meaning is quite hidden, and I do not know whether it has been drawn forth and chiseled out by me with suitable words: why he would not cast out him who comes to him, for the very reason that he did not come to do his own will, but the will of him who sent him.

19. He said, "Now this is the will of him who sent me, the Father, that of all that he has given me, I should lose nothing of it." The one who keeps humility was given to him; he receives this one. But he who does not keep humility is far from the master of humility. "That of all that he has given me, I should lose nothing of it." "So it is not the will in the eyes of your Father that one of these little ones should perish."[66] Of the proud [one] can perish, but of the little ones none perishes; for "unless you are like this little one, you will not enter into the kingdom of heaven."[67] "Of all that the Father has given me, I should lose nothing of it; but I shall raise it up on the last day."

(2) See how also he delineates that twofold resurrection.[68] "He who comes to me," having become humble in my members, now rises; but also "I shall raise him up on the last day" according to the flesh. "For this is the will of my Father who sent me, that everyone who sees the Son, and believes in him, may have life everlasting; and I shall raise him up on the last day." Earlier he said, "He who hears my word and believes him who sent me,"[69] but now "He who sees the Son and believes in him." He did not say, "sees the Son and believes in the Father." For to believe in the Son is the same as to believe in the Father. For "as the Father has life in himself, so he has given to the Son also to have life in himself."[70]

---

66. Cf. Mt 18.14.
67. Cf. Mt 18.3–4.
68. Cf. *Tractates* 19.8–18; 23.12–15.
69. Cf. Jn 5.24.
70. Jn 5.26.

(3) "That everyone who sees the Son and believes in him shall have life everlasting," by believing and passing to life, as by that first resurrection. And because [that] is not the only [resurrection], he says, "And I shall raise him up on the last day."

TRACTATE 26

On John 6.41–59

HEN, AS WE HEARD in the gospel when it was read, our Lord, Jesus Christ, had said that he was the bread which came down from heaven, the Jews murmured and said, "Is this not Jesus, the son of Joseph, whose father and mother we know? How then does he say, 'I have come down from heaven?'" These men were far from the bread of heaven and they did not know how to hunger for it. They had weak jaws of the heart; they were deaf with open ears; they saw and stood blind. For indeed this bread searches out the hunger of the interior man; wherefore in another place he says, "Blessed are they who hunger and thirst for justice, for they shall have their fill."[1]

(2) But the Apostle Paul says that Christ is justice for us.[2] And, by reason of this, he who hungers for this bread, let him hunger for justice, but the justice which comes down from heaven, the justice which God gives, not which man makes for himself. For if man did not make justice for himself, the same Apostle would not say of the Jews, "for, not knowing of the justice of God, and seeking to establish their own, they have not submitted to the justice of God."[3] Hence, there were those who did not understand the bread coming down from heaven, because, sated with their own justice, they did not hunger for the justice of God. What does this mean, the justice of God and the justice of man? Here [that] is called the justice of God, not by which God is just but which God gives to man that man may be just through God. But what

1. Mt 5.6. 2. Cf. 1 Cor 1.30.
3. Rom 10.3.

was their justice? [That] by which they put confidence in their
own strength and spoke of themselves as if they were the ful-
fillers of the Law from their own power.

(3) But no one fulfills the Law except he whom grace, that
is, the bread which comes down from heaven, has helped.
For, as the Apostle says briefly, "Love is the fulfillment of the
Law,"[4] not love of money, but of God, not love of earth, not
of heaven, but of him who made heaven and earth.[5] Whence
is this love for man? Let us hear him. He says, "The love of
God is poured forth in our hearts by the Holy Spirit who has
been given to us."[6]

(4) Therefore, the Lord, who was about to give the Holy
Spirit, said that he himself was the bread which has come
down from heaven, encouraging us to believe in him. For to
believe in him is to eat the living bread. He who believes eats;
he is nourished[7] invisibly because he is reborn invisibly. He is
an infant within; he is new within. Where he is renewed,
there he is sated.

2. What, then, did Jesus answer such murmurers? "Do not
murmur among yourselves." As if saying, "I know why you
do not hunger and do not understand nor seek this bread."
"Do not murmur among yourselves. No one can come to me
unless the Father who sent me draw him." A great commendation of grace! No one comes unless drawn!

(2) Whom he draws and whom he does not draw, why he
draws one and does not draw another, do not wish to judge
unless you wish to be wrong. Receive it once, and understand.

---

4. Cf. Rom 13.10.   5. Cf. Ps 120.2; 123.8.
6. Cf. Rom 5.5.

7. The Latin word here is *saginare* which in secular Latin meant "to fatten
animals for eating" or "to feed lavishly." The Christian Latin meaning of "to
nourish" or "to fortify" occurs as early as Tertullian and is used in several
senses. Its use in connection with the Eucharist is found in Tertullian, *De
Resurrectione Mortuorum* 8.3 (CCL 2.931), as well as by Augustine here and in
Tractate 27.12 and in *Sermo* 112.5.5 (PL 38.645) where he refers to Jn 6.41
and indicates spiritual nourishment through the Eucharist. It is also used by
Cyprian, *Epistula* 31.1 (PL 4.298; CSEL 2.557; and ACW 44.33) for nourish-
ment through a written letter and by Augustine, *Epistula ad Catholicos* 5.10
(PL 43.398; CSEL 52.241–242; BA 28.503ff.) for nourishment through the
Gospels. See Blaise, 733, and Berrouard, *Homélies XVII–XXXIII*, 484.

Are you not yet drawn? Pray to be drawn. What are we saying here, brothers? If we are drawn to Christ, therefore, we believe unwillingly. Therefore force is applied, will is not aroused. One can enter the Church unwillingly, one can approach the altar unwillingly, one can receive the sacrament unwillingly; no one can believe except willingly. If one believed with the body, it would occur in those unwilling; but one does not believe with the body. Hear the Apostle, "With the heart a man believes unto justice." And what follows? "But with the mouth confession is made unto salvation."[8]

(3) From the root of the heart this confession[9] rises. Sometimes you hear a man confessing, and you do not know him as a believer. But you ought not to call him confessing whom you judge not believing. For this is to confess, to say what you have in your heart; but if you have one thing in your heart [and] you say another, you speak, you do not confess. Therefore, since a man believes in Christ with his heart, a thing which no one, of course, does unwillingly, but he who is drawn seems as though he is being compelled against his will, how do we solve this question, "No one comes to me unless the Father who sent me draws him"?

3. If he is drawn, someone says, he comes unwillingly. If he comes unwillingly, he does not believe; if he does not believe, he does not come. For, we do not run to Christ by walking, but by believing; nor do we approach by movement of the body but by the will of the heart. And so, that woman who touched the fringe of his garment touched him more than the crowd which pressed upon him.[10] For that reason the Lord said, "Who touched me?" And the disciples in astonishment said, "The crowds press upon you and do you say, 'Who touched me?'" And he repeated, "Someone has touched me." She touches, the crowd presses. What does "touched" mean except believed?

(2) Wherefore also after his resurrection to that woman who wished to fall at his feet he said, "Do not touch me, for

8. Rom 10.10.
9. I.e., profession of faith, not confession of sins.
10. Cf. Lk 8.42–46.

I have not yet ascended to my Father."[11] You think that only this which you see is I; do not touch me. What is it? You think that only this which I appear to you is I; do not so believe, that is, "Do not touch me, for I have not yet ascended to my Father." To you, I have not ascended; for I have never withdrawn from there. She did not touch him standing on earth; how would she touch him ascending to the Father?

(3) So nevertheless, so he wanted himself to be touched; so he is touched by those by whom he is well touched; he, ascending to the Father, remaining with the Father, equal to the Father.

4. In accordance with that [is] also [the statement] here, if you direct your mind to it, "no one comes to me except whom the Father draws." Do not think that you are drawn unwillingly; the mind is drawn also by love. Neither ought we to fear that we may, perhaps, in this evangelistic word of the Holy Scriptures be rebuked by men who examine the words and are far removed from understanding the especially divine things, and it may be said to us, "How do I believe by will, if I am drawn?"

(2) I say, it is not enough by will, you are also drawn by pleasure. What does it mean to be drawn by pleasure? "Take delight in the Lord, and he will grant you your heart's requests."[12] There is a certain pleasure of the heart to which that heavenly [bread] is sweet bread. Moreover, if it was allowed to a poet to say, "His own pleasure draws each man,"[13] not need but pleasure, not obligation but delight, how much more forcefully ought we to say that a man is drawn to Christ who delights in truth, delights in happiness, delights in justice, delights in eternal life—and all this is Christ? Or is it rather that the senses of the body have their own pleasures and the intellect is without its own pleasures? If the intellect does not have its own pleasures, how is it said, "But the children of men will hope under the covering of your wings; they

---

11. Cf. Jn 20.17.　　　　12. Ps 36.4.

13. Vergil, *Ecl.* 2.65; see H. Hagendahl, *Augustine and the Latin Classics* (Stockholm, 1967), 459–460.

will be inebriated by the richness of your house, and you will give them to drink of the torrent of your pleasure."

(3) "For with you is the fountain of life and in your light we shall see light"?[14] Give me one who loves, and he feels what I am saying. Give me one who desires, give me one who hungers, give me one traveling and thirsting in this solitude and sighing for the fountain of an eternal homeland, give me such a one, and he knows what I am saying. But if I speak to someone coldly unresponsive, he knows not what I speak.[15] Such were these who were murmuring among themselves. "He whom the Father draws," he said, "comes to me."

5. But what does it mean "whom the Father draws" when Christ himself draws? Why did he want to say, "whom the Father draws"? If we must be drawn, let us be drawn by him to whom a certain woman who loves him says, "We will run after the odor of your ointments."[16] But let us observe, brothers, what he wanted to be understood, and let us grasp it as far as we can. The Father draws to the Son those who believe in the Son for the reason that they think that he has God as his Father. For God the Father begot a Son equal to himself, so that one who thinks and in his faith perceives and ponders that he in whom he has believed is equal to the Father, him the Father draws to the Son.

(2) Arius[17] believed [him to be] a created being; the Father did not draw him because he does not take the Father into consideration who does not believe the Son an equal. What do you say, O Arius? What, heretic, do you speak? What is Christ? Not, he says, true God, but one whom the true God made. The Father has not drawn you; for you have not understood the Father whose Son you deny. You think something else: it is not the Son himself. You are neither drawn by the Father nor are you drawn to the Son. For, the Son is one thing, what you say [is] something else.

14. Cf. Ps 35.8–10.
15. The codices and some editions omit "he knows not" and read simply, "What do I say?"
16. Cf. Cant (Song) 1.3 (LXX) (NAB 1.4).
17. Cf. *Tractate* 1.11, note 27.

(3) Photinus[18] said, "Christ is only man, he is not also God."
The Father has not drawn him who so believes. He whom the
Father has drawn says, "You are the Christ, the Son of the
living God."[19] Not as a prophet, not as John, not as some
great just man, but as the only one, as an equal, "You are the
Christ, the Son of the living God." See that he has drawn and
he has been drawn by the Father. "Blessed are you, Simon
Bar-Jona, for flesh and blood has not revealed it to you, but
my Father who is in heaven."[20]

(4) This revelation itself is what draws.[21] You show a green
branch to a sheep and you draw her. Nuts are shown to a boy
and he is drawn. And he is drawn by what he runs to, by
loving he is drawn, without injury to the body he is drawn,
by a chain of the heart he is drawn. Therefore, if those things
which amid earthly delights and pleasures are revealed to
those who love them draw them, because it is true that "his
own pleasure draws every man," does not Christ, revealed by
the Father, draw? For what does the soul desire more strongly
than the truth? Why ought it to have greedy jaws, with which
to desire that the inner palate [which is] the judge of true
things may be healthy, except that it may eat and drink wisdom, justice, truth, eternity?

6. But where [does it do] this? There better, there more
truly, there more fully. For here we can more easily hunger,
and this if we have good hope, than be sated; for he says,
"Blessed are they who hunger and thirst after justice"—but
here!—"for they shall have their fill"[22]—but there! And so

18. Photinus of Sirmium, fl. 344–351 A.D., held that Christ did not exist
before conception and that he was a human like all of us except for his
miraculous birth, but that he gradually acquired a plenitude of grace
through moral perfection and became our model. See Augustine, *De Haeresibus* 44–45 (CCL 46.311–312); Optatus of Milevis, *De Schismate Donatistarum*
4.5 (CSEL 26.107–109); G. Bardy, "Photin de Sirmium," DThC 12.2.1532–
1536; ODCC², 1087. For other references to Photinus in Augustine see Berrouard, *Homélies XVII–XXXIII*, 809. Augustine seems to have used Photinus
as his example of those who thought Christ to be only human.

19. Cf. Mt 16.17.   20. Ibid.

21. See R. Hardy, *Actualité de la révélation divine*, Théologie historique 28
(Paris, 1974) 53–56.

22. Mt 5.6.

when he said, "No one comes to me unless the Father who sent me draw him," what did he add? "And I will raise him up on the last day." I deliver to him what he loves, I deliver what he hopes for; he will see what he has believed in while still not seeing. He will eat what he hungers for; he will be filled with that for which he thirsts. Where? In the resurrection of the dead, for "I will raise him up on the last day."

7. "For it has been written in the prophets, 'And they all shall be taught of God.'" Why have I said this, O Jews? The Father has not taught you. How can you recognize me? All the men of that kingdom shall be taught of God, they will not hear from men. And if they hear from men, still what they understand is given within, it gleams within, it is revealed within.[23] What do men who proclaim from without do? What am I now doing when I speak? I bring the noise of words to your ears. Unless he who is within should reveal, what do I say, or what do I speak?

(2) The planter of a tree is outside; its creator is inside. He who plants and he who waters work from the outside; we are doing this. But "neither he who plants is anything, nor he who waters, but God who gives the growth."[24] That is, "they all shall be taught of God." Who are "all"? "Everyone who has listened to the Father and has learned comes to me." See how the Father draws. By teaching he delights, not by imposing necessity. See how he draws. "They all shall be taught of God." This is God's drawing. "Everyone who has listened to the Father and has learned comes to me." This is God's drawing.

8. What then, brothers? If everyone who has listened to the Father and has learned, himself comes to Christ, has Christ taught nothing here? Why is it that men have not seen the Father, their teacher, [but] have seen the Son? The Son spoke but the Father taught. I, since I am a man, whom do I teach? Whom, brothers, but him who has listened to my word? If I,

---

23. Whoever preaches, whoever teaches, it is the interior master, who is Christ (who is God), who gives understanding. On the interior master see *Tractate* 1.7, note 23.

24. 1 Cor 3.7.

since I am a man, teach him who listens to my word, the Father, too, teaches that man who listens to his Word. Seek what Christ is and you will find his Word. "In the beginning was the Word."[25]

(2) Not, in the beginning God made the Word, as "in the beginning God made heaven and earth."[26] See that he is not a creature. Learn to be drawn to the Son by the Father; let the Father teach you, hear his Word. What Word of his, you say, do I hear? "In the beginning was the Word"—not was made, but was—"and the Word was with God, and the Word was God."[27] How do men, who are of flesh, hear such a Word? Because "the Word was made flesh, and dwelt among us."[28]

9. And he himself explains this and shows us what he said: "He who has listened to the Father and has learned comes to me." Immediately he added what we would be able to conceive, "not that anyone has seen the Father, but he who is from God, he has seen the Father"; you have not seen the Father; and yet, you do not come to me unless you are drawn by the Father. But what is it for you to be drawn by the Father except for you to learn from the Father? What is to learn from the Father except to listen to the Father? What is to listen to the Father except to hear the Father's Word, that is, me? Therefore, when I say to you, "Eveyone who has listened to the Father and has learned," that you may not, perhaps, say among yourselves, "But we have never seen the Father; how could we have learned from the Father?" hear from me, "Not that anyone has seen the Father, but he who is from God, he has seen the Father." I know the Father, I am from him, but as a word from that man whose word it is; not one which sounds and passes, but one which remains with the speaker and draws the hearer.

10. Let what follows instruct. "Amen, amen, I say to you, he who believes in me has life everlasting." He wanted to reveal himself, what he was; for he could have said briefly, "He

25. Cf. Jn 1.1.   26. Gn 1.1.
27. Jn 1.1.   28. Cf. Jn 1.14.

who believes in me has me." For Christ himself is the true God and life everlasting.[29] "Therefore," he says, "he who believes in me goes into me;[30] and what goes into me has me." But what does "to have me" mean? To have life everlasting. Life everlasting has taken upon itself death; life everlasting wanted to die, but on your account, not his own. He received from you that whereby he might die for you. For he took upon himself flesh from men, but not in the manner of men. For having the Father in heaven, he chose a mother on earth; and there [he was] born without a mother, here without a father. Therefore, life took upon itself death that life might kill death.[31]

(2) For "he who believes in me," he says, "has life everlasting," not that which lies open, but that which is hidden. For life everlasting "in the beginning was the Word with God, and the Word was God, and the life was the light of men."[32] He himself, life everlasting, has also given life everlasting to the flesh which he had taken. He came to die, but on the third day he rose. Between the Word taking on [flesh] and the flesh rising, death, in the middle, was annihilated.

11. He says, "I am the bread of life." And what were they proud about? "Your fathers," he says, "ate manna in the desert, and have died." What is it about which you are proud? "They ate manna, and have died." Why did they eat and die? Because they believed what they saw, but did not understand what they did not see. For that reason [they are] your fathers because you are like them. For, my brothers, as far as pertains to this visible and corporeal death, do not we who eat the bread coming down from heaven die? So they, too, have died, as we shall die, as far as concerns, as I said, the visible and fleshly death of this body. But as far as pertains to that death with which the Lord frightens, by which their father died, Moses, too, ate manna, Aaron ate manna, Phinees, too, ate

29. Cf. 1 Jn 5.20.
30. I.e., enters the body of Christ, becomes a member of his body: "the body of Christ is the Church." See *Tractate* 15.31.
31. Cf. *Tractates* 8.8, 12.8, and 14.2.
32. Cf. Jn 1.1, 2, and 4.

manna, many there who pleased the Lord ate it, and they have not died.[33] Why? Because they understood the visible food spiritually, they hungered spiritually, they tasted spiritually, that they might be filled spiritually.

(2) For we, too, today receive visible food; but the sacrament is one thing, the efficacy of the sacrament another.[34] How many receive from the altar and die, and by receiving die? For this reason the Apostle says, "He eats and drinks judgment to himself."[35] For the morsel of the Lord was not poison to Judas. And yet he received it; and when he received it, the enemy entered into him,[36] not because he received an evil thing but because an evil man received a good thing evilly.[37] See to it, therefore, brothers; eat the heavenly bread spiri-

33. On Moses and Aaron and the manna, see Ex 16; on Phinees (Phinehas) see Nm 25.1–13.

34. Berrouard argues convincingly that both the manna and the Eucharist are sacraments, visible signs of an underlying reality, Christ, and that for those who accept these sacraments properly, they effect, through grace, Christ's saving work in the believers, whether Old Testament Jews or New Testament Christians. Hence, Augustine here emphasizes that sacraments are always signs; whatever else one may say about the reality of Christ in the Eucharist, its significative character always remains. See M.-F. Berrouard, "Pour une refléxion sur le 'sacramentum' augustinien la manne et l'eucharistie dans le *Tractatus* XXVI, 11–12 in Iohannis Evangelium," in *Forma Futuri: Studi in onore del Cardinale Michele Pellegrino* (Torino, 1975), 830–844. Note also that the word "sacrament" here is used in a different and vaguer sense than its modern use. A sacrament is a sign that can both signify a reality and be the reality at the same time. Likewise the "sacraments" are not fixed rituals with set forms. Augustine's treatment of the Eucharist here is difficult to interpret since he passes back and forth between literal, allegorical and anagogical senses of the Scripture without clarity; see Comeau, 101. A very detailed analysis of *Tractates* 26 and 27, and other places where Augustine deals with the Bread of Life passage from Jn 6, can be found in E. Siedlecki, *A Patristic Synthesis of John VI, 54–55* (Mundelein, Ill., 1956), 1–119. In these *Tractates* Augustine emphasizes the sacramental, i.e., significative, nature of the Eucharist as signifying the reality of the immanent union of Christ with the believer and the believer with Christ and the union of all the believers in the body of Christ, as well as the spiritual effect of the sign, the attainment of eternal life; Augustine is not here arguing against the real presence but against a literalist anthropophagic interpretation, called Capharnaitic from the fact that those who see cannibalism here in John are from Capharnaum. See E. Portalié, *A Guide to the Thought of Saint Augustine*, tr. R. Bastian (Chicago, 1960), 247–260, esp. 255–257.

35. Cf. 1 Cor 11.29.   36. Cf. Jn 13.26–27.

37. Cf. *Tractate* 6.15.

tually. Carry innocence to the altar. Even if there are daily sins, at least let them not be mortal. Before you approach the altar, observe what you are to say, "Forgive us our debts, as we also forgive our debtors."[38] You forgive; you will be forgiven. Approach without anxiety; it is bread, not poison. But see to it that you forgive; for if you do not forgive, you lie, and you lie to him whom you do not deceive. You can lie to God; you cannot deceive God. He knows what he does.[39] He sees you within, he examines you within, he inspects you within, he judges you within, he either damns or crowns you within.

(3) But they were the fathers of these men, that is, the evil father of evil men, the unbelieving father of unbelievers, the murmuring fathers of murmurers. For that people was said to have offended the Lord in no way more than by murmuring against God.[40] And so the Lord too, wishing to show that they were sons of such men, began to speak to them with this, "Why are you murmuring among yourselves," murmurers, sons of murmurers? "Your fathers ate the manna in the desert, and have died," not because the manna was an evil thing, but because they ate it evilly.

12. "This is the bread which comes down from heaven." Manna signified[41] this bread; the altar of God signified this

38. Cf. Mt 6.12; Lk 11.4; also *Tractate* 7.11.
39. Some texts read, "what you do."
40. Cf., e.g., Ex 16.2, 6–8 and 12.
41. Most of the codices read *significavit*, "signified," with manna and *significat*, "signifies," with the altar of God. Willems, with the Maurists and Migne, prefers the perfects in both places as rendering the text more logical. Berrouard, however, in the article cited in note 34, 832–835, argues for the present tense in the second place. As here translated, the altar of God is the altar of holocausts; hence, both the manna and the altar were mystical significations of the Christian Eucharist and altar, but the saving effects of both pairs were the same. Berrouard sees the present tense as the *lectio difficilior* and explains it by making the altar of God the Christian Eucharistic altar; he then takes the following phrase, "those were sacraments," as an inconsistency stemming from the extemporaneous character of the sermons. Berrouard's approach emphasizes the sacramental character of both sets of signs, the spiritual effect bestowed by grace; my approach, accepting the perfect tenses of the editors, focuses, here in this sermon, on the significative function of the Old Testament precedents. Nevertheless, Berrouard is right to insist that both the Old and the New have the same spiritual effect—Christ, the underlying reality, working the salvation of human persons through signs.

bread. Those were mysteries;[42] in signs they are different, in the thing which is signified they are alike. Hear the Apostle: He says, "For I would not have you ignorant, brethren, that our fathers were all under the cloud, and all passed through the sea, and all were baptized into Moses, in the cloud and in the sea. And all ate the same spiritual food."[43] The same spiritual food, of course; for corporeally it was another thing, because they ate manna, we something else, but [they ate] the spiritual [food] which we [eat]. But our fathers, not those men's fathers, those to whom we are like, not those to whom they were like.

(2) And he added, "And all drank the same spiritual drink."[44] They, one thing, we another, but in its visible aspect, but which, nevertheless, would signify this same thing in spiritual efficacy. For how "the same drink"? He says, "They drank from the spiritual rock that was following them, and the rock was Christ."[45] From there the bread, from there the drink. The rock is Christ in a sign, the true Christ in the Word and in the flesh. And how did they drink? The rock was struck twice with a rod.[46] The double striking signifies the two pieces of wood on the cross.

(3) Therefore, "this is the bread coming down from heaven, that if anyone eat of it, he will not die." But as pertains to the efficacy of the sacrament, not as pertains to the visible sacrament: he who eats within, not without; he who eats with his heart, not he who crushes with his teeth.

13. "I am the living bread, who have come down from heaven."[47] Living for the reason that I have come down from heaven. The manna also came down from heaven; but the manna was shadow, he is truth. "If anyone eat of this bread, he shall live forever; and the bread that I will give is my flesh, for the life of the world." When would flesh comprehend

---

42. I.e., sacraments (*sacramenta*).   43. 1 Cor 10.1–3.
44. 1 Cor 10.4.   45. Ibid.
46. Cf. Nm 20.11.
47. The Latin text has a relative clause with a first person verb; the relative clause thus modifies "I" (*ego*) rather than "bread." In the Greek text there is an attributive participial phrase modifying "bread."

flesh—that which he said was bread? It is called flesh, that
which flesh does not comprehend; and flesh does not comprehend it, therefore, all the more because it is called flesh.
For they were horrified at this; they said that this was too
much for them, they thought this could not be. "It is my flesh,"
he said, "for the life of the world." The faithful know the body
of Christ if they should not neglect to be the body of Christ.
Let them become the body of Christ, if they want to live from
the Spirit of Christ. Nothing lives from the Spirit of Christ
except the body of Christ.

(2) Understand, my brothers, what I have said. You are a
man; you have a spirit, and you have a body. I say spirit which
is called the soul, because of which it is substantiated that you
are a human being; for you are a substance composed of body
and soul. Tell me what lives from what. Does your spirit live
from your body, or your body from your spirit? Everyone who
lives answers (but he who cannot answer this, I do not know
if he lives); what does everyone who lives answer? "My body,
of course, lives from my spirit." Do you therefore also wish to
live from the Spirit of Christ? Be in the body of Christ. For
does my body live from your spirit? Mine lives from my spirit,
yours from your spirit. The body of Christ can only live from
the Spirit of Christ. It is for this reason that the Apostle Paul,
explaining this bread to us, says, "We though many, are one
bread, one body."[48]

(3) O mystery of true faith![49] O sign of unity! O bond of
love! He who wishes to live has the place to live, has the means
to live. Let him approach, let him believe, let him be embodied, that he may be given life. Let him not shrink back from
the coalition of members, let him not be a rotten limb which
deserves to be cut off, let him not be a deformed one on
account of which there is embarrassment. Let him be a beautiful limb, let him be a fitting one, let him be a healthy one,

---

48. Cf. 1 Cor 10.17.

49. *O sacramentum pietatis! O signum unitatis! O vinculum caritatis!* Berrouard, *Homélies XVII–XXXIII*, 814–815 points out how this memorable
rhymed phrase renders the mystery even more mystical. The first phrase is
perhaps borrowed from 1 Tm 3.16 and the third adapted from Col 3.14.

let him adhere to the body, let him live for God from God. Let him now labor on earth that afterwards he may reign in heaven.

14. "The Jews therefore argued with one another, saying, 'How can this man give us his flesh to eat?'" Of course, they argued with one another because they did not understand the bread of concord, neither did they want to take it. For they who eat such bread do not argue with one another, because "we though many, are one bread, one body."[50] And through it "God makes those of one kind to dwell in a house."[51]

15. But what they are seeking in arguing with one another, how the Lord can give his own flesh to eat, they do not hear at once, but it is still said to them, "Amen, amen, I say to you, unless you eat the flesh of the Son of man, and drink his blood, you shall not have life in you." You do not, indeed, know how it is eaten and what is the manner of eating this bread; nevertheless "unless you eat the flesh of the Son of man, and drink his blood, you will not have life in you." He was speaking these things, of course, not to corpses, but to living men. Wherefore, that they might not also argue about this matter, understanding it as this life, he continued and added, "He who eats my flesh and drinks my blood has life everlasting." Therefore, he who does not eat this bread nor drink this blood does not have this [life]; for men can have temporal life without that [bread], but they cannot at all have eternal life. Therefore he who does not eat his flesh nor drink his blood does not have life in him; and he who eats his flesh and drinks his blood has life. But to both he answers what he said, "everlasting."

(2) For it is not so in the case of this food which we take for the sake of sustaining this temporal life. For he who does not take it will not live, yet neither will he who does take it live. For very many even who take it die possibly of old age, or disease, or some accident. But in this true food and drink, that is, the body and blood of the Lord, it is not so. For both he who does not take it[52] does not have life; and he who takes

---

50. Cf. 1 Cor 10.17.   51. Cf. Ps 67.7.
52. The Latin has a singular pronoun, *eam,* which refers to the body and

it does have life, and this [life which is], of course, everlasting.

(3) And so he wants this food and drink to be understood as the society of his body and his members, that which is the holy Church[53] in its saints who were predestined, and called, and justified, and glorified,[54] and in its believers. The first of these things has already happened, that is, predestination. The second and third have happened, are happening, and will happen, that is, vocation and justification. But the fourth exists in hope now, but will be in fact, that is, glorification. The sacrament of this reality, that is, of the unity of the body and blood of Christ, is provided at the Lord's table, in some places daily, in other places with certain intervals of days;[55] and it is taken from the Lord's table: for some, for life, for some, for destruction. But the reality of which it is the sacrament is for every man for life, for no man for destruction, whoever shall have been a sharer in it.

16. But that they might not think that eternal life is promised in this food and drink in such a way that they who take it would not even now die in body, he deigned to come to grips with this thought. For when he had said, "He who eats my flesh and drinks my blood has life everlasting," immediately he added, "and I will raise him up on the last day." [He said this] that he may meanwhile have eternal life according to the spirit in the rest which receives the spirits of the saints; but

---

the blood together as the food, *esca,* a word used several times in this section. For a thorough analysis of the texts and teaching of Augustine on the reality and symbolism of the Eucharist, emphasizing the complexity of his concept of a symbol as both embodying a reality and often serving as a sign of eternal things, see P.-T. Camelot, "Réalisme et symbolisme dans la doctrine eucharistique de saint Augustin," *Revue des sciences philosophiques et théologiques* 31 (1947) 394–410.

53. The Eucharist is both in reality the body and blood of Jesus and a ritual sign of the reality of the unity of the Christian community; this community exists in the widest sense as it includes all Christians, living and dead, and the reality of this community is embodied in the Church. See Berrouard, *Homélies XVII–XXXIII,* 817–819 and Portalié, 256–260.

54. Cf. Rom 8.3.

55. The evidence for the frequency of the Eucharistic ritual is occasional and indirect; in general it supports Augustine's statement here. Berrouard, *Homélies XVII–XXXIII,* 819–822 gives a brief summary of the evidence; see also J. Jungmann, *The Mass of the Roman Rite,* tr. F. Brunner (New York, 1951) 1.245–252.

as pertains to the body, that he may not be cheated of its eternal life, but [be] in the resurrection of the dead on the last day.

17. He says, "For my flesh is food indeed, and my blood is drink indeed." For although by food and drink men strive for this, that they hunger not and thirst not, only this food and drink truly offer this; for it makes those by whom it is taken immortal and incorruptible, that is, the very society of saints, where there will be peace and full and perfect unity. For this reason, indeed, even as men of God knew this before us, our Lord, Jesus Christ, manifested his body and blood in those things which are reduced from many to some one thing. For the one is made into one thing from many grains, the other flows together into one thing from many grapes.[56]

18. Now, finally, he explains how what he is saying happens and what it is to eat his body and to drink his blood. "He who eats my flesh and drinks my blood, abides in me and I in him." Therefore, to eat that food and to drink that drink is to abide in Christ and to have him abiding in oneself. And, as a result, he who does not abide in Christ and in whom Christ does not abide, beyond doubt neither eats his flesh nor drinks his blood,[57] but rather eats and drinks the sacrament of so great a thing to judgment for himself,[58] because he presumed to approach unclean to the sacraments of Christ which one takes worthily only if he is clean. And about these it is said, "Blessed are the clean of heart, for they shall see God."[59]

56. Cf. Cyprian, *Epistula* 63.13.4 (PL 4.395–396; CSEL 2.711–712) and also 69.5 cited as *Epistola S. Cypriani ad Magnum* 6 (PL 3.1189; CSEL 2.753–754, mentioned as 76 in PL 4.427); cf. FOTC 51.211 and 247–248. See also John Chrysostom, *In Epistulam Primam ad Corinthios* 24.2 (PG 61.200); *Didache* 9.4 (K. Lake, *The Apostolic Fathers*, The Loeb Classical Library (Cambridge, Mass., 1912) 1.322–323; and ACW 6.20 and 160); and Augustine, *Sermo* 227 (PL 38.1100) and 272 (PL 38.1247–1248); and Berrouard, *Homélies XVII–XXXIII*, 822–823.

57. Some editions read: "neither eats his flesh spiritually nor drinks his blood although he crushes carnally with his teeth the sacrament of the body and blood of Christ."

58. The rest of this section is found in many editions but not in the codices; it is, as the sentence cited in the previous note, probably an interpolation. See Browne, 412–413 and Berrouard, *Homélies XVII–XXXIII*, 823–824.

59. Mt 5.8.

19. He says, "As the living Father has sent me, and I live because of the Father, so he who eats me, he also shall live because of me." He did not say, "As I eat the Father and I live because of the Father, so he who eats me, also shall live because of me." For the Son who was begotten equal does not become better by participation in the Father, as by participation in the Son through the unity of his body and blood, the thing which that eating and drinking signify, we are made better. Therefore we, eating him, live because of him, that is, by receiving him as eternal life which we do not have from ourselves; but he lives because of the Father, sent by him because he emptied himself, becoming obedient even to the death of the cross.[60]

(2) For if we take "I live because of the Father" according to what he said elsewhere, "The Father is greater than I,"[61] as we also live because of him who is greater than we, this happened from the fact that he was sent. His sending, of course, is his emptying of himself, and his receiving of the servant's form; and this is rightly understood, if the equality of the Son's nature with the Father is preserved. For the Father is greater than the human son, but he holds the God Son equal, since the very same one is both God and man, Son of God and Son of man, one Christ Jesus. And in this sentence if these words are rightly understood, he so said, "As the living Father has sent me, and I live because of the Father, so he who eats me, he also shall live because of me," as if he were to say, "That I may live because of the Father, that is, that I may refer my life to that so much greater one, my emptying in which he sent me effected that, but that anyone may live because of me, his participation by eating me effects that. And so I live, humbled, because of the Father; he, elevated, lives because of me."

(3) But if "I live because of the Father" was so said that he is from the Father [and the Father] not from him,[62] it was said without loss of equality. And yet by saying, "so he who eats

60. Cf. Phil 2.7–8. 61. Cf. Jn 14.28.
62. Cf. *Tractate* 19.3.

me, he also shall live because of me," he did not signify the same equality of himself and us, but he showed the grace of the mediator.[63]

20. "This is the bread that has come down from heaven," so that by eating it we may live because we cannot have eternal life from ourselves. He said, "Not as your fathers ate the manna and have died. He who eats this bread shall live forever." Therefore the fact that they died he wishes to be understood thus, that they do not live forever. For, indeed, these too, who eat Christ, shall die in time, but they live forever because Christ is life everlasting.

63. Cf. Rom 5.2.

TRACTATE 27

On John 6.60–72

E HAVE HEARD from the gospel the words of the Lord which follow his previous discourse. From these a discourse is owed to your ears and minds, and it is not unsuitable for today;[1] for it is about the body of Christ which he said that he was giving for eating because of life everlasting. Moreover, he explained the method of this bestowal and his gift, how he would give his flesh to eat, saying, "He who eats my flesh, and drinks my blood, abides in me, and I in him."[2] This is the sign that he has eaten and drunk, if he abides and is abided,[3] if he dwells and is dwelt in, if he adheres that he may not be abandoned.[4] Therefore, he instructed and taught us this in mystical words, that we may be in his body, under himself as the head, in his members, eating his flesh, not leaving behind unity with him.

(2) But the majority of those who were present, because of not understanding, were scandalized; for, on hearing these words, they thought only of the flesh which they were themselves. But the Apostle says, and he says the truth, "To be wise according to the flesh is death."[5] The Lord gives us his own flesh to eat, and "to be wise according to the flesh is death," although he says about his own flesh that therein is life everlasting. Therefore we ought not to be wise about the flesh according to the flesh, as in these words:

2. "Many therefore," not of his enemies, but "of his disciples, hearing it, said, 'This is a hard saying. Who can hear

---

1. This sermon was delivered on the feast of St. Lawrence, August 10; see section 10.

2. Cf. Jn 6.57 (NAB 6.56).   3. Cf. *Tractate* 26.18.
4. Cf. *Tractate* 2.8.   5. Cf. Rom 8.6.

it?'" If his disciples held that to be a hard saying, what about his enemies? And yet, so it was necessary that that be said which would not be understood by all. A secret of God ought to make us attentive, not antagonistic. But these men quickly defected, when the Lord Jesus spoke such words; they did not believe him although he was saying something great and veiling some grace with these words. But just as they wanted, and in a human way, so they understood that Jesus could, or that he was proposing, because the Word had been clothed in flesh, to cut himself up, as it were, and distribute himself to those believing in him.[6] "This is," they say, "a hard saying. Who can hear it?"

3. "But Jesus knew in himself that his disciples were murmuring at this." For they said these words among themselves so that they might not be heard by him; but he knew them in themselves, hearing in himself, answered and said, "This scandalizes you," because I said, "I give you my flesh to eat and my blood to drink." Of course this scandalizes you. "What then if you should see the Son of man ascending where he was before?" What does this mean? By this did he resolve what had disturbed them? By this did he make clear why they had been scandalized? Clearly he did this, if they understood. For they thought that he was going to disburse his body; but he said that he was going to ascend to heaven, whole, of course. "When you see the Son of man ascending where he was before," surely then, at least, you will see that

6. Augustine distinguishes the material reality from a spiritual reality and a symbolic reality, according to M. F. Berrouard, "L'être sacramental de l'eucharistie selon saint Augustin: Commentaire de Io 6, 60–63 dans le *Tractatus* XXVII, 1–6 et 11–12 in Ioannis Evangelium," *Nouvelle revue théologique* 99 (1977) 702–721. The Eucharist presents a paradox and a mystery; there is no literal eating of the actual body of Christ which he had in his historical life on this earth and yet unless we eat his body we cannot attain eternal life. What we eat is the living flesh, spiritualized by the Resurrection and Ascension, which takes its power from its union with the Word; this living spiritualized flesh and blood united with the Word constitutes a mode of being totally original. Christ thus unites with us this spiritual reality through the symbolic reality of the sacrament, gives us the Holy Spirit through it, and through the Spirit brings unity to the body of Christ. Cf. also *Tractate* 26.11, note 34, and Siedlecki in the article cited there, 28–31.

he does not disburse his body in the way in which you think; surely then, at least, you will understand that his grace is not consumed in bite-sized pieces.

4. And he said, "It is the spirit which gives life; the flesh profits nothing." Before we explain this, as the Lord bestows, those other words of his, "What if you should see the Son of man ascending where he was before?" should not be passed by negligently. For the Son of man is Christ, of the Virgin Mary. Therefore the Son of man began to be here on earth where he took on himself flesh from the earth. For this reason in prophecy it had been said, "Truth has arisen out of the earth."[7] What, then, does it mean, "when you see the Son of man ascending where he was before"? For there would be no question if he had said it thus: "If you should see the Son of God ascending where he was before." But when he said the Son of man ascending where he was before, was the Son of man in heaven before the time when he began to be on earth? Here he said, "where he was before," as if then he were not there when he was speaking these words. But in another place he said, "No man has ascended into heaven except he who has descended from heaven: the Son of man who is in heaven."[8] He did not say, "was," but he said, "The Son of man who is in heaven." He was speaking on earth and said he was in heaven. And he did not say it thus, "No one has ascended into heaven except he who has descended from heaven; the Son of God who is in heaven."

(2) Where does this lead except that we understand—as also in my previous sermon[9] I showed you, my beloved people—that Christ, God and man, is one person, not two, so that our faith is only a Trinity and not a Quaternity? Therefore Christ is one, the Word, soul and flesh, one Christ; the Son of God and the Son of man, one Christ. The Son of God always, the Son of man in time, nevertheless, one Christ according to the unity of person. He was in heaven when he was speaking on earth. So the Son of man was in heaven as

7. Cf. Ps 84.12.   8. Jn 3.13.
9. Cf. *Tractate* 26.19; see also *Tractate* 12.8.

the Son of God was on earth; the Son of God was on earth in the flesh he had taken, the Son of man was in heaven in the unity of person.

5. Why, then, does he add, "It is the spirit that gives life; the flesh profits nothing"? Let us say to him (for he allows us if we do not contradict him but desire to know): "O Lord, good teacher, how 'does the flesh profit nothing' when you have said, 'Unless a man eat my flesh and drink my blood, he shall not have life in him'?[10] Or does life profit nothing? And because of what are we what we are except that we have life everlasting which you promise by your flesh? What, then, does it mean, 'the flesh profits nothing'?" It profits nothing, but as they understood it; for, of course, they so understood flesh as [something that] is torn to pieces in a carcass or sold in a meat market, not as [something that] is enlivened by a spirit. Accordingly, it was said, "The flesh profits nothing," just so as it was said, "Knowledge puffs up."[11] Ought we, therefore, to hate knowledge? Far from it. And what does "knowledge puffs up" mean? Alone, without love. Thus he added, "but love edifies."[12] Therefore, add love to knowledge, and knowledge will be useful, not in itself but through love. So too, now, "flesh profits nothing," but flesh alone; let spirit be added to flesh, as love is added to knowledge, and it profits very much. For if flesh profited nothing, the Word would not have become flesh to dwell among us.[13]

(2) If Christ profited us much through his flesh, how does flesh profit nothing? But through the flesh the Spirit has accomplished something for our salvation. The flesh was a vessel; observe what it had, not what it was. The apostles were sent; did their flesh profit us nothing? If the flesh of the apostles profited us, could the flesh of the Lord have profited nothing? For from where does the sound of a word [come] to us except through the voice of the flesh? From where [comes] the pen, from where the writing? All these things are works of the flesh, but with the spirit playing it, its musical instru-

10. Cf. Jn 6.54 (NAB 6.53).   11. Cf. 1 Cor 8.1.
12. Ibid.   13. Cf. Jn 1.14.

ment, as it were. Therefore, "It is the spirit that gives life; the flesh profits nothing." As they understood flesh, not so do I give my flesh for eating.

6. Accordingly, he says, "The Words that I have spoken to you are spirit and life." For we have said,[14] brothers, that the Lord had shown, in the eating of his flesh and the drinking of his blood, that we abide in him and he in us. But we abide in him when we are his members; but he abides in us when we are his temple. But that we may be his members, unity joins us together. That unity may join together, what causes it except love? And whence is the love of God? Ask the Apostle! He says, "The love of God has been poured forth in our hearts by the Holy Spirit who has been given to us."[15] Therefore, "it is the spirit that gives life"; for the spirit produces living members. And the spirit produces living members only which it has found in the body which the spirit itself enlivens. For the spirit which is in you, O man, by which it is clear to you that you are a man, does it give life to a member which it has found separated from your flesh? I call your soul your spirit. Your soul gives life only to the members which are in your flesh; if you should remove one, it is no longer given life from your soul because it is not bound to the unity of your body.

(2) These words are said that we may love unity and fear separation. For a Christian ought to dread nothing so much as to be separated from the body of Christ. For, if he is separated from the body of Christ, he is not a member of him; if he is not a member of him, he is not enlivened by his Spirit. The Apostle says, "But whoever does not have the Spirit of Christ, he does not belong to him."[16] Therefore "it is the spirit which gives life; but the flesh profits nothing. The words that I have spoken are spirit and life."

(3) What does "are spirit and life" mean? They must be understood spiritually. Did you understand them spiritually? "They are spirit and life." Did you understand them carnally? Even so they "are spirit and life," but they are not to you.

14. Cf. section 1 and *Tractate* 26.18 on Jn 6.57.
15. Cf. Rom 5.5.   16. Cf. Rom 8.9.

7. He says, "But there are some among you who do not believe." He did not say, "There are some among you who do not understand" but he stated the cause why they do not understand. "For there are some among you who do not believe." And they do not understand precisely because they do not believe. For the prophet said, "Unless you believe, you will not understand."[17] We are joined together through faith; we are given life through understanding. Let us first adhere through faith that there may be that which may be given life through understanding. For he who does not adhere stands opposed; he who stands opposed does not believe. For he who stands opposed, how is he given life? He is an adversary to the ray of light by which he must be penetrated; he does not turn aside eyes but closes his mind. Therefore "there are some who do not believe." Let them believe and open up; let them open up and they will be enlightened. "For Jesus knew from the beginning who they were who believed,[18] and him who would betray him."

(2) For Judas, too, was there. For some were scandalized; but he remained for treachery, not for understanding. And because he had remained for that reason, the Lord did not keep quiet about him. He did not expressly name him, but neither did he hold silence, that all might fear, though only one was lost. But after he spoke and distinguished the believers from the non-believers, he expressly stated the cause why they do not believe; he said, "This is why I have told you that no one can come to me unless it is granted him by my Father."

(3) Therefore it is also granted us to believe; for it is not nothing to believe. But if it is something great, rejoice that you have believed, but do not be overly elated; for what do you have which you have not received?[19]

8. "From this time many of his disciples went back and no longer walked with him." "They went back," but behind sa-

17. Cf. Is 7.9 (LXX).
18. Augustine omits the "not" of the scriptural text: "who did not believe."
19. Cf. 1 Cor 4.7.

tan, not behind Christ. For one time the Lord Christ called Peter satan, more because he wanted to precede his Lord and to advise him that he should not die who had come to die that we might not die forever. And he said to him, "Go behind me, satan, for you do not savor the things of God, but those of men."[20] He did not compel him to go behind satan and called him satan, but he made him go behind himself that, by walking behind his Lord, he might not be satan. But these men turned back in the same way as the Apostle says about some women: "For some have turned aside after satan."[21] They went about with him no more. Look, cut off from the body, they lost life, because perhaps they were not even in the body. These, too, must be accounted among the unbelievers even though they were called disciples. They went back, not a few, but many.

(2) Perhaps this happened for consolation, because sometimes it happens that a man says the truth, and what he says is not grasped, and they who hear are scandalized and depart. But the man is sorry that he said what is true; for the man says to himself, "I ought not to have spoken thus; I ought not to have said this." Look, it happened to the Lord. He said it, and he lost many; he remained for the few. But he was not troubled because he knew from the beginning both who they were who believed and who they were who did not believe; if it should happen to us, we are very distressed. Let us find solace in the Lord, and nevertheless, let us utter our words cautiously.

9. And to the few who had remained, "Jesus, therefore, said to the Twelve," that is, to those twelve who remained, he said, "Do you also wish to go?" Judas did not depart, not even he. But why he remained was already clear to the Lord; later it was revealed to us. Peter answered for all, one for many, unity for all of them: "Simon Peter therefore answered him, 'Lord, to whom shall we go?'" You thrust us from you; give us the other you. "To whom shall we go?" If we depart from you, to whom shall we go? "You have words of life everlast-

20. Cf. Mk 8.33; Mt 16.23.   21. Cf. 1 Tm 5.15.

ing." See how Peter understood, God granting, the Holy Spirit renewing. Whence, except that he believed? "You have words of life everlasting." For you have life everlasting in the ministration of your body and your blood.

(2) "And we have believed and known." Not we have known and believed, but "we have believed and known." For we have believed that we might know; for if we were to wish to know first and then to believe, we could neither know nor believe.[22] What have we believed, and what have we known? "That you are the Christ, the Son of God,"[23] that is, that you are life everlasting itself, and you do not give in your flesh and blood but what you are.

10. Therefore, the Lord Jesus said, "Have I not chosen you twelve, and one of you is a devil?" Should he have said, therefore, "Have I not chosen you eleven"? Or is a devil also chosen, and is a devil among the chosen? They are accustomed to be called "chosen" in praise; was this one also chosen from whom, although unwilling and unknowing, some great good would happen? This is characteristic of God, contrary to wicked men. For as the wicked use the good works of God evilly, so, on the other hand, God uses the evil works of wicked men in a good way. How good a thing it is that the members of the body exist in such a way that they cannot be disposed except by God, their maker! And yet how evilly does wantonness use the eyes? How evilly does deceit use the tongue? Does not a false witness first slaughter his own soul by his tongue, and try to wound another when he is himself destroyed? He uses the tongue evilly, but the tongue is not, therefore, an evil thing; the tongue is a work of God, but that wickedness uses the good work of God evilly.

(2) How do they who race to crimes use the feet? How do murderers use the hands? And how evilly do evil men use those good creations of God which lie about outside [them]?

---

22. Cf. *Tractates* 8.6–7, 15.24, 18.1, and 22.2.

23. This is the text of the *Vulgate* and some Greek manuscripts; the best Greek text reads, "God's Holy One." Perhaps the Latin texts were influenced by Mt 16.16. See Berrouard, *Homélies XVII–XXXIII*, 554–555; Brown 29.298; and M.-J. Lagrange, *Évangile selon saint Jean* (Paris, 1948), 191.

With gold they corrupt courts, they oppress the innocent. Evil men use the very daylight evilly; for by living evilly they even employ the daylight itself by which they see as an aid to their crimes. For an evil man to do some evil wants it to be light for him that he might not hurt himself, who has already hurt himself within and fallen; what he fears for his body, he already falls into in his heart. Therefore an evil man uses evilly all the good works of God—I shall not run through each one of them; it would take too long—on the other hand, a good man uses well the evils of evil men.

(3) And what is so good as the one God? Seeing that the Lord himself said, "No one is good but God alone."[24] Therefore as much as he is better, so much the better does he use even our evils. What is worse than Judas? Among all those adhering to the master, among the Twelve, their purse was entrusted to him and the stewardship of the poor was assigned to him.[25] Ungrateful for so great a privilege, so great an honor, he accepted money, lost his justice, and himself dead, delivered up life. Him whom he had followed as a disciple he persecuted as an enemy. This whole evil was Judas', but the Lord used his evil well. He suffered himself to be delivered up that he might redeem us. See, the evil of Judas has been converted into a good! How many martyrs has satan persecuted? If satan stopped persecuting, we would not today be celebrating the so glorious crown[26] of Saint Lawrence.[27] Therefore if God uses well the evil works of the devil himself, what an evil man does, using something evilly, harms himself and is not a contradiction to the goodness of God. The maker uses him; and the great maker, if he did not know how to use him, would not even permit him to be.

(4) Therefore "one of you is a devil," he said, although I

24. Cf. Mk 10.18; Lk 18.19.   25. Cf. Jn 12.6.
26. I.e., the eternal happiness merited by martyrdom.
27. The feast day of St. Lawrence was August 10. A deacon of Rome, Lawrence was martyred by being roasted on a gridiron on August 10, 258 A.D., during the persecution of Valerian. A church was built on the spot and became a center of pilgrimage, and the cult of St. Lawrence was widespread throughout Christendom by the early fourth century. See J. Bruckmann, "St. Lawrence," NCE 8.566.

have chosen you twelve. That he said, "I have chosen twelve" could also be understood in such a way that the number is mystical. For the honor of that number was not taken away because one of them perished; for in the place of the one who perished another was substituted. The mystical number remained, the number twelve, because through the entire world, that is, through the four cardinal points of the world,[28] they were going to announce the Trinity. Thus three times four. Therefore Judas committed suicide; he did not damage the number twelve. He abandoned his teacher, for God appointed a successor to him.

11. Because the Lord spoke all of this about his flesh and blood, and because he promised us life everlasting in the grace of his bestowal, and because from this he wanted it to be understood that the eaters[29] and drinkers of his flesh and blood abide in him and he in them, and because, knowing spiritual things carnally, they were scandalized, and because when they were scandalized and falling away, the Lord was present as a comfort to the disciples who had remained, for the testing of whom he asked, "Do you also wish to go?" so that the answer of their remaining might become known to us (for he knew that they remained), therefore let all of this have this effect on us, most beloved people, that we not only eat the flesh of Christ and the blood of Christ in the sacrament as many evil men also do, but that we eat and drink for participation in the spirit, that we may abide as members in the body of the Lord, that we may be enlivened by his spirit and not be scandalized even if many now eat and drink the sacraments temporally with us, who will have eternal torments at the end.

(2) For now the body of Christ has been mixed, so to speak,

---

28. I.e., north, south, east, west; see *Tractates* 9.14, 10.12.

29. The Latin word is *manducatores,* a very rare word in surviving Latin texts, cited only two other times, once in the *Itala* and once in Julianus Pomerius, a Christian writer of the late fifth century. See Blaise, 512; TLL 8.272; Berrouard, *Homélies XVII–XXXIII,* 560; and Mohrmann, *Die Altchristliche Sondersprache,* 1.192–193.

on the threshing floor;[30] but the Lord knows who are his.[31] If you know what you are threshing, that there is substantial matter hiding there, and the threshing does not squander what the winnowing will cleanse, we are certain, brothers, that all of us, who are in the body of Christ and abide in him, that he, too, may abide in us, find it necessary in this world to live among evil men even to the end. I do not say among those evil men who blaspheme Christ, for very few are found now who blaspheme with the tongue, but many who [do so] by their life. Therefore, it is necessary that we live among those even to the end.

12. But what do his words mean, "who abides in me and I in him"?[32] What, except what the martyrs heard: "He who shall persevere to the end, he shall be saved"?[33] How did Saint Lawrence, whose feast we celebrate today, abide in him? He abided even in face of temptation, he abided even in face of tyrannical interrogation, he abided even in face of the harshest threats, he abided even in face of killing. It is not enough he abided even in face of cruel torment. For he was not killed swiftly, but was tortured with fire; he was allowed to live long, nay, rather, he was not allowed to live long, but compelled to die slowly. Thus in that drawn-out death, in those torments, because he had eaten well and drunk well, as if nourished by that food and intoxicated with that cup,[34] he did not feel the torments.

(2) He was there who said, "It is the spirit that gives life." For the flesh was aflame, but the spirit enlivened his soul. He did not yield, and he went up into the kingdom. Moreover, Saint Xystus, the martyr,[35] whose day we celebrated five days

30. Augustine frequently refers to the notion of the mixed congregation, as was indicated in the Introduction. He often uses the concept of the grain and the chaff from Mt 3.12 and Lk 3.17, as, e.g., in *Tractates* 6.12 and 11.8.

31. Cf. 2 Tm 2.19.

32. Cf. Jn 6.57 (NAB 6.56).				33. Cf. Mt 10.22 and 24.13.

34. Perhaps with Ps 22.5 (LXX) in mind since a similar phrase occurs in the direct interpretation of this Psalm verse in *En in Ps* 35.14 (CCL 38.332–335).

35. Sixtus II, Pope, 257–258 A.D., was beheaded with four of his deacons

ago,[36] had said to him, "Do not grieve, my son." for [Xystus] was a bishop, and he was a deacon. "Do not grieve," [Xystus] said, "you will follow me after three days." Now he said three days intervening between the day of the suffering of Saint Xystus and the day of today's suffering of Saint Lawrence. There are three days intervening. O consolation! He did not say, "Do not grieve, son; the persecution will stop, and you will be safe." But, "Do not grieve, where I precede you will follow, and your following is not delayed, three days will intervene and you will be with me."[37] He accepted the prophecy, he conquered the devil, he attained triumph.

on August 6, 258 A.D. He supported the view that baptism by heretics was valid. See E. Weltin, "Sixtus II, Pope, St.," NCE 13.271.

36. The Romans used inclusive dates; we would say four.

37. This dialogue is found in Ambrose, *De Officiis* 1.41. 204–206 (PL 16.90–92); see Berrouard, *Homélies XVII–XXXIII*, 565.

INDICES

GENERAL INDEX

Numbers Refer to Tractate, Section, and Paragraph

INDEX OF HOLY SCRIPTURE

(Books of the Old Testament)

(Books of the New Testament)